PHILONIC EXEGESIS IN GREGORY OF NYSSA'S *DE VITA MOYSIS*

Program in Judaic Studies
Brown University
Box 1826
Providence, RI 02912

BROWN JUDAIC STUDIES

Series Editors 2001–
David C. Jacobson
Ross S. Kraemer
Saul M. Olyan

Number 333
Studia Philonica Monographs 5

PHILONIC EXEGESIS IN GREGORY OF NYSSA'S *DE VITA MOYSIS*

by
Albert C. Geljon

PHILONIC EXEGESIS IN GREGORY OF NYSSA'S *DE VITA MOYSIS*

Albert C. Geljon

Brown Judaic Studies
Providence

PHILONIC EXEGESIS IN GREGORY OF NYSSA'S *DE VITA MOYSIS*

by
Albert C. Geljon

Copyright © 2002 by Brown University

Written with the financial support of the
Netherlands Organization for Scientific Research (N. W. O.).
Published with the financial support of the Prof. dr. C. J. de Vogel Foundation.

Library of Congress Cataloging-in-Publication Data
Geljon, Albert C.
  Philonic exegesis in Gregory of Nyssa's De vita Moysis / Albert C. Geljon.
      p. cm. — (Brown Judaic studies ; no. 333) (Studia Philonica monographs ; 5)
Includes bibliographical references and index.
    ISBN 1-930675-12-7 (cloth bdg. : alk. paper)
  1. Gregory, of Nyssa, Saint, ca. 335-ca. 394. De vita Moysis. 2. Philo, of Alexandria. I. Title. II. Series. III. Brown Judaic studies. Studia Philonica monographs ; 5.
  BR65.G75 D485 2002
  222'. 1092—dc21   2002007303

08 07 06 05 04 03 02   5 4 3 2 1

Printed in the United States of America
on acid-free paper

STUDIA PHILONICA MONOGRAPHS

STUDIES IN HELLENISTIC JUDAISM

EDITOR
David M. Hay
Coe College, Cedar Rapids, Iowa

The Studia Philonica Monographs series accepts monographs in the area of Hellenistic Judaism, with special emphasis on Philo and his *Umwelt*. Proposals for books to be published in the Monographs series should be sent to Prof. David M. Hay, 1428 Airline Road,, McDonough, GA 30252, U.S.A.

Article-length contributions should be sent to the American Editor of *The Studia Philonica Annual,* Prof. Gregory E. Sterling, Department of Theology, University of Notre Dame, Notre Dame, IN 46556. Books for review in the Annual should be sent to Alan Mendelson, Book Review Editor, Department of Religion, McMaster University, Hamilton, Ontario, L8S 4K1, CANADA.

Parentibus meis

CONTENTS

III. Gregory's *De vita Moysis* 63
   1. The title of the treatise 63
   2. The theme of the treatise 64
   3. Moses as example 66
   4. Allegorical and typological interpretations 68
   5. Previous research on Gregory and Philo 69

PART THREE:

THE PHILONIC BACKGROUND OF GREGORY'S
DE VITA MOYSIS

I. Method of research 73
II. Analysis of Gregory's *De vita Moysis* 79
   0. Introduction (I.1-15) 79
   1. Moses' birth and the tyrant (I.16, II.1-5) 80
      1.1. The metaphor of giving birth to virtue 81
      1.2. The symbolic explanation of male and female 82
   2. Moses' basket in the river (I.17, II.6-9) 83
      2.1. The stream of life 84
      2.2. Exegesis of Moses' basket 85
   3. Moses adopted by Pharaoh's daughter (I.17-18, II.10-12) 87
      3.1. Moses' royal education 87
      3.2. Interpretation of Pharaoh's daughter 88
      3.3. The image of the woman being in labour 89
   4. Moses kills an Egyptian (I.18, II.13-16) 90
   5. Moses in Midian (I.19, II.17-18) 91
      5.1. Description of Moses' father-in-law 91
      5.2. The image of the shepherding of the movements of
         the soul 92
   6. Moses' encounter with God (I.20-21, II.19-34) 93
      6.a. The shining of the truth (I.20, II.19-25) 93
         6.a.1. The description of the burning bush 94
         6.a.2. The exegetical tradition of God's appearance in
            the burning bush 95
      6.b. The covering of skin (II.22) 97
      6.c. Deliverance from tyranny (II.26-34) 98
   7. Moses' return to Egypt (I.22, II.35-53) 100
      7.1. Interpretation of Pharaoh and Egypt 101
      7.2. The comparison of Moses to an athlete 102
      7.3. The interpretation of Moses' wife 103

PREFACE

This study is a revised version of my doctoral thesis, defended at Leiden University in December 2000. Now that this study is being published in a definitive version, it is a great pleasure to express my thanks to the persons who helped and stimulated me. During my study at the Free University in Amsterdam Prof. A. P. Box filled me with enthusiasm for ancient and patristic philosophy and drew my attention to Philo of Alexandria. Later on Prof. D. T. Runia from Leiden University agreed to become my dissertation advisor. I would like to thank him sincerely for his critical and stimulating supervision. Dr. A. van den Hoek of the Harvard Divinity School gave me a warm welcome in Cambridge, Massachusetts and at her home in Dedham. I remember our discussions with pleasure. Prof. G. E. Sterling, chair of the Philo of Alexandria Group of the Society of Biblical Literature, gave me the opportunity to present a paper on Philo at the meeting in Orlando in November 1998. Prof. D. M. Hay gave me valuable comments on an earlier version of my dissertation and approved the final manuscript for publication in the Studia Philonica Monograph Series. A. P. Runia corrected my English and Ms. Gonni Runia-Deenick prepared the camera-ready copy. The management of the CSG Oude Hoven in Gorinchem generously allowed me to do research while I was employed as a teacher.

Finally I would like to express my gratitude to my parents. They gave me the freedom to pursue my studies in a field which I liked and supported my research in many different ways. I dedicate this monograph to them.

INTRODUCTION

During recent years the ancient city of Alexandria has been frequently in the news.[1] New excavations, both in the harbour and on the mainland, have yielded exciting discoveries about the classical city, founded by Alexander the Great in 332 BC. The building of the new Library at the present time has the aim of celebrating and even recapturing some of the original one's intellectual brilliance.

Shortly after its foundation Alexandria became an important centre of learning due to the initiatives of the Ptolemies, the kings of Egypt. Moreover it was what we would now call a multicultural city, including a great number of Jewish inhabitants. The exegete and philosopher Philo (ca. 15 BC – ca. 45 AD) held a prominent place in this Jewish community. The vast majority of his writings offer allegorical exegesis of the five books of Moses in the Hebrew Bible or Old Testament, the so-called Pentateuch.[2] For this reason Philo should be regarded first and foremost as an exegete of Scripture.[3] He based his exegesis on the Septuagint (LXX), the Greek translation of the Hebrew Bible, made in Alexandria.[4]

The figure of Moses was for Philo, as a Jewish believer, of vital importance, and he devoted a separate treatise to Moses' life, *De vita Moysis* (*Mos.*). In this work he describes Moses' life under the four headings of Moses as king, legislator, high priest, and prophet. Dealing with Moses as leader in the exodus from Egypt, he gives an encomium on Moses (*Mos.* 1.148-162), in which he writes that Moses has set himself and his life as an example for those who wish to imitate it (1.158).

Philo's thought and allegorical interpretation of the Bible had an enormous impact on the writers of the early Church. Philo's influence on

---

[1] See, for instance, *NRC/Handelsblad, Cultureel Supplement*, 12-6-98, 1; 11-6-99, 1; 22-10-99, 7.

[2] For Philo's life and works, see the introductions of Sandmel (1979), Id. (1984), Borgen (1984b), Morris (1984), Williamson (1989); Borgen (1984a) gives a survey of Philonic research after 1945. Runia (1986) 5-20 gives a short history of Philonic scholarship. Borgen (1997) 1-13 offers an overview of different views on Philo. Bibliography up to 1937 is given by Goodhart-Goodenough (1938). Radice-Runia (1988) offers an annotated bibliography for the period 1937-1986. Runia (2000) covers the period 1987-1996. Supplements to the Radice-Runia bibliography appear regularly in *SPhA*.

[3] Representatives of this approach are V. Nikiprowetzky, P. Borgen, and D.T. Runia. See especially Nikiprowetzky (1977).

[4] For the LXX, see Schürer-Vermes (1973-87) 3.1.474-480, Tov (1987).

the early Church fathers has been thoroughly investigated by D.T. Runia in his study *Philo in Early Christian Literature,* published in 1993. Philo's influence began with Clement of Alexandria and, via Origen and his pupil Gregory Thaumaturgus, reached the region of Cappadocia in Asia Minor. Like Philo, the Cappadocian theologian and philosopher Gregory of Nyssa wrote a treatise on Moses' life, *De vita Moysis* (*VM*), in which he presents Moses as an example of the virtuous life. In the first book he narrates Moses' life, basing himself on the scriptural account, while in the second book he explains it in an allegorical way. Although this treatise bears nearly the same title as Philo's work, there are important differences between the two treatises. The second part of Gregory's *VM* offers many allegorical interpretations, whereas in Philo's *Mos.* allegorical exegesis is virtually absent. Gregory's *VM* is written for an audience consisting of monks, whereas Philo wrote his *Mos.* for gentile readers who are interested in Judaism. Despite these differences Gregory makes use of the writings of Philo, not only of *Mos.*, but also of other Philonic works. References to the Jewish author are routinely offered in modern editions of Gregory's treatise, but a detailed examination of the links between that work and Philo's writings has not been attempted until now.

The aim of the present study is to offer such a detailed examination and compare Gregory's *VM* with Philo's *Mos.* and other writings. Philo's treatise on Moses is the focus of attention in Part I of our study. Its place in the Philonic corpus, its goal, and its readership are all matters of dispute. In nearly all editions it is placed between *De Iosepho* and *De decalogo*, as part of the so-called Exposition of the Law. The Exposition is a series of writings that gives a systematic presentation of the Mosaic legislation. In these writings Philo alternates literal exposition with allegorical interpretations.[5] There are, however, good reasons to assume that this placement is incorrect, and that *Mos.* does not belong to the Exposition of the Law. It can be argued that *Mos.* has significant points of contact with the genre of philosophical introductory *bioi.* Such a *bios* gives a sketch of the philosopher's life and an overview of his writings. It functions as a first introduction to the philosopher in question.[6] We think that a comparison of Philo's *Mos.* with this genre can be useful for a better understanding of its purpose. When we have elucidated the aim and goal of Philo's *Mos.* we will be in a better position to compare it with Gregory's *VM*.

Part II focuses on Gregory and his *De vita Moysis.* For our subject it is important to know more about Gregory's knowledge of Philo and

---

[5] See Morris (1987) 840.
[6] See Mansfeld (1994) 6.

therefore we begin by discussing Philo's influence in several writings of Gregory. Because Philo himself was a convinced Jew — and Gregory was aware of this fact — we research Gregory's general attitude towards Judaism. Part II ends with a discussion of some general aspects of *VM*, such as its contents and aim.

In Part III — the real heart of our study — we will examine how and why Gregory makes use of Philo. It is our aim to offer answers to the following questions:

— What is the relationship between Gregory's *VM* and Philo's writings and especially his treatise on Moses? Which treatises of Philo have special significance for Gregory? Does Gregory make use of all Philo's writings?

— In what ways does Gregory borrow from Philo? Does he, for instance, quote Philo *verbatim*, or does he only make allusions that are hardly recognizable as Philonic?

— For which exegetical themes does Gregory employ Philo's writings? Does he take over Philonic exegesis without making alterations, or does he make adaptations in order to use Philo's material for his own purposes? In order to answer these questions we make an analysis of Gregory's *VM* in which we research Philonic exegesis that is employed by Gregory. Our method of research is set out at the beginning of Part III. We conclude with a summation concerning Gregory's use of Philo and his working method.

PART ONE

THE PLACE OF PHILO'S *DE VITA MOYSIS* WITHIN HIS ŒUVRE

INTRODUCTION

The Jewish exegete and philosopher Philo of Alexandria was a very prolific author, and the large number of his surviving writings is usually divided into three main groups:[1]

(a) The exegetical works, which are subdivided into the following three series:

(1) The so-called Allegorical Commentary, in which Philo gives an allegorical explanation of Genesis in the form of a running commentary on the biblical text. This series consists of *Leg.* 1-3, *Cher.*, *Sacr.*, *Det.*, *Post.*, *Gig.*, *Deus*, *Agr.*, *Plant.*, *Ebr.*, *Sobr.*, *Conf.*, *Migr.*, *Her.*, *Congr.*, *Fug.*, *Mut.*, *Somn.* 1-2.

(2) The so-called Exposition of the Law,[2] in which Philo mainly uses literal exposition, but offers allegorical exegesis as well. It is formed by the following works: *Opif.*, *Abr.*, *Ios.*, [*Mos.* 1-2], *Decal.*, *Spec.* 1-4, *Virt.*, *Praem.*[3]

(3) *The Questions and Answers on Genesis and Exodus*, in which a literal exposition parallels an allegorical exegesis.

(b) The philosophical treatises, in which there are hardly any biblical references: *Prob.*, *Aet.*, *Prov.*, *Anim.*

(c) The historical-apologetic treatises, which describe contemporary issues and events concerning the Jewish community in Alexandria: *Contempl.*, *Flacc.*, *Legat.*, *Hypoth.*

In nearly all editions *Mos.* is placed between *Ios.* and *Decal.* as part of the Exposition, but, as we have already remarked in the introduction, there are good reasons to assume that this place is not correct. Before we look in more detail at the order of Philo's writings and especially at the place of *Mos.*, we deal with two preliminary issues concerning the treatise, namely the presentation of Moses, and its contents.

---

[1] Massebieau (1889), Cohn (1899), Schürer (1909) 644-687, Borgen (1984a) 117-121, Morris (1987) 826-854. Nikiprowetzky (1977) 202 regards the Allegory and the Exposition as one grand commentary.

[2] The term 'Exposition of the Law' is not used by Philo. To my knowledge it was used for the first time by Massebieau (1889) 33. Schürer calls the Exposition 'eine systematische Darstellung der mosaischen Gesetzgebung' (1909) 659.

[3] For the placing of *Opif.* in the Exposition, see Terian (1997).

Philo's treatise on Moses' life consists of two books: in the first book Philo narrates Moses' life in chronological order, describing him as a philosopher-king; the second book deals with Moses in his qualities as legislator, high priest, and prophet. Philo explains these four offices at the beginning of book 2.[4] He refers with an anonymous reference ('some say.') to Plato who said that states can only make progress in well-being if either kings are philosophers or philosophers are kings (*Rep.* 473D). Moses, however, possessed not only these two faculties, but also three others (*Mos.* 2.2). Through God's providence he became king, lawgiver, high priest and prophet. Next Philo explains why these four functions are combined in the same person (4). He states that it is the task of a king to command what should be done and to forbid what not should be done.[5] To command and to forbid is the duty of the law, so that the king is a living law, and the law a just king.[6] Philo proceeds to say that it behoves a king and lawgiver to oversee not only human, but also divine affairs. Because the affairs of kings and subjects cannot flourish without God's directing care, the king needs to become high priest, so that he may request averting of evil and participation in good for himself and his subjects from him who is gracious (5). Because many human and divine things are unclear for the king, lawgiver, and high priest, Moses necessarily obtained prophecy as well, in order that through God's providence he might discover what by reasoning he could not grasp (6). The union of these faculties is beautiful. Intertwined and clinging to each other, they imitate the virgin Graces, whom an immutable law of nature forbids to be separated. One may justly say of them what is often said of the virtues, that to have one is to have all (7).[7]

It may be asked what the background of these four functions is. The American scholar H.A. Wolfson points to some scriptural verses and post-biblical Palestinian literature.[8] Moses is called prophet in Deut. 34:10, king in Deut. 33:5, priest in Ps. 98:6, and Deut 33:4 speaks about the law which

---

[4]   The same treatment of the four offices is found in *Praem.* 53-56, see I § 4.

[5]   The distinction between commanding and forbidding is Stoic (SVF 2.1003, 3.314, 613, 614). This notion also in *Mos.* 2.46, 49, 187, *Leg.* 1.93, *Deus* 53, *Migr.* 130, *Congr.* 120, *Fug.* 95, *Ios.* 29, *Spec.* 1.299, *Praem.* 55.

[6]   Moses is also called living law at 1.162. The notion of the king as living law occurs in Pythagorean fragments on kingship from the Hellenistic age (Archytas (Stobaeus *Eclogae* 4.1.135), Diotogenes (Ibid. 4.7.61)). For the law as a just king, cf. Plato *Symp.* 196C.

[7]   For this dictum, cf. Plato *Protagoras* 329E, SVF 3.295-304. At *Abr.* 52-54 Philo refers to the three Graces, with whom he compares the three virtues of Abraham, Isaac, and Jacob. Because there are three Graces, Wolfson suggests that lawgiver and king are two phases of the same function, (1947) 2.17.

[8]   Wolfson (1947) 2.16-17.

Moses commanded.[9] Wolfson concludes that Philo, presenting Moses as king, lawgiver, high priest, and prophet, has 'native Jewish views in mind, fortified undoubtedly also by Greek conceptions as to relation of priesthood to kingship'.[10] The references to scriptural verses are, however, not very convincing. The Hebrew text of Deut. 33:5 uses the word *melek*, which is rendered in the LXX as ἄρχων, not as βασιλεύς. Furthermore, in *Mos.* Philo never refers explicitly to these verses. It can be more convincingly argued that Philo derives Moses' four functions from Greek philosophy, and in particular from views held by the Stoic school. He portrays the Jewish leader with the characteristics of a Stoic sage (σοφός), who is σπουδαῖος and τελεῖος (*Leg.* 2.91, 3.100, *Sacr.* 9, *Post.* 28, 169, *Mos.* 1.1,157 etc.).[11] Philo refers to Moses with the Stoic term ἀστεῖος, which is applied to Moses in Ex. 2:2 (*Conf.* 106, *Her.* 19, *Congr.* 132, *Somn.* 2.227, 230, *Mos.* 1.9).[12] Like a perfect Stoic, Moses bridles the passions, practising self-restraint and self-control (*Mos.* 1.25-26, 154). He has one aim: to live according to the right reason of nature (*Mos.* 1.48). In *Leg.* 3.129-137 Philo presents a contrast between Moses and Aaron. Aaron tries to cure the spirited element, but Moses thinks that it is necessary to cut it out of the soul. He is not content with moderation of passions (μετριοπάθεια), but only with complete absence of passions (ἀπάθεια; 129). God gave to the wise man the power of cutting out the passions. The perfect man studies for absence of passions, but Aaron, who makes gradual progress (προκόπτων), practises moderation of passions, and he is not able to cut out the breast and the spirited element (3.131-132, cf. 134). Philo even depicts Moses as a super-sage, who surpasses the Stoic sage.[13] Moses is close to the divine mind, and he even has the divine spirit at his side leading him in every right way (*Gig.* 55).

Clement of Alexandria remarks that the Stoics assign kingship, priesthood, prophecy, legislation, richness, true beauty, noble birth, and freedom to the wise man alone (*Strom.* 2.19.4 = SVF 3.619).[14] It is very striking that the first four features are exactly the offices that Philo ascribes to Moses, the most wise man. The first four characteristics differ from the last,

---

[9] Deut 34.10 καὶ οὐκ ἀνέστη ἔτι προφήτης ἐν Ισραηλ ὡς Μωυσῆς.
Deut. 33:5 καὶ ἔσται ἐν τῷ ἠγαπημένῳ ἄρχων συναχθέντων ἀρχόντων λαῶν.
Ps. 98:6 Μωυσῆς καὶ Ααρων ἐν τοῖς ἱερεῦσιν αὐτοῦ.
Deut. 33:4 νόμον, ὃν ἐντείλατο ἡμῖν Μωυσῆς.
[10] Wolfson (1947) 2.16.
[11] See the references in Earp PLCL 10.387-389, SVF 4 s.v. σοφός.
[12] See SVF 4 s.v. ἀστεῖος.
[13] Winston (1995).
[14] SVF 3.619 Τούτοις ἀκόλουθα οἱ Στωϊκοὶ φιλόσοφοι δογματίζουσιν, βασιλείαν, ἱερωσύνην, προφητείαν, νομοθητικήν, πλοῦτον, κάλλος ἀληθινόν, εὐγένειαν, ἐλευθερίαν μόνῳ προσάπτοντες τῷ σοφῷ.

because they are functions that can be performed. Therefore, Philo can attribute them to Moses. These offices are also ascribed to the wise man in other Stoic fragments. Chrysippus says that wise men are kings, and kingship is a rule without responsibility, which can only be maintained by the wise (SVF 3.617).[15] Philo himself is familiar with this Stoic view, as appears from passages where he states that the wise man is a king (*Migr.* 197, *Mut.* 152). According to the Stoics the wise man is also a priest, because he has knowledge of the service of God (SVF 3.544, 604).[16] Proclus reports the Stoic view that only the wise man is a king and ruler, and that all things which belong to the wise man belong also to the gods, for 'what belongs to friends is common' (SVF 3.618).[17] The proverb 'what belongs to friends is common' is also referred to by Philo, who applies it to Moses because he is called 'friend of God' (*Mos.* 1.156; Ex. 33:11). Because Philo is acquainted with Stoic views, we can conclude that he is inspired by Stoic ideas when he presents Moses as king, priest, prophet, and lawgiver.

Moses' four functions determine the structure of the treatise, as appears from the following overview, in which we also indicated the biblical source of Philo's material:

Book I: Moses as philosopher-king

1- 4	Preliminary remarks	
5-7	Moses' descent	
8-17	Moses' birth	Ex. 2:1-10
18-24	Moses' education	
25-31	Moses restrains the passions	
32-39	Moses' return to his own people; the Israelites' labour	Ex. 2:11
40-46	Moses kills an Egyptian	Ex. 2:11-12
47-59	Moses in Midian	Ex. 2:15-21
60-64	Moses as shepherd	Ex. 3:1
65-70	The burning bush	Ex. 3:2
71-84	Moses' calling	Ex. 3:6-4:17
85-90	Moses' actions in Egypt	Ex. 4:10-31
91-95	The wonder of the serpent	Ex. 7:10-13
96-139	The ten plagues (1)	Ex. 7:14-12:30
140-142	The deprivation of the Egyptians	Ex. 11:2-3

---

[15] SVF 3.617 οὐ μόνον δὲ ἐλευθέρους εἶναι τοὺς σοφούς, ἀλλὰ καὶ βασιλέας, τῆς βασιλείας οὔσης ἀρχῆς ἀνυπευθύνου, ἥτις περὶ μόνους ἂν τοὺς σοφοὺς ⟨συ⟩σταίη, καθά φησι Χρύσιππος.

[16] SVF 3.544 καθ' ἅ φασι μόνον καὶ πάντα τὸν σοφὸν εἶναι ἱερέα, τῷ μόνον καὶ πάντα τόν σοφὸν ἐπιστήμην ἔχειν τῆς τοῦ θεοῦ θεραπείας.

[17] SVF 3.618 μόνος ἄρχων ὁ σπουδαῖος, μόνος δυνάστης, μόνος βασιλεύς, μόνος ἡγεμὼν πάντων, μόνος ἐλεύθερος, καὶ ὅτι πάντα τῶν σπουδαίων ἐστίν, ὅσα καὶ τῶν θεῶν· κοινὰ γὰρ τῶν φίλων.

In his retelling of Moses' life Philo bases himself mainly on the biblical account in Exodus and Numbers, but he also reports what he has heard from the elders of the nation (*Mos.* 1.4). Some details and explications given by Philo and not found in the biblical account occur in the Midrash, like the symbolic interpretation of the burning bush (1.67; *Midr. Rab. Ex.* 2.5),[18] the cooperation of the four elements in performing the ten plagues (1.96),[19] and of the palms and springs at Elim (1.189).[20]

---

[18] Kugel (1997) 301-302.
[19] Ginzberg (1909-38) 2.341.
[20] Ginzberg (1909-38) 3.14.

CHAPTER ONE

THE DISCUSSION ON THE PLACE OF *DE VITA MOYSIS*

The aim of this chapter is to report on the scholarly discussion about the place of Philo's *Mos.* within his entire œuvre. It begins with a historical overview, in which the focus of attention is the transmission of the Philonic corpus, and the place of *Mos.* in the medieval manuscripts and in the first printed editions. Attention is also paid to the opinions of the first scholars on Philo until the end of the 19th century, when the critical edition of Philo's writings appeared. Thereafter the internal evidence for the place of *Mos.* is analysed. The question whether *Mos.* is a biography, which is involved in the discussion about its place in the corpus, is also dealt with. The chapter ends with a summary and an evaluation of the discussion.

1. *The Transmission of the Philonic Corpus in the Early Church*

The first Christian writer who was demonstrably acquainted with Philo's writings was Clement of Alexandria (ca. 145 - ca. 220), a member of the catechetical school in Alexandria.[1] In *Strom.* 1.151-157 he narrates Moses' birth and youth, giving lengthy quotations from Philo's *Mos.*[2] Speaking on Moses' education at Pharaoh's court, he remarks 'as Philo says in his Life of Moses' (1.153.2). Clement uses the Jewish author in his retelling of the biblical account of Moses' life, taking over Moses' role as prophet and legislator, but omitting his function as high priest. Simultaneously he had an apologetic intention, wishing to show that the Mosaic law was older than any other philosophy.[3] Clement also makes use of Philo's symbolic interpretation of the tabernacle, its furnishings, and the high priest's vestments in *Mos.*, reshaping the Philonic interpretation in a Christian sense.[4] It is probable that the library of the catechetical school possessed copies of Philo's writings, and on some occasions, in all likelihood,

---

[1] For Clement's use of Philo, see Van Winden (1978), Van den Hoek (1988), (1990) esp. 232-233, Runia (1993) 132-156, (1995b).

[2] Van den Hoek (1988) 48-68

[3] Van den Hoek (1988) 218.

[4] Van den Hoek (1988) 116-147.

Clement had the copies on his desk.[5] In any case, it is clear that Clement had access to Philo's *Mos.*

A major role in the transmission of the Philonic corpus was played by Origen (185-253), teacher in the catechetical school after Clement.[6] In his allegorical exegesis he makes use of Philonic allegorical interpretation; for the most part he refers to Philo in an anonymous way.[7] Origen was acquainted with Philo's *Mos.* At five places in his writings we find a highly probable borrowing from this work.[8] His use of Philo shows that the Jewish exegete was important for him because of his biblical interpretation and allegorization of the Law.

When Origen moved from Alexandria to Palestinian Caesarea in 233, he took his personal copies of the writings of the Jewish exegete with him, and later on the works obtained a place in the Episcopal Library, which was established by the priest Pamphilus (died 310).[9] This admirer of Origen — he had studied in Alexandria— was eager to preserve Origen's manuscripts and to enlarge the library with valuable and important works. In his task as a librarian he was helped by his pupil Eusebius (ca. 263 - ca. 340), the later bishop of Caesarea. In his *Historia Ecclesiastica* Eusebius presents Philo as a witness to the existence of a Christian community in Alexandria in Philo's days, claiming that the Therapeutae Philo describes in *Contempl.* are early Christians converted to the gospel by Mark (*HE* 2.16-17.2).[10] He also gives a list of Philo's writings, based on the holdings of the Episcopal Library. This list is of particular interest for our subject, the classification and order of Philo's treatises. Eusebius writes as follows (*HE* 2.18):[11]

> He (sc. Philo) first went through the subject of the events in <u>Genesis</u> in connected sequence, in the books which he entitled 'The allegories of the Sacred Laws.' He then made detailed arrangement into chapters of the difficulties in the Scriptures and gave their statement and solution in the books to which he gave the suitable title of 'The problems and solutions in Genesis and in Exodus.' There are, besides this, some specially elaborated treatises of his on certain problems, such as the two books 'On agriculture,' and as many 'On drunkenness,' and others with various appropriate titles,

---

[5] Runia (1993) 134-135. For the controversial question of the library and the catechetical school in Alexandria, see Grant (1986), Van den Hoek (1990), (1997), Sterling (1999a) 160-163.

[6] The transmission of Philo's writings is dealt with by PCW 1.i-iv, Runia (1993) 16-31, id. (1996).

[7] Runia (1993) 157-183, Van den Hoek (2000).

[8] *Ex. hom.* 3.1 (*Mos.* 1.83), 4.3 (*Mos* 1.96-97), 4.6 (*Mos.* 1.108), 9.4 (*Mos.* 2.135), *Num. hom.* 20.1 (*Mos.* 1.294ff.), see Borret (1985) 88 n. 1, 122 n. 1, 134 n. 3, 294 n. 2.

[9] For the library in Caesarea, see Gamble (1995) 155-160.

[10] Runia (1993) 216-221.

[11] Translation Lake (LCL).

such as 'The things which the sober mind desires and execrates,' 'On the confusion of tongues,' 'On flight and discovery,' 'On assembly for instruction,' and 'On the question who is heir of the divine things,' or 'On the distinction between odd and even,' and further 'On the three virtues which Moses describes with others,' in addition to this, 'On those whose names have been changed and why they were,' in which he says that he has also composed Books I. and II. 'On the covenants.' There is also a book of his 'On migration and the wise life of the man initiated into righteousness, or unwritten laws,' and also 'On giants or the immutability of God,' and Books I., II., III., IV., V., 'On the divine origin of dreams according to Moses.' These are the books which have come down to us dealing with Genesis. On Exodus we know Books I., II., III., IV., V. of his 'Problems and solutions,' the book 'On the tabernacle,' and that 'On the Ten Commandments,' and Books I., II., III., IV., 'On the laws specially referring to the principal divisions of the Ten Commandments,' and the book 'On animals for sacrifice and the varieties of sacrifice,' and 'On the rewards fixed in the law for the good and the penalties and curses for the wicked.' In addition to all this there are also some single volumes of his, such as the book 'On providence,' and the treatise composed by him 'On the Jews,' and 'The statesman,' moreover 'Alexander, or that irrational animals have reason.' In addition to this the 'That every wicked man is a slave,' to which is appended the 'That every good man is free.' After these he composed the book 'On the contemplative life, or suppliants,' .

There are many points connected with this list that can be discussed,[12] but we confine ourselves to two remarks. First, Eusebius does not distinguish between what is now called the Exposition of the Law and what is now named the Allegorical Commentary. Further, he does not see the Questions and Answers as a separate genre. Philo's works are partly ordered according to the biblical book they comment on. Eusebius begins with the treatises that deal with Genesis, followed by those on Exodus, and finally some single volumes (see underlinings above). Second, *Mos.* is absent in the list but this fact, as Runia suggests, may be due to oversight.[13] We can assume with certainty that Origen had a copy of this work and that it had a place in the library at Caesarea. Regarding Eusebius' possible acquaintance with Philo's *Mos.* the suggestion of Chesnut is worth noting. He thinks that the Christian historian, comparing emperor Constantine to Moses, was inspired by Philo 'who treated Moses in his Life of Moses as the ideal philosopher ruler of Hellenistic kingship theory'.[14] As a New Moses Constantine freed his people. If this suggestion holds good — and very

---

[12] Runia (1993) 17-21, (1996) 485-489.
[13] Runia (1993) 19.
[14] Chesnut (1986) 162-163. Chesnut's opinion that Eusebius borrowed his theories on kingship directly from Philo is doubted by Runia, but the hypothesis that Philo's *Mos.* was an example for Eusebius is regarded as very plausible by the same scholar, (1993) 221-222.

likely it does — it indicates the importance and influence of Philo's treatise
on Moses' life.

That Philo's *Mos.* was widely known appears also from the fact that the
pagan author Heliodorus gives a nearly literal quotation from this work in
the description of Egypt in his novel *Aethiopica* (9.9.3; Philo *Mos.* 2.195).[15]
We do not know when Heliodorus lived, but most plausibly in the fourth
century. He originates from Emesa in Syria, and we can assume that he
became acquainted with Philo's work via the library in Caesarea.[16] This is
the only case in which it can be proved with certainty that Philo was read
by a pagan author.

A century and a half after Origen's move to Caesarea, the Philonic
manuscripts in the Episcopal Library begin to deteriorate. Therefore,
Euzoius, bishop of Caesarea from about 376 to 379, had copies made on
parchment.[17] Nearly all the medieval manuscripts we possess today derive
from an archetype from the library in Caesarea.[18]

2. *The Medieval Manuscripts*

The Philonic manuscripts show a great variety — or one could say chaos —
in the arrangement of the treatises. In order that the reader may get an
impression of the situation, a few codices are discussed.[19] The Codex
Monacensis graecus 459 (A in PCW, GG no 35) dates from the 13th
century, and contains 38 works of Philo.[20] *Mos.* is placed in the following
context:

> 11. περὶ ἀρῶν (= *Praem.* 127-172)[21]
> 12. περὶ ἀνδρίας (= *Virt.* 1-50)
> 13. - 15. περὶ τοῦ βίου Μωσέως (libri I - III = *Mos.*)[22]

---

[15] Runia (1990) 134-139, Hilhorst (1992), Sterling (1999b) 20-21.

[16] For the work of Heliodorus, see Hägg (1983) 54-73.

[17] PCW 1.iii-iv, Runia (1993) 21-22. In the Codex Vindobonensis Theologicus graecus 29
the statement is found that 'Euzoius the Bishop had new copies made in codices'.

[18] PCW 1.xlix.

[19] Cohn-Wendland divide the codices that they collected for *Mos.* 1 into four classes: (1)
BEMA, (2) KZ, (3) CVO, (4) FGHP; the codices of *Mos.* 2 are divided into three classes:
(1) BEM, (2) VOK, (3) AFGHP (PCW 4.xxix-xxxi).

[20] PCW 1.iv-vii.

[21] In the manuscripts and the editions until Cohn-Wendland *Spec.*, *Virt.* and *Praem.* are
divided into separate treatises with separate titles; see GG 131-136, and the list of abbrevia-
tions of Philo's works.

[22] In the manuscripts *Mos.* is divided into three books, book three beginning at what is
now 2.66. Since the edition of Cohn-Wendland it is printed into two books, based on

16. περὶ τῆς Μωσέως κοσμοποιίας (= *Opif.*)
17. εἰς τὴν (sic) δεκάλογον Μωσέως (= *Decal.*)

Ios. stays in the 23th place and *Abr.* is the last work listed in the codex. A different sequence is seen in the Codex Venetus graecus 40 (H in PCW, GG no 84) from the 14th century.[23] It contains 46 treatises, beginning with *Opif.* and *Decal.* The treatises on Joseph and Abraham are listed in the 10th and 18th place. *Mos.* (no 26-28) is preceded by *Legat.* and followed by *Nob.* The Codex Parisinus graecus 435 (C in PCW, GG no 49), dating from the 11th century, covers the following works:[24]

1. Φίλωνος βίος σοφοῦ τοῦ κατὰ διδασκαλίαν τελειωθέντος ἢ νόμων
   ἀγράφων· ὅ ἐστι περὶ ἀβραάμ (= *Abr.*)
2. Φίλωνος βίος πολιτικοῦ ὅπερ ἐστὶ περὶ ἰωσήφ (= *Ios.*)
3. Φίλωνος περὶ τοῦ βίου μωσέως α' (= *Mos.* 1)
4. περὶ φιλανθρωπίας (= *Virt.* 51-174)
5. περὶ μετανοίας (= *Virt.* 175-186)
6. περὶ εὐγενείας (= *Virt.* 187-227)
7. excerpts from *Mos.* 2 and 3.
8. Φίλωνος ἀρετῶν α' ὅ ἐστι τῆς αὐτοῦ πρεσβείας πρὸς Γάϊον (= *Legat.*)
9. Φίλωνος ἱκέται ἢ περὶ ἀρετῶν δ' (= *Contempl.*)

Our final example is the Codex Vaticano-Palatinus graecus 248 (G in PCW, no 83 in GG), dating from the 14th century, and containing 29 writings of Philo.[25] It begins with *Mos.* 1-3, followed by *Opif.* and *Decal.*, while *Ios.* is no 12, and *Abr.* no 13.[26]

Because nearly every manuscript offers a different sequence of treatises, it is clear that the manuscripts do not provide a sound basis for a classification nor for an order of the Philonic writings.

3. *The First Printed Editions and Scholarship until the End of the 19th Century*

The editio princeps of Philo's œuvre was edited by Adrianus Turnebus (1512-1565), director of the Press Royale in France, and published in Paris

---

Philo's remark in *Virt.* 52 ...δεδήλωται πρότερον ἐν δυσὶ συντάξεσιν, ἃς ἀνέγραψα περὶ τοῦ βίου Μωυσέως. Only two mss. read τρισί, see PCW 4.xxx-xxxi, Wendland (1896) 440 n. 2, Cohn (1899) 416.

23 PCW 1.xi-xiv.
24 PCW 4.i-ii.
25 PCW 4.xxxiv-xxxv.
26 Codex B and E begin with *Mos.* followed by *Fort.* and *Abr.* In V and O *Mos.* 1-3 is followed by *Fort.* and *Ios.* K has the following sequence: *Mos.* 2,3,1, *Ios.*, *Abr.*, *Fort.* In codex M *Abr.* occupies the 8th place, *Mos.* the 18th - 20th place, and *Ios.* the 22nd place.

in 1552.[27] In his edition he divides the writings into four main groups: τὰ κοσμοποιητικά, τὰ ἱστορικά, τὰ νομοθετικά, and τὰ μονοβίβλια. The first three groups are, as Turnebus himself declares in the preface directed to cardinal Charles of Lorraine, derived from Philo's tripartition of the Pentateuch given in *Praem.* 1-3.[28] His division is as follows:

> τὰ κοσμοποιητικά: *Opif., Leg.* 1, 3, *Cher., Sacr., Det., Agr., Plant., Ebr., Sobr., Gig., Deus, Conf.*
> τὰ ἱστορικά: *Abr., Migr., Her., Congr., Fug., Ios., Somn.* 1, *Mos.* 1.2.3,[29] *Hum., Iud., Consti., Fort.*
> τὰ νομοθετικά: *Decal., Mon.* 1. 2, *Merced., Cir., Sac. hon., Vic., Sacrif., Spec.* 2.1-38, *Spec.* 3.1-209, *Praem.*
> τὰ μονοβίβλια: *Prob., Nob., Contempl., Incor., Flacc., Legat.*

Turnebus' criteria for his division are not very clear; the first group of writings covers the events described in Genesis up to the building of the tower of Babel. The historical treatises begin with the story of Abraham. Works that deal with the prescripts of the law are also placed among the historical writings. The French scholar based his edition on three codices, namely Parisinus graecus 433 (L in PCW, GG no 99; related to codex H), 434 (GG no 88), and 435 (GG no 49), which were available at the Royal Library in Fontainebleu.[30] The works that are absent in these codices (*Mut., Leg.* 2, *Somn.* 2) were subsequently edited by the German scholar David Hoeschelius (1556-1617) on the basis of codex A in 1614.[31]

One of the first scholarly accounts of Philo's life and writings was given by the classicist J.A. Fabricius (1668-1736) in his voluminous work *Bibliotheca Graeca*, consisting of twelve volumes. He begins his list of Philo's treatises with the writings dealing with Genesis, among which *Abr.* and *Ios.* Thereafter he mentions the works on Exodus starting with *Mos., QE* and *Decal.* [32]

Nearly two centuries after Turnebus a new text was established by T. Mangey (1688-1755), and printed in London in 1742.[33] This edition

---

27 PCW 1.lxx-lxxii.
28 For *Praem.* 1-3, see below § 4.
29 It is striking that Turnebus printed *Mos.* in three books, while at *Virt.* 52 he read δυσὶ συντάξεσιν.
30 Omont (1889) 162-163.
31 PCW 1.lxxii-lxxiii. Hoeschelius was also editor of the editio princeps of the Greek text of Gregory's *VM* published in Leiden in 1593. Musurillo (1964) xviii and Daniélou (1968) 38 give 1586 as year of publication. The copy in the Library of the University of Leiden dates from 1593, and this edition is listed in Altenburger-Mann (1988) 42.
32 Fabricius (1795) 727-743. The work was first published in 1705-28. The edition from 1795 contains supplementary notes by C.G. Harles.
33 PCW 1.lxxiv-lxxviii.

includes *Post.* and *Spec.* 4, which were absent in the editions of Turnebus and Hoeschelius. Mangey introduces the arrangement of the Philonic writings in which the exegetical treatises are divided into the so-called Allegorical Commentary and the Exposition of the Law, and which is used today in nearly all editions and translations of Philo.[34]

The place of *Mos.* between *Ios.* and *Decal.* given by Mangey was disputed by several scholars, among whom was A.F. Gfrörer (1803-1861). In his monograph entitled *Philo und die jüdisch-alexandrinische Theosophie* (1835) he argues that *Decal.* fits immediately in with *Ios.*, basing himself on the opening section of *Decal.* Further, Moses is not mentioned as a living law at the beginning of *Abr.*[35] He does, however, count *Mos.* among the 'historisirende Abhandlungen', to which *Opif., Abr., Ios., Decal., Spec., Virt.*, and *Praem.* also belong. He refers to *Spec.* 4.135, where Philo remarks that he has spoken earlier of the virtue of piety or holiness. On the basis of this reference Gfrörer concludes that Philo wrote a separate treatise on piety, and he argues that this work can be linked with *Mos.*[36] The treatise on humanity, *Hum.*, can also be connected with *Piet.* and *Mos.* because Philo refers to Moses' humanity at the beginning of *Hum.* (=*Virt.* 51), where humanity is called the sister of piety.[37]

The opinion of Gfrörer is partly shared by Louis Massebieau (1840-1904), who considers *Mos.* the first and the most important work of a short series of writings. In this series *Mos.* is followed by the lost work *Piet.*, and the treatise *Hum.* together with *Paen.* The series ends with *Nob.*[38] Massebieau argues that a work on piety fits in well with *Mos.*, because piety is a virtue common to the high priest and prophet.[39] Just as Philo connects humanity with piety in the description of Abraham's life (*Abr.* 208), so he links these two virtues in the presentation of Moses (*Virt.* 51, 95). Massebieau regards *Piet.* as a work of transition between *Mos.* and *Hum.* Furthermore, there is a point of contact between *Hum.* and *Mos.* in the presentation of Moses' life as a model (*Mos.* 1.158, *Virt.* 51(= *Hum.* 1)). Finally, Massebieau remarks that in *Paen.* Philo urges pagans to convert and to serve the true God, and in *Nob.* he defends the rights of proselytes, upholding the view that εὐγένεια is not based on birth. So the series, beginning with the instruction of the pagans, ends with the defence of

---

[34] Viewing *Nob.* as a separate work, Mangey placed it after *Praem.* In PCW it is printed as the last part of *Virt.*

[35] Gfrörer (1835) 11-12.

[36] See for *Piet.*, Runia (1991) 132-133. Fragments of the work are in Harris (1886) 10-11.

[37] Gfrörer (1835) 18-23, see also Dähne (1833) 1031.

[38] Massebieau (1889) 40. He follows the manuscripts by dividing *Mos.* into three books.

[39] Massebieau refers to the mention of Moses' piety in *Mos.* 2.66, 284.

their rights.[40] Whereas Gfrörer and Massebieau conceive of *Mos.* as being part of a larger series, Emil Schürer (1844-1910) regards *Mos.* as a separate work, but, in his view, it has to be connected with the writings of the Exposition, because in *Mos.* Philo narrates the life of the legislator, and in the treatises of the Exposition the law is explained.[41]

Massebieau's view that the lost *Piet.*, *Hum.*, *Paen.*, and *Nob.* are supplements to *Mos.* was disputed by Paul Wendland (1864-1915). He rightly argues that in the second book of *Mos.* Moses' piety is not the prevailing idea, as Massebieau assumes, and that it is not possible to prove that the lost *Piet.* forms a transition between *Mos.* and *Hum.* Furthermore, *Hum.* should be connected with the works on the laws, because Philo, having discussed proofs of Moses' humanity, proceeds to deal with the prescripts that belong to humanity. Finally, the way Clement of Alexandria extensively quotes from *Hum.*, *Paen.*, and *Nob.* in the second book of the *Stromateis* shows that for him the writings belong together.[42]

Finally, we mention the opinion of Leopold Cohn (1856-1915), who, together with Wendland, was the editor of the critical edition of Philo's writings, and who laid the foundation for the classification that has become customary today. He argues that *Mos.* belongs to the historical-apologetic treatises, together with *Hypoth.* (with *Contempl.* as part of it), *Flacc.*, and *Legat.*[43] The apologetic intention can be seen in the first sentence, in which Philo declares that he wishes to make known Moses' life to those who deserve not to be ignorant of it. Cohn makes the assumption that the occasion for the composing of *Mos.* was the accusation of misanthropy against the Jews.[44] The German scholar does not regard *Mos.* as a part of the Exposition, because there is no reference to treatises of the Exposition in *Mos.* Rather, much of what is told in the Exposition is repeated in *Mos.*[45] In contrast to Schürer, Cohn excludes any relationship between *Mos.* and the Exposition, because *Mos.* is written for educated Greeks, and the Exposition is directed towards a Jewish audience.[46] In his critical edition of Philo's writings he follows, however, the order of Mangey, placing *Mos.* between *Ios.* and *Decal.*[47] He does so for practical

---

[40]   Massebieau (1889) 49-54.
[41]   Schürer (1909) 674-675.
[42]   Wendland (1896) 438-456.
[43]   Cohn (1899) 31-40, PCH 1.7.
[44]   PCH 1.217-219.
[45]   He does not give examples, but he may be thinking of the story of the Flood (*Mos.* 2.59-65, *Abr.* 40-46, *Praem.* 22-23), the story of the golden calf (*Mos.* 2.161-173, 270-274, *Spec.* 1.79, 3.125-7), or the rebellion of Korah (*Mos.* 2.275-287, *Praem.* 74-78).
[46]   Cohn (1899) 33.
[47]   PCW 4.xxix.

reasons, as he himself explains.[48] In the German translation, published in 1909, the treatises of the Exposition, including *Opif.* and *Mos.*, precede the Allegorical Commentary.[49]

4. *Internal Evidence*

After the historical survey in the previous section, it is high time to have a closer look at Philo's texts on which the scholars base their views on the place of *Mos.* As appears from the previous section, an important role in the discussion is played by the opening passages of the treatises that form the Exposition. In the beginning of *Abr.* Philo, having discussed the title of the first book of the Pentateuch, Genesis, continues:

[2] ὃν μὲν οὖν τρόπον ἡ κοσμοποιία διατέτακται, διὰ τῆς προτέρας συντάξεως,[50] ὡς οἷόν τε ἦν, ἠκριβώσαμεν. [3] ἐπεὶ δὲ τοὺς νόμους κατὰ τὸ ἑξῆς ⟨καὶ⟩ ἀκόλουθον ἀναγκαῖον διερευνᾶσθαι, τῶν ἐπὶ μέρους καὶ ὡς ἂν εἰκόνων ὑπέρθεσιν ποιησάμενοι τοὺς καθολικωτέρους καὶ ὡς ἂν ἀρχετύπους προτέρους διερευνήσωμεν. [4] οὗτοι δέ εἰσιν ἀνδρῶν οἱ ἀνεπιλήπτως καὶ καλῶς βιώσαντες ... [5] οἱ γὰρ ἔμψυχοι καὶ λογικοὶ νόμοι ἄνδρες ἐκεῖνοι γεγόνασιν, οὓς δυοῖν χάριν ἐσέμνυεν·[51]

In what follows he sketches the lives of the three men Enos (7-16), Enoch (17-26), and Noah (27-46), who represent hope, repentance, and justice respectively. He then introduces a second triad consisting of Abraham, Isaac, and Jacob, after which he discusses the life of Abraham in the rest of the treatise. In addition to a literal account, he gives an allegorical explanation of the events in Abraham's life. The two triads of men are presented as living laws and types of soul (4, 47, 52). Abraham, Isaac, and Jacob are examples of men who gained perfect virtue through teaching, nature and practice respectively.

At the beginning of the next treatise, *Ios.*, Philo refers to these men and announces that he will describe a fourth life, that of the statesman:

---

48 PCH 1.vi.

49 PCH 1.

50 I.e. *Opif.*; cf. Nikiprowetzky (1977) 197, Morris (1987) 844-845, Terian (1997).

51 *Abr.* 1.2-5 'The story of the order in which the world was made has been set forth in detail by us as well as was possible in the preceding treatise; but, since it is necessary to carry out our examination of the law in regular sequence, let us postpone consideration of particular laws, which are, so to speak, copies, and examine first those which are more general and may be called the originals of those copies. These are such men as lived good and blameless lives...for in these men we have laws endowed with life and reason, and Moses extolled them for two reasons.' (translation Colson).

[1] Τρεῖς μέν εἰσιν ἰδέαι, δι' ὧν τὸ ἄριστον τέλος, μάθησις, φύσις, ἄσκησις,
τρεῖς δὲ καὶ σοφῶν οἱ πρεσβύτατοι κατὰ Μωυσῆν ἐπώνυμοι τούτων· ὧν τοὺς
βίους ἀναγεγραφώς, τόν τε ἐκ διδασκαλίας καὶ τὸν αὐτομαθῆ καὶ τὸν
ἀσκητικόν, τέταρτον κατὰ τὸ ἑξῆς ἀναγράψω τὸν πολιτικόν. [52]

It is striking that together with the first triad the total number of men
described is seven, which is a most holy number for Philo.[53] Joseph is a
symbol of the sage who is involved in political matters. The lives of Isaac
and Jacob must have been lost early, since they are not mentioned by
Eusebius in his catalogue of Philonic writings (*HE* 2.18).[54]

In contrast to the beginnings of *Abr.* and *Ios.*, Philo does not refer to
previous treatises or announce following writings in the opening section of
Mos. Nor are there references to the other treatises of the Exposition in
Mos. He opens this work as follows:

[1] Μωυσέως τοῦ κατὰ μέν τινας νομοθέτου τῶν Ἰουδαίων, κατὰ δέ τινας
ἑρμηνέως νόμων ἱερῶν, τὸν βίον ἀναγράψαι διενοήθην, ἀνδρὸς τὰ πάντα
μεγίστου καὶ τελειοτάτου, καὶ γνώριμον τοῖς ἀξίοις μὴ ἀγνοεῖν αὐτὸν
ἀποφῆναι.[55]

The opening section of *Decal.*, in which Philo refers to the lives of wise
men he has described, links well up with *Ios.* and *Abr.*:

[1] Τοὺς βίους τῶν κατὰ Μωυσέα σοφῶν ἀνδρῶν, οὓς ἀρχηγέτας τοῦ ἡμετέρου
ἔθνους καὶ νόμους ἀγράφους αἱ ἱεραὶ βίβλοι δηλοῦσιν, ἐν ταῖς προτέραις
συντάξεσι μεμηνυκὼς κατὰ τὰ ἀκόλουθα ἑξῆς τῶν ἀναγραφέντων νόμων τὰς
ἰδέας ἀκριβώσω....[56]

At the beginnings of the four parts of *Spec.*, Philo points to the previous
treatises as well.[57] In the opening lines of *Virt.* he refers to the previous

---

[52] *Ios.* 1. 'The factors which produce consummate excellence are three in number:
learning, nature, practice. And these names are represented in three of the wise men to
whom Moses gives the senior place. Since I have described the lives of these three, the life
which results from teaching, the life of the self-taught and the life of practice, I will carry
on the series by describing a fourth life, that of the statesman.' (translation Colson).
[53] Cohn (1899) 24.
[54] Cohn (1899) 25, Morris (1987) 847.
[55] *Mos.* 1.1 'I purpose to write the life of Moses, whom some describe as the legislator of
the Jews, others as the interpreter of the Holy Law. I hope to bring the story of this
greatest and most perfect of men to the knowledge of such as deserve not to remain in
ignorance of it.' (translation Colson).
[56] *Decal.* 1 'Having related in the preceding treatises the lives of those whom Moses
judged to be men of wisdom, who are set before us in the Sacred Books as founders of our
nation and in themselves unwritten laws, I shall now proceed in due course to give full
descriptions of the written laws.' (translation Colson).
[57] *Spec.* 1.1 διὰ τῆς προτέρας συντάξεως, 2.1 ἐν τῇ πρὸ ταύτης συντάξει, 3. 7 ἔπει δὲ τῶν

discussion of the virtue of justice (cf. 22), and in § 3 of the last work of the Exposition, *Praem.*, a reference is found to the discussion of virtues in the preceding treatises.

From this overview of the opening sections of the treatises belonging to the Exposition of the Law, it appears that at the beginnings of *Abr.* and *Ios.* Philo does not refer explicitly to a life of Moses. In the opening section of *Mos.* he does not mention the lives of the patriarchs and Joseph or refer to following treatises.[58] As Gfrörer saw, the first sentence of *Decal.* links up very well with *Abr.* and *Ios.*, but not with *Mos.*[59] It also seems rather odd that Moses the lawgiver should himself be included in the men who are living laws according to Moses.[60] The French scholar V. Nikiprowetzky, who vigorously maintains that *Mos.* is part of the Exposition, argues against this view that Philo refers twice to Moses as νόμος ἔμψυχος (*Mos.* 1.162, 2.4) and that it is not impossible to think that the expression τοὺς βίους τῶν κατὰ Μωυσέα σοφῶν ἀνδρῶν includes Moses.[61] He regards the first two sections of *Mos.* as a transition between *Ios.* and *Decal.* Philo there finishes the treatment of the living and unwritten laws and before dealing with the written law he wants to describe the life of the lawgiver himself.[62]

Besides the opening sections, a few other passages have to be examined. First, *Mos.* 2.46-47, where Philo gives a division of the sacred books of Moses. He writes:

[46] τούτων τοίνυν τὸ μέν ἐστιν ἱστορικὸν μέρος, τὸ δὲ περὶ τὰς προστάξεις καὶ ἀπαγορεύσεις, ὑπὲρ οὗ δεύτερον λέξομεν τὸ πρότερον τῇ τάξει πρότερον ἀκριβώσαντες. [47] ἔστιν οὖν τοῦ ἱστορικοῦ τὸ μὲν περὶ τῆς τοῦ κόσμου γενέσεως, τὸ δὲ γενεαλογικόν, τοῦ δὲ γενεαλογικοῦ τὸ μὲν περὶ κολάσεως ἀσεβῶν, τὸ δ' αὖ περὶ τιμῆς δικαίων.[63]

In the following sections he explains why Moses commences his legislation with the genesis of the universe (2.47-51), and then he retells the

---

δέκα λογίων (. .) πέντε μὲν εἴρηται, 4.1 λέλεκται πρότερον.
[58] Morris (1987) 847 n. 137, 854-855, Colson PLCL 6.xiv.
[59] See also Botte (1954) 57.
[60] Colson PLCL 6.xvi n. a, Morris (1987) 855.
[61] Nikiprowetzky (1977) 195, see also Colson PLCL 6.xvi.
[62] Nikiprowetzky (1977) 220 n. 177.
[63] *Mos.* 2.46 'They (= the sacred books) consist of two parts: one the historical, the other concerned with commands and prohibitions, and of this we will speak later, after first treating fully what comes first in order. [47] One division of the historical side deals with the creation of the world, the other with particular persons, and this last partly with the punishments of the impious, partly with the honouring of the just.' (translation Colson). Regarding the term γενεαλογικόν Colson remarks that it is used in the grammatical schools. It concerns that part of history or literature that deals with persons, PLCL 6.606.

punishments for the wicked and the rewards for the just as recorded in the historical part (52-65).[64] It seems that Philo does not keep his promise to treat the legislative part fully in *Mos.*, and for this reason a lacuna is assumed, in which Philo would have discussed it.[65] The lacuna has to be placed after 2.65, where book two ends in the manuscripts. In a separate article devoted to *Mos.* and the Exposition, E.R. Goodenough observes that the division of the Pentateuch in *Mos.* 46-47 is 'exactly the plan of the Exposition — in substance, purpose, and method'.[66] The first treatises deal with the historical part, whereas the law and the special prescripts are treated in the writings after *Mos.* and there Philo fulfils his promise to discuss the legislation. In the lacuna Philo would have referred to a companion document, namely the Exposition. Goodenough concludes that *Mos.* is a treatise independent of the Exposition, but *Mos.* can be connected with the Exposition.[67] The two works are companion pieces, 'like Luke's gospel and the Acts, in which the earlier work was independent, yet is assumed in the later work to have been read.'[68] *Mos.* and the writings of the Exposition are intended for gentile readers who are interested in Judaism. The treatises do not suppose familiarity with Scripture. The gentile reader with sympathy for the Jews should first read *Mos.*, and thereafter, having become more interested in Judaism, the writings of the Exposition.[69] So, Goodenough considers *Mos.* as an introductory work that should be read before studying the other writings of Philo.

Nearly the same division of the books of Moses is given in *Praem.* 1-3, where Philo writes that the oracles of Moses are of three kinds. The first kind deals with the creation of the world, the second with history, and the third with legislation. The story of the creation of the world begins with the genesis of heaven, and ends with the framing of man. The historical part describes good and bad lives, and rewards and punishments. The legislative section is divided into two parts: one covers the Ten Commandments, the other the specific laws (1-2). In the following Philo goes on to discuss the rewards assigned to individual persons, starting with a triad of men, consisting of Enos, Enoch, and Noah.[70] Enos, representing hope, obtains the name 'man' as a reward (14). A new home and a life of solitude are the

---

[64] Morris (1987) 845 n. 134.
[65] Massebieau (1889) 47, Cohn (1899) 416, PCW 4.xxxi, see also Colson PLCL 6.606-607.
[66] Goodenough (1933) 112.
[67] Goodenough (1933) 112-113, see also Sandmel (1979) 49, Morris (1987) 855.
[68] Goodenough (1933) 110.
[69] Gooudenough (1933) 124-125.
[70] The same triad is treated in *Abr.* 7-46.

prizes for Enoch, symbol of repentance (15-21). Noah, attaining to justice, receives two rewards: he was saved from the deluge, and was made the founder of a new generation (22-23). Next Philo discusses a second triad, made up of Abraham, Isaac, and Jacob. Abraham, who acquired virtue by teaching, is rewarded with faith in God (28-30). Abraham's son, Isaac, the self-thaught, receives life-long joy as reward (31-35), and the man of practice, Jacob, obtains the highest prize, the vision of God (36-48).

Having set out two triads of men, Philo devotes a few sections to Moses (52-56), who was the winner of the crown in the sacred games. He possessed the virtue of piety in a high degree (53). In addition to this he was king, lawgiver, prophet, and high priest (54-56). These four offices were found and embodied in the same person. He who falls short in any of the four is unsuited for rule. It is important to note that the two triads together with Moses form a total of seven persons, just as the two triads in *Abr.* with Joseph are seven men. Having dealt with the offices of Moses, Philo discusses the prizes for whole households and families (57-60).

In this part of *Praem.* there are two relevant passages. First, at the beginning of § 52 Philo writes:

> Ἑνὸς ἔτι μνησθεὶς ἀνδρός, στοχαζόμενος τοῦ μὴ μακρηγορεῖν, ἐπὶ τὰ ἀκόλουθα τῶν λόγων τρέψομαι. ὁ δ' ἀνὴρ οὗτος τοὺς ἱεροὺς ἀγῶνας ἐξῆς στεφανωθεὶς ἐκηρύχθη.[71]

Nikiprowetzky sees in this sentence a support for his view that *Mos.* belongs to the Exposition, because Philo himself remarks that Moses' life is connected with the lives of Abraham, Isaac, and Jacob.[72] Second, in § 53 Philo gives a reference to *Mos.*:

> ...ἡ εὐσέβεια, ἣν ἐκληρώσατο διαφερόντως ὁ θεολόγος Μωυσῆς, δι' ἣν μετὰ μυρίων ἄλλων, ἅπερ ἐν τοῖς γραφεῖσι περὶ τοῦ κατ' αὐτὸν βίου μεμήνυται, τεττάρων ἄθλων ἐξαιρέτων τυγχάνει, [τυχὼν] βασιλείας, νομοθεσίας, προφητείας, ἀρχιερωσύνης.[73]

Writing about Moses' four offices, which he received as rewards, Philo refers to *Mos.* This reference does not give us any information about the

---

[71] *Praem.* 52 'One other man I will mention and then, as I wish to avoid prolixity, proceed to the next part of the subject. This man is he who in the sacred contests one after the other was proclaimed the winner of the crown'. (translation Colson).

[72] Nikiprowetzky (1977) 195.

[73] *Praem.* 53 '. . piety, which Moses, the teacher of divine lore, in a special degree had for his own, and through it gained among a multitude of other gifts, which have been described in the treatises dealing with his life, four special rewards, the offices of king, legislator, prophet and high priest. (translation Colson).

place of *Mos.*, and whether it is part of the Exposition or a separate treatise. In the following sections (54-56) Philo gives a treatment of the four functions that can be compared well with the discussion in *Mos.* 2.1-7.[74] Another reference to *Mos.* is found in *Virt.* 52. Philo writes about Moses as follows:

τὰ μὲν οὖν ἐκ πρώτης ἡλικίας ἄχρι γήρως εἰς ἐπιμέλειαν καὶ κηδεμονίαν ἑνὸς ἑκάστου καὶ πάντων ἀνθρώπων πεπραγμένα αὐτῷ δεδήλωται πρότερον ἐν δυσὶ συντάξεσιν, ἃς ἀνέγραψα περὶ τοῦ βίου Μωυσέως.[75]

In what follows Philo describes some achievements of Moses as proof of his humanity, which were not told in *Mos.* (*Virt.* 53-79). From this reference to *Mos.*, Cohn draws the conclusion that it is a work independent of the Exposition.[76] His argumentation does not seem to be very clear, and there are stronger arguments for seeing *Mos.* as a treatise independent of the Exposition. Cohn's view is followed by Goodenough, who adds that Philo could assume that the reader of the Exposition would already have read his work on Moses' life, because in *Virt.* Philo gives 'a supplement to the account of Moses' life in the earlier work.'[77]

Finally, there is a possible reference to *Mos.* in the Allegorical Commentary, namely in *Gig.* 57. Philo here poses the question why Moses died at the same age (namely 120 years) as the men of flesh mentioned in Gen. 6:3 (cf. Deut. 34:7). He remarks:

τὸν δὲ ἀκριβῆ λόγον τῶν εἴκοσι καὶ ἑκατὸν ἐτῶν ὑπεθησόμεθα εἰς τὴν τοῦ προφητικοῦ βίου παντὸς ἐξέτασιν, ὅταν αὐτὸν ἱκανοὶ γενώμεθα μυεῖσθαι, νυνὶ δὲ τὰ ἑξῆς λέγωμεν.[78]

The discussion promised here is not found in *Mos.*, however, and the French commentator A. Mosès thinks that the work Philo refers to was never written.[79] By contrast, Nikiprowetzky, assuming that Philo here does refer to *Mos.*, concludes that *Mos.* was written after *Gig.* and before *Virt.* and *Praem.* He, however, admits that a discussion of the 120 years is not found

---

[74] See the Introduction above.
[75] *Virt.* 52 'Now the actions which he performed from his earliest years to old age for the care and protection of each single man and of them all have been set forth already in two treatises in which I wrote about the life of Moses.' (translation Colson).
[76] Cohn (1899) 417.
[77] Goodenough (1933) 110.
[78] *Gig.* 57 'But the closer discussion of this matter of a hundred and twenty years we will postpone till we inquire into the prophet's life as a whole, when we have become fit to learn its mystery. Now let us speak of the words which follow the text'. (translation Colson).
[79] Mosès (1963) 48 n. 2

in *Mos.*[80] It should be noticed that the sentence 'when we have become fit to learn its mystery' indicates that the promised treatment would have been complicated. This complicated discussion would not have fitted in well with the introductory character of *Mos.* The only thing we can safely say is that Philo does not fulfil his promise in the surviving works.

5. *De Vita Moysis as a Biography*

In an article devoted to Philo's *Mos.*, Bernard Botte calls attention to the difference in contents between *Abr.* and *Ios.* on the one hand and *Mos.* on the other. The first two treatises are not biographies in the strict sense, but an explanation of the Genesis narrative presented as an expression of the unwritten laws. Hence, Philo also describes the lives of Enos, Enoch, and Noah in *Abr.* The full title of *Abr.* runs: βίος σοφοῦ τοῦ κατὰ διδασκαλίαν τελειωθέντος ἢ νόμων ἀγράφων, ὅ ἐστι περὶ ἀβραάμ (The life of the wise man made perfect through teaching or on unwritten laws, that is On Abraham).[81] We find, Botte argues, a different situation in *Mos.*, in which Moses' life itself holds a prominent place, and not the legislation. For this reason *Mos.* is a biography in its literal sense.[82]

Nikiprowetzky rejects Botte's view, pointing to the title of *Mos.* given by Mangey περὶ βίου Μωυσέως ὅπερ ἐστὶ περὶ θεολογίας καὶ προφητείας.[83] This is in accordance with what Philo writes on his forthcoming life of Moses in *Gig.* 57 τὴν τοῦ προφητικοῦ βίου παντὸς ἐξέτασιν. According to Nikiprowetzky this title shows that the life of Moses, being a προφητικὸς βίος, is a counterpart of the life of Joseph, which is a βίος πολιτικός. The prominent role of the law in *Mos.* (in the description of the tabernacle and the Jewish cult) indicates that the work is an integral part of the Exposition. Furthermore, the structure of the treatise, determined by the four offices of Moses, shows that it is a philosophical treatise rather than a biography. This also explains the 'mépris de la chronologie' and the repetition of some stories (e.g., the crossing of the Red Sea, told in 1.176-180 in the context of Moses' kingship, and in 2.247-257 as an example of one of his prophecies). Nikiprowetzky also thinks that the series of the lives is incomplete without the life of Moses.[84]

---

[80] Nikiprowetzky (1977) 216.
[81] PCW 4.xxviii-xxxixi.
[82] Botte (1954) 57, see also Arnaldez-Mondésert *at al.* (1967) 12-13.
[83] The title given in the majority of the manuscripts is περὶ τοῦ βίου Μωυσέως, see Part II. III § 1.
[84] Nikiprowetzky (1977) 196-197, see also Colson PLCL 6.xvi.

6. *Evaluation and Conclusion*

From the foregoing sections a few conclusions can be drawn. As we have seen, the list of Philo's works in Eusebius does not offer a clear basis for classification of the treatises. The medieval manuscripts also do not provide a sound basis for the arrangement of the writings or for the place of *Mos.* The first editor, A. Turnebus, was quite right when he wrote that he found a great σύγχυσις of the writings in the manuscripts. Because the external evidence does not yield results, we have to look to the internal evidence. We have observed that in the opening sections of the treatises of the Exposition, Philo refers to preceding or following treatises, whereas in *Mos.* he does not do so. This can be regarded as a very strong argument in favour of a place of *Mos.* outside the Exposition.

Actually, Nikiprowetzky is virtually the only modern scholar who upholds the place of this treatise within the Exposition between *Ios.* and *Decal.*[85] One of his arguments is based on *Praem.* 53, where Philo links Moses' life with the lives of Abraham, Isaac, and Jacob.[86] It goes, however, too far to conclude from this connection that *Mos.* is part of the Exposition. Furthermore, Joseph is not mentioned here between Jacob and Moses, and the treatise on his life does clearly belong to the Exposition. Nikiprowetzky himself admits this, and he suggests that Philo, writing *Praem.*, had not yet included *Ios.* among the lives.

Regarding the notion of Moses as living law, it can be suggested that there is a difference between the patriarchs as living laws and Moses as embodiment of the law. Moses is twice called living law, at *Mos.* 1.162 and 2.4, and both occurrences are in the context of Moses as king and leader: he is a living law, because he is king. In *Mos* 1.162, at the end of the digression of Moses as leader, Philo writes that Moses, since he was destined to be a legislator by divine providence, earlier became a law endowed with life and reason. As we have seen in the Introduction, at *Mos.* 2.4 Philo states that it is the task of a king to command and to forbid, which is the function of the law. It follows that the king is a living law, and the law a just king. In the case of the patriarchs the living law is not combined with royalty and legislation. They were living laws because they were obedient to the law before it was written down. The patriarchs show that the written law is consistent with the law of nature (*Abr.* 5, 275-276).[87]

---

[85] Colson also defends this place, PLCL 6. xvi.

[86] Nikiprowetzky (1977) 195.

[87] See Martens (1994) 326: 'Yet the 'living law' designation for Patriarchs does not attribute royal exclusivity to them in the same way it does for Moses .(...) Thus (...) Philo creates two levels of *nomoi empsychoi*, those of king and of sage.' I thus disagree with

Another argument that Nikiprowetzky uses is that in *Mos.* the legislation holds a prominent place, and this shows that it is part of the Exposition.[88] Philo does indeed discuss the legislation in *Mos.*, but we should bear in mind that Moses' prophecies, for instance, also play an important role. The attention paid to the legislation is a result of the depiction of Moses as lawgiver.

We have seen that the question whether *Mos.* can be regarded as a biography is also involved in the discussion. According to Momigliano, a biography is 'an account of the life of a man from birth to death'.[89] Philo's *Mos.* match this definiton exactly. Philo himself sees it as a biography, declaring that it is his goal to describe Moses' life (1.1, 4). The title also affirms that it is primarily a biography, and the final sentence says 'such was the life and such was the death of (...) Moses (...)'. Botte is right in arguing that *Mos.* is a biography in the strict sense, in which Moses' life is narrated. *Abr.* and *Ios.* are not primarily meant as biographies, because in these treatises the lives of the patriarchs are presented as types of soul and as unwritten laws (*Abr.* 4, 47, 52). The titles refer also to types of soul.[90] *Abr.* and *Ios.* are not meant as descriptions of the lives of Abraham and Ioseph. Furthermore, *Abr.* is not a biography in the strict sense, because the lives of Enos, Enoch, and Noah are also discussed.

In addition to this point there is another noticeable difference between *Abr.* and *Ios.* on the one hand and *Mos.* on the other. In *Abr.* and *Ios.* a literal narrative and an allegorical interpretation run parallel. For instance, Philo discusses Abraham's migration in *Abr.* 60-67 and explains it allegorically in 68-88. The transition from a literal explanation to allegory is noted explicitly (68, cf. 99, 119, 147, 200, 217, 236). This also applies at least partly to *Ios.*, for up to § 156 the two different kinds of interpretation parallel each other, but from § 156 a literal exposition only is given. This parallelism does not occur in *Mos.*, in which allegorical exegesis is virtually absent.

The most important conclusion we draw is that *Mos.* is a separate treatise and does not belong to the Exposition of the Law. Although more than 100 years ago, Cohn argued that *Mos.* is a work independent of the Exposition, it is placed in the middle of the Exposition in nearly all editions and

---

Richardson (1957), who claims that Moses 'pre-eminently filled the rôle of Νόμος ἔμψυχος', and does not distinguish between the patriarchs and Moses. See for 'unwritten law' in Philo, Heinemann (1927) 149-159.

[88] Nikiprowetzky (1977) 196.

[89] Momigliano (1993) 11.

[90] The full title of *Ios.* is βίος πολιτικοῦ ὅπερ ἐστὶ περὶ Ἰωσήφ (The life of the statesman, that is On Joseph), see PCW 4.xxix. For the title of *Abr.*, see above § 5.

translations; a place where it does not belong. Fortunately, the recent translation of the Philonic corpus in modern Hebrew is an exception: volume two (Exposition of the Law, part one) contains: *Opif.*, *Abr.*, *Ios.*, and *Spec.* 1.[91]

---

91 See Satran (1995).

CHAPTER TWO

THE GENRE OF INTRODUCTORY *BIOI*

From the foregoing chapter it has emerged that there are solid arguments to support the view that *Mos.* is not a part of the Exposition, and that it should be regarded as a separate work. The next question is what kind of work *Mos.* is and what its relationship is with the other Philonic writings. It can well be argued that it has significant points of contact with the genre of philosophical lives, which gives it an introductory function. The aim of Philo's *Mos.* is to introduce the reader to Mosaic philosophy, as written down in the Pentateuch and explained by Philo. Because of its introductory character the *Life of Moses* should be read before studying Philo's other treatises. The genre of philosophical βίοι is related to the so-called *schema isagogicum* found in Late Neoplatonic commentators on Aristotle, like Olympiodorus, Philoponus, and David.[1] This schema, which has been thoroughly investigated by the Dutch scholar J. Mansfeld, consists in a set of preliminary questions that are discussed at the beginning of the commentary, such as the theme of the work, its position in the corpus, its utility, and its authenticity. The life of the philosopher is also narrated. Such a *bios* has an introductory function, and treats preliminary issues concerning the author. It should be read before studying the writings of the author himself, and hence it was often placed at the beginning of an edition of his writings, but it could circulate separately as well.[2]

A study which is highly relevant to our hypothesis concerning Philo's *Mos.* is the monograph by Richard Burridge on the genre of the gospels. He argues that the gospels show a great resemblance to the genre of *bioi*, and that they can in fact be regarded as *bioi*.[3] The genre of *bioi* can be divided into several subgenres, like political βίοι, literary βίοι, βίοι of philosophers and so forth. The gospels bear a similarity to the subgenre of religious or philosophical βίοι.[4] In his argumentation Burridge discusses five examples of early Graeco-Roman *bioi*, among which Philo's *Mos.* is included. The other examples are: Isocrates' *Evagoras*, Xenophon's *Agesilaos*,

---

[1] For the *schema isagogicum*, see Mansfeld (1994).
[2] Mansfeld (1994) 6, Saffrey (1992) 32.
[3] Burridge (1992) 242-243.
[4] Burridge (1992) 247.

Satyrus' *Euripides*, and Nepos' *Atticus*.[5] On the basis of these examples he presents generic features of *bioi*, divided into (1) opening features, (2) subject, (3) external features, (4) internal features. The title, containing the subject's name, and the preface belong to the opening features. With regard to the subject, the *bioi* concentrate on the protagonist. External features are that the *bioi* are written in prose narrative, have a chronological structure, and that the writers make use of several sources. Internal features are concerned with the setting and the topics that are discussed. The aim and purpose of a βίος also belong to the internal features.

1. *Examples of Philosophical bioi*

Our first example is Xenophon's *Agesilaos*, written in about 360 BC.[6] Agesilaos was king of Sparta, not a philosopher, but for Plato and Philo good kings have to be philosophers as well. We should note that Philo presents Moses as a philosopher-king in *Mos.* In the first sentence of the βίος Xenophon states that it is difficult to write an appreciation of Agesilaos that shall be worthy of his virtue and glory. The first topic that he discusses is Agesilaos' ancestry and family (1.2-4). He then narrates the campaigns of the Spartan king (1.6-2.31). A great part of the βίος is devoted to Agesilaos' virtues, like piety, justice, self-control, courage and wisdom (3-10). The king is presented by Xenophon as a man who is perfect in goodness (1.1, 10.1). His virtue is an example to be imitated by those who wish to practice ἀνδραγαθία (10.2). Xenophon narrates the military activities of Agesilaos because 'his deeds will throw the clearest light on his qualities.' (1.6). The emphasis on the moral character of the protagonist and the long discussion of his virtues nearly make the *Agesilaos* a philosophical βίος.

We now turn to what is characteristic of the introductory *bios*, namely the combination of biography with bibliography. It has its provenance in the city of Alexandria.[7] The famous Hellenistic poet Callimachus (c 305-240 BC), who worked at the Library in Alexandria, composed a catalogue of the holdings of the library, in which he combined bibliography with biographical information. This work, the so-called *Pinakes*, was divided into several categories, in which he deals with, for instance, historians, philosophers, epic and lyric poets.[8] The full title was Πίνακες τῶν ἐν πάσῃ

---

[5] Burridge (1992)129-133.
[6] See Momigliano (1993) 50-51.
[7] Mansfeld (1994) 60.
[8] See Regenbogen (1950) 1420-1424, Pfeiffer (1968) 127-133, Fraser (1972) 452-453.

παιδείᾳ διαλαμψάντων καὶ ὧν συνέγραψαν. In addition to this great work Callimachus wrote a special pinax on Democritus: Πίναξ τῶν Δημοκρίτου γλωσσῶν καὶ συνταγμάτων. This research, the results of which were drawn up in the Pinakes, was one of the causes of the development of biography.[9]

Callimachus' pupil Hermippus of Smyrna, who can be connected with the Peripatos, lived in Alexandria around 200, and wrote many βίοι. As appears from the quotations by Diogenes Laertius, he wrote, among other things, about the Seven Sages, Pythagoras, Empedocles, Plato, and Aristotle.[10] The lives can be divided into three main groups: Περὶ νομοθετῶν, Περὶ τῶν ἑπτὰ σοφῶν, Περὶ τῶν ἐν τῇ παιδείᾳ διαλαμψάντων. In composing these lives, he made use of the files of Callimachus. He had a preference for anecdotes, and was especially interested in death scenes.[11] From the overview of the contents of his life on Aristotle, reconstructed by Düring, it appears that it dealt with Aristotle's descent and family, and contained his will and a list of his books.[12] Another Peripatetic biographer was Satyrus, who probably lived in the third century BC in Alexandria.[13] His work, entitled βίων ἀναγραφή, is referred to and quoted by Athenaeus and Diogenes Laertius. In his work he deals with philosophers, tragedians, generals, kings, and orators. The βίοι were epitomized by Heraclidus Lembus during the reign of Ptolemy VI (181-146 BC). Fragments from his life of Euripides, written in dialogue form, were discovered on papyrus in Oxyrhynchus.[14] Like Hermippus, he seems to have been eager to relate anecdotes. Anecdotes can be used to characterize the person.[15] The lives of philosophers written by Hermippus and Satyrus did not have the specific purpose of being introductions to the thoughts of the philosophers in question, but a description of the philosopher's life naturally has a introductory and preliminary function. A modern scholar like W.K.C. Guthrie also deals first with a philosopher's life, date, and writings before discussing the philosopher's thought.

---

[9] Fraser (1972) 453-454, Momigliano (1993) 13.
[10] Diogenes Laertius 1.33, 42, 72, 101, 106, 117, 3.2, 8.1, 51. The fragments are collected in FHG 3.34-50. For Hermippus, see Heibges (1913), Momigliano (1993); Josephus refers to him in *C. Ap.* 1.163-165.
[11] Cf. Diogenes Laertius 2.109, 120, 3.2, 4.44, 9.4, 27, 10.15.
[12] Düring (1957) 464-466. The life of Aristotle was also dealt with by Andronicos in the first century BC in his work *On Aristotle's Writings*, which is characterized by Düring as a 'catalogue raisonné'. Besides a list and discussion of Aristotle's works, it contains a biography, the will, and letters (Düring (1957) 421-425, 467, Regenbogen (1950) 1442-43).
[13] See Momigliano (1993) 80-81.
[14] Hunt (1972).
[15] Burridge (1992) 141.

Thrasyllus (died 36 AD), the astrologer of emperor Tiberius, also came from Alexandria. He wrote an introductory work on Democritus, of which we find traces in Diogenes Laertius.[16] According to this writer Thrasyllus wrote that Democritus was truly versed in philosophy, for he trained himself in physics and ethics, and in mathematics and the general education (ἐγκύκλιοι λόγοι; 9.37). The historian of the philosophers' lives adds that the saying 'word is the shadow of deed' derives from Democritus. Diogenes also remarks that it is clear from his writings what kind of man he was, and he goes on to quote Thrasyllus. 'He (sc. Democritus) seems to be an admirer of the Pythagoreans. He mentions Pythagoras himself, praising him in a work with the same title. He seems to have taken all his views from him and to have been his disciple, if it was not against chronology.' (9.38). Discussing Democritus' year of birth, Diogenes gives the title of Thrasyllus' work *Prolegomena to the reading of the works of Democritus* (Τὰ πρὸ τῆς ἀναγνώσεως τῶν Δημοκρίτου βιβλίων; 9.41). Further, Diogenes reports that Thrasyllus made an ordered catalogue of Democritus' works, arranging them in tetralogies (9.45). From these citations and references it appears that Thrasyllus' *bios* on Democritus dealt with his birth and his education, and that it contained a list of his works.

Thrasyllus was also used as a source by Diogenes Laertius in his account of Plato in 3.48-66.[17] As is evident from 3.1 Thrasyllus dealt with Plato's origin, and Mansfeld remarks that such facts 'belong with a standard part of a biography, viz. the protagonist's origin or *genos*'.[18] The biography was combined with a bibliography (3.47), as in the case of the *bios* on Democritus, since Thrasyllus recorded that Plato published his dialogues in tetralogies, and Thrasyllus himself gave a double title to each of the works. The first tetralogy has a common plan underlying it, for Plato wishes to describe what the life of a philosopher will be (3.56-57).[19] The question of authenticity was also treated (3.57). The works of Thrasyllus on Democritus and Plato were clearly meant to function as an introduction to the study of the works of the philosopher.[20]

---

[16] For Thrasyllus, see Krappe (1927), Dillon (1977) 184-185, Tarrant (1993) 7; for his work on Demetrius, see Regenbogen (1950) 1441-1442, Mansfeld (1994) 97-98. As stated by Porphyry, Thrasyllus wrote about Pythagorean and Platonic principles as well (*Vita Plot.* 20).

[17] Regenbogen (1950) 1441, Tarrant (1993) 19-27, Mansfeld (1994) 59.

[18] Mansfeld (1994) 59.

[19] Mansfeld (1994) 68-69.

[20] Mansfeld (1994) 98, 108. Theon of Smyrna (2nd century AD) wrote a work entitled *Sequence of Reading Plato's Books and the Titles of his Compositions*, which contained a *genos* and a bibliography (see Mansfeld [1994] 59 n. 102, Dillon (1996) 397-399).

Finally, we mention two introductory lives written by pupils on their masters. Arrian (2nd century AD) wrote a *bios* on his Stoic master Epictetus, which is lost, but Simplicius informs us about it. In the beginning of his commentary on the *Enchiridion*, he writes that Arrian, 'who arranged the *Diatribes* of Epictetus in books containing many lines, wrote about the life and death of Epictetus. From him (sc. Arrian) one may learn what sort of man he was to his life.' (translation Mansfeld). This *bios* has a paradigmatic function, and was also combined with an arrangement of the works of Epictetus.[21]

This work by Arrian on his master Epictetus can be well compared to the treatise on Plotinus written by his pupil Porphyry (234-301) and placed before his edition of Plotinus' works as a tool for the study of Plotinus.[22] The *Vita Plotini* should, according to Mansfeld, 'be placed in the same category as the two introductory essays by Thrasyllus'.[23] In the title of this work *On the life of Plotinus and the arrangement of his books* (Περὶ Πλωτίνου βίου καὶ τῆς τάξεως τῶν βιβλίων αὐτοῦ) we find the same combination of the life and the order of the books of the philosopher as in the other *bioi* discussed. This combination is explicitly expressed in c. 24, where Porphyry writes that hitherto he has described Plotinus' life, and will now go on to deal with the arrangement of his books. In the description of Plotinus' life Porphyry treats Plotinus' γένος, remarking that his master could not bear to speak about it (1). He discusses the chronology of the writings (4-6), and their style as well (8). Regarding Plotinus' personality he tells some anecdotes, and describes his manner of delivering his lectures (14-15). Accusations that Plotinus was guilty of plagiarism are also discussed (17).

2. *Features of Philosophical bioi*

Basing ourselves on the studies by Mansfeld and Burridge, we can establish a list of features of philosophical βίοι. As Burridge has shown, the genre has some flexibility with regard to its features.[24]

(1) The βίοι show variety in their titles.[25] In some of them the introductory function is explicitly mentioned (Thrasyllus on Democritus), other titles consist only of the subject's name (Agesilaos). The lives written by Hermippus are simply named βίοι.

---

21 Mansfeld (1994) 109-110.
22 Mansfeld (1994) 108-113.
23 Mansfeld (1994) 109, see also Regenbogen (1950) 1444, Safrey (1992) 31.
24 Burridge (1992) 138.
25 Burridge (1992) 133.

(2) The βίος of a philosopher has an introductory character.[26] This implies that extensive discussions of philosophical issues are absent.

(3) The introductory character entails that a general readership is assumed, they are not only written for philosophical specialists.

(4) The aim of a βίος may be informative: to give information about the life of the philosopher and to provide some introductory remarks about his thought. A βίος may also have an apologetic purpose, i.e. it is intended to defend the ideas of the philosopher.[27]

(5) Standard topics that are discussed are the subject's ancestry, family, birth, death, and funeral.[28] Thrasyllus deals with Plato's origin (D.L. 3.1), and according to Simplicius Arrian wrote about Epictetus' life and death.

(6) The education of a philosopher occupies a prominent place in the description of his life. Thrasyllus writes that Democritus trained himself in the subjects of the general education (D.L. 9.37).

(7) The events are narrated in a chronological sequence, but the sequence can be interrupted by topical material.[29]

(8) The βίος is an encomium on the protagonist. His great deeds are recorded, and his virtues are discussed to show the character of the person.[30] Xenophon, for instance, deals at great length with Agesilaos' virtues.

(9) A βίος shows what kind of person the protagonist was, and that his deeds were in harmony with his words.[31] Arrian's βίος of Epictetus shows what sort of man Epictetus was.

(10) The description of the life has a paradigmatic function: his virtue has to be imitated.[32] Xenophon refers explicitly to the paradigmatic function of Agesilaos (*Age.* 10.2). Arrian's βίος of Epictetus has also a paradigmatic function.

(11) An annotated bibliography is given, combined with a discussion of the order and chronology of the writings. Their authenticity may be also discussed.[33] Callimachus combined biography with bibliographical information; Thrasyllus does the same and discusses the authenticity of some Platonic dialogues (D.L. 3.56-57). Porphyry, too, referring to the arrangement of Plotinus' writings in his title, deals with their chronology.

---

[26] Mansfeld (1994) 98, 108.
[27] Burridge (1992) 149-152.
[28] Burridge (1992) 145-147, Mansfeld (1994) 59.
[29] Burridge (1992) 139-141.
[30] Burridge (1992) 148-149.
[31] Mansfeld (1994) 179-180.
[32] Mansfeld (1994) 9, 110, 183.
[33] Mansfeld (1994) 6.

CHAPTER THREE

PHILO'S *DE VITA MOYSIS* AS AN INTRODUCTORY PHILOSOPHICAL *BIOS*

A short overview of the genre of introductory *bios* of a philosopher was given in the previous chapter, and we ended with a list of features of an introductory philosophical life. Using these features as a basis, we are in a position to formulate the hypothesis that *Mos.* is a philosophical life with an introductory aim. It can be well compared to the βίοι written by Thrasyllus, Arrian, and Porphyry. We have seen that the introductory βίος has its provenance in the city of Alexandria, where Callimachus, Hermippus, and Satyrus were working. Thrasyllus also came from this city, which played an important role in the development of Hellenistic biography. In all likelihood, the Alexandrian Philo was acquainted with the genre of the introductory *bioi* of philosophers. An important observation was made in this regard by Monique Alexandre, when she demonstrated that Philo's writings display formal characteristics typical of pagan genres. Philo's title Νόμων ἱερῶν ἀλληγορίαι, for instance, can be compared with the title given to Heraclitus' work in some manuscripts *Allegories of Homer*.[1] In what follows we apply the characteristics of an introductory philosophical βίος to Philo's *Mos.*

(1) The full title of Philo's treatise is Περὶ τοῦ βίου Μωύσεως. This shows clearly that *Mos.* is meant as a biography.[2] Regarding the title Burridge remarks: 'Philo uses a formula often found in the title of philosophical and other treatises, namely περὶ τοῦ. . ; this may suggest that the *Moses* also has elements of the philosophical treatise about it.'[3] Although there are elements of a philosophical treatise in *Mos.* the title and the opening lines suggest that it is primarily a biography rather than a philosophical treatise.

(2) That *Mos.* has an introductory character appears from the absence of thorough philosophical discussions. Philo never elaborates a philosophical

---

[1] Alexandre (1997) 265.
[2] See I § 5.
[3] Burridge (1992) 133.

idea. As an example we can take the theme of seeing God, which occupies a central place in his thought.[4] He repeatedly discusses this theme in the Allegorical Commentary, in the Exposition of the Law, and in the Questions and Answers, but he does not do so in the treatise on Moses' life. In *Spec.* 1.41-50, for instance, he deals with this notion in commenting on Ex. 33, where Moses' request to God that he manifest himself is recorded.[5] This episode from Moses' life is not narrated in *Mos.*, presumably because the philosophical interpretation does not fit in very well with the introductory character of the treatise. Philo very often connects 'seeing God' with the name of Israel, which he interprets as 'one who sees God' (*Leg.* 2.34, 3.186 etc.).[6] As Birnbaum indicates, Philo most frequently uses the name Israel, combined with the notion of seeing God, in the Allegorical Commentary, but rarely in the Exposition; in *Mos.* it is totally absent. To indicate the Israelites Philo uses Ἰουδαῖος, Ἑβραῖος, or Χαλδαῖος in *Mos.*[7]

The absence of philosophical ideas accords with the almost complete lack of any complicated allegorical exegesis in *Mos.* The words ἀλληγορία or ἀλληγορέω do not occur in it. A symbolic interpretation is, however, found in the following cases: the burning bush (1.67),[8] the springs and trees at Elim (1.189),[9] Moses' hands at the victory over Amalek (1.217),[10] and the nut of Aaron's staff (2.180-183).[11] The discussion of the tabernacle, its furnishings, and of the vestments of the high priest consists largely of symbolic interpretation (2.80-140). These interpretations, however, represent symbolism rather than allegory.[12] We do, however, find examples of allegorical exegesis, namely the interpretation of the Cherubim as God's two powers, and the explanation of the mercy seat of the ark as God's gracious power (2.96, 99).[13]

---

[4] For the idea of seeing God in Philo, see Birnbaum (1995), (1996) 61-90.

[5] See Part III. II § 19.a.

[6] For this etymology, see Birnbaum (1996) 67-77.

[7] See Birnbaum (1995) 45-50. In the Allegorical Commentary the name Israel occurs over seventy times; in the Exposition only twice, namely at *Abr.* 57 and *Praem.* 44, where Philo discusses the figure of Jacob, whose name was altered to Israel. An allusion to the interpretation of the name is found in *Mos.* 2.196, where an Israelite is indicated as τις τῶν ὁρατικοῦ καὶ ἐπιστημονικοῦ γένους. Perhaps it is a slip of the pen. For Philo's use of the title of Chaldaioi, see Wong (1992).

[8] See Part III. II § 6.a.2.

[9] See Part III. II § 14.

[10] See Part III. II § 17.

[11] See Part III. II § 26.

[12] See Arnaldez-Mondésert *et al.* (1967) 13.

[13] *Mos.* 2.99 ἐγὼ δ᾽ ἂν εἴποιμι δηλοῦσθαι δι᾽ ὑπονοιῶν τὰς πρεσβυτάτας καὶ ἀνωτάτω δύο τοῦ ὄντος δυνάμεις. See Part III. II § 18.c.2.

Furthermore, it should be noticed that many events presented in a literal way in *Mos.* are explained in allegorical terms in other treatises, e.g., the crossing of the Red Sea and the destruction of the Egyptian army. In *Mos.* that event is twice described literally, whereas an allegorical exegesis occurs at *Ebr.* 111.[14] In *Mos.* Philo does not translate and interpret biblical names, as he does in other treatises. The name of Amalek, for instance, who is overcome by the Israelites (Ex. 17:8-16), is neither mentioned nor interpreted in the description of the victory (*Mos.* 1.214-219). Philo does translate Amalek as 'a people licking out' and interpret him as passion at *Leg.* 3.186. The absence of philosophical themes and of allegorical exegesis, combined with interpretation of names, is an indication of the introductory character of *Mos.*

In a recent article Sterling deals with the question whether Philo taught in an institutional environment. He argues that the Allegorical Commentary can be placed in a setting of a school, in which the commentaries function as a guide, explaining the difficult text. Sterling draws a comparison with philosophical schools, where students read texts of philosophers with the help of a commentary.[15] It is possible to extend this comparison: just as in philosophical schools the life of the philosopher was read before studying the writings with the help of a commentary, so in Philo's school *Mos.* may have been read before studying the Pentateuch with the help of Philo's commentaries.

(3) The question of the readership of Philo's treatises is a matter of scholarly dispute. One of the first scholars who discussed this issue was M.L. Massebieau, who also made a classification of Philo's writings.[16] He argued that the Exposition has two readerships: the lives of the patriarchs and Joseph are intended for a broad audience, whereas the writings on the laws and prescripts are addressed to Jewish readers. He based his view on a general impression, but also on some remarks in the text. For instance, Philo's expression τοῦ ἡμετέρου ἔθνους (*Decal.* 1) implies that the reader is also Jewish.[17] In contrast to the Exposition, *Mos.* was written for gentiles, who do not know the life of the Jewish legislator.[18]

In his article on the Exposition and *Mos.*, Goodenough offers several arguments for the view that the Exposition is intended for gentiles

---

14 See Part III. II § 12.4.
15 Sterling (1999) 159-160.
16 See I § 3.
17 Massebieau (1889) 34, 38 n. 1.
18 Massebieau (1889) 38.

interested in Judaism. First, he argues that the positive presentation of the statesman Joseph in *Ios.*, which contrasts with the negative depiction in the Allegory, accords with the political views of gentile readers. Furthermore, the interpretation of the prescripts from the Pentateuch is in harmony with gentile jurisprudence in contemporary Egypt; the exhortations to proselytes point to a gentile audience. Finally, the Exposition does not presuppose any knowledge of Scripture. Goodenough himself, however, observes that there is a difficulty in his view, because the last part of *Praem.*, that is *Bened.* and *Exsecr.*, is obviously intended for Jews, and he goes on to argue that *Bened.* and *Exsecr.* are not a part of the Exposition. Like the Exposition, *Mos.* is also written for gentiles who are interested in the Jews, and the Exposition and the life of Moses are companion pieces.[19]

As an introductory treatise *Mos.* seems to be intended for a general readership. The chief argument is that no special knowledge of the Penta-teuch is assumed. In this respect, it differs clearly from the Allegorical Commentary, which seems to be written for those who are more advanced in Mosaic philosophy. The broad audience of *Mos.* may consist of Jews and non-Jews.

(4) Philo's *Mos.* aims at furnishing information, as appears from the preface, where Philo remarks that he wishes to make known Moses' life to those who deserve not to remain in ignorance of it. Moses' laws are known all over the world, but only a few people know his life (1.1-2). At the same time, *Mos.* has an apologetic purpose. Philo presents Moses as the greatest of all legislators and his laws as most excellent (2.12). To prove this view he refers to the fact that the laws are firm and remain secure from the day when they were first enacted to now (2.14). Further, he remarks that the laws attract the attention of the whole inhabited world. The argument he gives is that everyone shows respect for the sacred seventh day by abstaining from work (2.20-21). The same argument is found in Josephus' apologetic *Contra Apionem* (2.282).[20]

(5) In *Mos.* Philo deals with standard topics that belong to a βίος, like descent, ancestry, birth, education, great deeds, and death. In the beginning of his narrative, he tells us that Moses was Chaldean by race,

---

[19] Goodenough (1933) 114-125, (1962) 33. For his view on *Mos.*, see I § 4. Same opinion regarding the audience of *Mos.* in Schürer (1909) 675 and Botte (1954) 60. See also Birnbaum (1996) 18-20. She argues that the Allegory has an audience with a sophisticated knowledge of Scripture and philosophy, and that the Exposition does not assume any familiarity with Scripture.

[20] Goodenough regards *Mos.* as an apology for the Jews, Goodenough (1962) 33.

explaining that his ancestors migrated from Chaldea to Egypt (1.5). He also narrates the circumstances of Moses' birth and exposure (1.7-11). At the end of book 2 Moses' death is related. In his treatment Philo relies on the scriptural account, but sometimes he goes beyond the biblical narrative, for instance in the treatment of Moses' education (1.21-24). With regard to his sources, Philo indicates that he not only makes use of the Bible, but also of what he has heard from the elders of the people (1. 4).

(6) A philosopher's βίος deals with his education. Philo extensively describes the schooling of Moses at Pharaoh's court: teachers came from Egypt, Greece, and the neighbouring countries to educate the young Moses. He was an excellent disciple: in a short time he surpassed the capacities of his teachers. Alluding to Plato's theory of learning as ἀνάμνησις, Philo remarks that Moses' knowledge seems to have been gained by remembering rather than by learning. The Egyptian teachers taught him arithmetic, geometry, rhythm, metre, harmony, and music. They also educated him in the philosophy conveyed in symbols, which is shown in the so-called holy inscriptions. Greek men taught him the rest of the ἐγκύκλιος παιδεία, whereas men from the neighbouring countries instructed him in the Assyrian letters and the Chaldean science of heavenly bodies. During his education he sought only for truth, and his mind did not accept any falsehood (1.21-24).

(7) Philo narrates Moses' life in a chronological sequence, beginning with his birth and ending with his death. The chronological structure is combined with a thematic approach: in book one the events in Moses' life are told under the heading of Moses as philosopher-king, although many of the events are not relevant to Moses' role as king or philosopher. Book two deals with Moses' functions as lawgiver, high priest, and prophet. The consequence is that some events are told twice, for instance the crossing of the Red Sea (1.169-173; 2.247-257), and the story of the golden calf (2.161-173; 270-274).

(8) In *Mos.* there are elements of an encomiastic style.[21] In the opening lines Moses is already called the greatest and most perfect of men (1.1). Philo frequently tells us about Moses' virtues. In his youth he bridled the passions with the reins of self-control and self-restraint. Everyone was surprised at Moses' attitude, wondering whether his mind was human or

---

[21] See Shuler (1990) 90-97.

divine or a mixture of both. Wishing to live for his soul only, not for his
body, he especially practised frugal contentment and treated the luxurious
life scornfully (1.25-29). After his flight to Midian, Moses carried out the
exercises of virtue, using his reason as trainer. He trained himself for the
highest forms of life, the theoretical and the practical (1.48).

In the narrative of the exodus of the Israelite people from Egypt, Philo
makes a digression on Moses as leader of the people (1.148-162). Moses
was appointed as leader on the basis of his virtue and goodness. He
received his office as a reward from God, the lover of virtue and goodness.
As a leader he did not enrich himself or his family, but he wished only to
benefit his subjects. He despised material wealth as blind, but pursues the
wealth of nature that can see.[22] Philo lists several treasures that Moses
possessed, such as self-restraint, self-control, good sense, knowledge,
endurance of toil and hardships, contempt of pleasure, and justice (1.154).

In the part dealing with Moses as legislator, Philo speaks first about the
legislative condition of mind. There are four virtues which the legislator
should have: love of humanity, of justice, of goodness, and hatred of evil.
Moses possessed all these virtues (2.8-11). Discussing Moses' priesthood,
Philo remarks that Moses shows piety in the highest degree (2.66, cf.
2.284).

Such an elaborate treatment of Moses' virtues does not have any scriptural basis. The emphasis on Moses' excellence and virtues is an aspect that
belongs to the philosophical βίοι. We are strongly reminded that
Xenophon deals with Agesilaos' virtues in the same way.

(9) In *Mos.* Philo shows that Moses' words are in harmony with his deeds.
In the description of Moses' bridling of the passions, he writes as follows:
'he (sc. Moses) demonstrates his philosophical tenets by his daily actions,
saying what he thought and acting in accordance with what he said in
order to achieve consistency between doctrine and life, so that the life was
found to be like the doctrine and the doctrine like the life.' (1.29).[23] The
same notion is found in the description of Moses in Midian. Moses read
the doctrines of philosophy and brought his personal conduct into
harmony with them, desiring truth rather than seeming (1.48).

Interpreting the high priest's vestments, the Jewish exegete explains why
the reason-seat (λογεῖον) is fastened to the high priest's ephod. God does
not consider it right that word (λόγος) should be separated from deeds
(ἔργα), and the shoulder is a symbol of work and activity (2.130, cf. 2.48,

---

[22] For the expression 'wealth not blind, but seeing', cf. Plato *Nomoi* 631C.
[23] Translation Mansfeld (1994) 186.

140).[24] A variation is found in Philo's assertion that words, thoughts, and actions should correspond to each other. He makes this statement in his interpretation of Deut. 30:11-14, where it is written that God's commandment is not far away, but very near, in your mouth, heart, and hands. Philo explains mouth, heart, and hand as symbols of words, thoughts, and actions. Happiness lies in these three. 'For when thoughts correspond to words and actions correspond to intentions, life is praise-worthy and perfect, but when they are at strife with each other, it is imperfect and a matter for reproach' (*Virt.* 183-184).[25] Philo reproaches the sophists for saying very good things, but doing the most shameful (*Post.* 86, cf. *Congr.* 67).

(10) As we have seen in the case of Arrian's life of Epictetus, a philosopher's vita has a paradigmatic function: the philosopher's life is depicted as a model to be imitated.[26] Philo too presents Moses' life as an example in *Mos.* 1.158, writing that Moses puts forward his own life as a παράδειγμα for those who are willing to imitate it. The Jewish exegete refers here to Ex. 20:21, where it is written that Moses entered into the darkness where God was. He interprets the darkness in a Platonic way as the invisible and paradigmatic essence of the existents. In other treatises Philo explains this verse as indicating the unknowability of God's essence (*Post.* 14, *Mut.* 7).[27] It is very likely that Philo does not discuss God's incomprehensibility in *Mos.*, because this doctrine is too difficult and complicated for an introductory treatise.

(11) In an introductory life the biography is combined with bibliographical information, containing remarks on the writings, their order, contents, and authenticity. Porphyry, for instance, discusses the writings of his master, their chronological order, and questions of plagiarism. Likewise Philo recounts the origin of the Greek translation of what was regarded as Moses' writings, the Pentateuch. He not only describes their

---

[24] Cf. *Fug.* 150, 152, *Mut.* 195, *Ios.* 230, *Spec.* 2.52, 4.134. The idea of the harmony between word and deed already occurs in Plato (*Laches* 188D, 193DE) and Xenophon (*Mem.* 4.3.18, 5.4.25). See Mansfeld (1994) 183-191.

[25] Translation Colson PLCL 8; same exegesis in *Post.* 85, *Mut.* 237-238, *Somn.* 2.180, *Praem.* 80-81, cf. *Mos.* 2.212.

[26] Cf. Diogenes Laertius 3.10-11, where he reports a decree of the Athenians that Zeno of Citium should be crowned. In the decree it is mentioned that Zeno 'presented his own life as a paradigm to all people, in perfect consistency with his doctrines.' (translation Mansfeld (1994) 189).

[27] See Part III. II § 18.b.2

origin, but also their classification, and he gives an overview of their contents (2.25-65).[28] The discussion about origin and structure is a preliminary question that has to be dealt with in an introductory philosophical life.

From the foregoing it appears that there are many points that suggest that *Mos.* can be regarded as an introductory philosophical life, but there remain some aspects of the treatise that do not fit in so well with an introductory life. The most important deviation is the thematic approach in *Mos.* Philo deals with the events in Moses' life on the basis of Moses' four functions: king-philosopher, lawgiver, high priest, and prophet. Within this thematic arrangement the events are told chronologically.

Furthermore, the extensive, detailed and sometimes difficult treatment of the tabernacle, its furnishings and of the high priest's vestments seems to be out of place in an introductory treatise. In this treatment Philo offers symbolic meanings of the numbers used in the tabernacle. These meanings are also mentioned in the Allegorical Commentary and the Exposition of the Law. Philo, for instance, explains that the number four is the essence of ten, which is the supremely perfect number (2.84, cf. *Opif.* 47, *Plant.* 123-125). It can, however, be said that Philo places the treatment of the tabernacle within the framework of Moses as high priest, and so it has its right place in the narrative of Moses' life.

Dealing with the furnishings of the tabernacle, Philo explains the two Cherubim allegorically as God's two highest powers (2.99), and this interpretation is also found in the Allegorical Commentary (*Cher.* 27, *Her.* 166). Philo speaks also about God's powers in a historical work, namely *Legat.* 6. For this reason, it can be argued that God's powers occupy a prominent place in Philo's thought and that they are too important to omit in a philosophical βίος with an introductory aim.

Despite some aspects that do not suit the genre of introductory philosophical βίος, it can very well be argued that Philo's *Mos.* belongs to this genre. It was intended to be an introduction to Philo's exegesis of Moses' writings, i.e., Mosaic philosophy. For this reason, it should be placed at the very beginning of the exegetical series, the Allegorical Commentary, the Exposition, and the Questions and Answers. It should be read before studying the exegesis of Moses' laws. From the reference to *Mos.* at *Virt.* 52 it appears that Philo presupposes knowledge of his treatise on Moses' life. The reference to the forthcoming life of Moses at *Gig.* 57

---

[28]   For Philo's account of the translation, see Borgen (1997) 140-143.

yields some problems.[29] Philo does not give the discussion about the notion of 120 years in *Mos*. Furthermore, the sentence 'when we have become fit to learn its mystery' shows that the discussion would have been at an advanced level, which does not suit the introductory character of *Mos*. Therefore, the reference cannot be to *Mos*.

The suggestion that *Mos*. should be situated before the exegetical writings is attractive for a number of reasons. First, it can explain the difference in approach between *Mos*. and the Exposition, for instance in the use of allegory, but it also offers an explanation of the overlaps in contents. It is quite understandable that Philo repeats in the Exposition what he has already told in the introduction. The placing of *Mos*. at the beginning does not, however, exclude the connection between it and the Exposition — a connection to which Goodenough pays attention, calling *Mos*. and the Exposition 'companion pieces'.

Furthermore, the suggestion does justice to the special status that the person of Moses occupies in Philo's thought. For Philo, Moses is the philosopher *par excellence*, who has reached the summit of philosophy (*Opif.* 8). He is called 'God to Pharaoh' (Ex. 7:1, *Leg.* 1.40, *Migr.* 84), and 'friend of God' (Ex. 33:11, *Mos.* 1.156). Moses is not presented as a type of soul, like the patriarchs, and Philo does not translate and interpret his name. Moses is the legislator of the Jews, and the writer of the Torah.[30]

Third, if *Mos*. does not belong to the Exposition, but is a separate work, we can assume different audiences. The treatise on Moses' life is intended for a broad readership, consisting of people — whether pagans or native Jews — who needed to be introduced to the life of the Jewish legislator. It seems that the Exposition is primarily written for Jews, without, however, excluding pagan readers.[31] The interpretation of the prescripts in *Spec.* seems to be directed to adherents of the Jewish faith, because non-Jews would not be interested in it.

Without *Mos*. the structure of the Exposition is very clear, and the treatises are linked well together. It begins with a treatment of the creation of the universe. Thereafter, Philo deals with the lives of six patriarchs (Enos, Enoch, Noah, Abraham, Isaac, Jacob) as types of ethical conduct. Their lives are explained in a literal way, but also interpreted in allegorical terms. Philo adds to them as seventh the life of Joseph as a model of one who is involved in political matters. Having thus described the living laws, Philo proceeds to deal with the written law. In *Decal.* he treats the

---

[29] See I § 4.
[30] For Moses as the writer of the Torah, see Amir (1983) 77-106.
[31] Seland (1995) 81-82.

Decalogue, while in *Spec.* he explains the special prescripts, dividing them into categories related to the Ten Commandments. From *Spec.* 4.133 onwards and in *Virt.* Philo discusses universal virtues, which are common to all the Ten Commandments. Next the Jewish exegete sets forth the rewards for the good, and the punishments for the wicked. The last part of *Praem.* describes the blessings and curses as related in the law.[32]

We may conclude that Philo's *Mos.* is an introductory *bios.* Moses' life is presented as an example which the reader is encouraged to follow, notably through a further and deeper study of his writings. The paradigmatic character of Moses' life is also found in Gregory of Nyssa's *De Vita Moysis,* which is the focus of attention in the following part of our study.

---

[32] Borgen (1997) 63-79.

PART TWO

GREGORY AND HIS *DE VITA MOYSIS*

INTRODUCTION

Gregory of Nyssa, his elder brother Basil, and their friend Gregory of Nazianzus are known as the great Cappadocian fathers. Each of them had his own speciality: Basil is best known for his organisation of the monastic life; Nazianzen had great rhetorical skills; Gregory of Nyssa was the most philosophically minded.[1]

Gregory was born in about 330 in a Christian family. His father, a famous rhetorician in Neocaesarea in Pontus, was a son of Macrina the Elder, who was a pupil of Gregory Thaumaturgus. Gregory first chose a worldly career and became a rhetor in 364, but later on, in 371, he was made, against his own will, bishop of the little town of Nyssa by his elder brother Basil. Due to Arian bishops and the Arian emperor Valens he was deposed in 376, but returned to his see two years later after the emperor's death. He was one of the leading members of the council of Constantinople in 381, convened by the emperor Theodosius, at which the Nicene creed was re-established. He had close contacts with the imperial family, and delivered funeral speeches for the princess Pulcheria and the empress Flaccilla in 385. His death took place not long after 394.[2]

He received his education from his brother Basil, whom he often calls 'teacher' (e.g., *Opif. Hom.* 126B).[3] Basil had studied in Constantinople under the famous rhetor Libanios and, together with Gregory of Nazianzus, in Athens under the Christian rhetor Prohaeresios and Himerios. It is evident that Basil was acquainted with the Philonic corpus, though he alludes to it sparingly. His exegesis of the creation story in *Homiliae in Hexaemeron* shows the influence of Philo's treatise on the same subject, *De opificio mundi*.[4] Basil stimulated Gregory to read and study the works of pagan and Christian authors, and Gregory's writings show that he had a profound and great knowledge of pagan culture.[5]

---

[1] A general introduction to the three Cappadocians and their thoughts is given by Meredith (1995).

[2] For Gregory's life and writings, see Bardenhewer (1913-32) 3.188-219, Daniélou (1955), (1956), (1965a), (1966), (1968) 8-16, Quasten (1950-86) 3.254-296, Aubineau (1966) 29-82 (Gregory's life until 371), May (1971), Dörrie (1983), Meredith (1999) 1-26. Bibliography in Altenburger-Mann (1988).

[3] Gregory *Ep.* 13.4, Aubineau (1966) 54-56, Runia (1993) 158, 244.

[4] Runia (1993) 235-241.

[5] Aubineau (1966) 44-49.

Together with the other Cappadocians, Gregory was a strong defender of the Nicene creed, and all three Cappadocians were engaged in the controversy with the Neo-Arian Eunomius.[6] In the years 363-365 Basil wrote his *Contra Eunomium* as a refutation of Eunomius' treatise *Apologia*.[7] Eunomius, in his turn, replied to Basil in his *Apologia apologiae* in 378.[8] After Basil's death in 379 Gregory of Nyssa took over Basil's job in defending the orthodox view against the Neo-Arians, and in the years 381-382 he composed his vast work *Contra Eunomium*, in which he refutes Eunomius.[9]

The most important matter of dispute concerns God's essence. Eunomius assumes a difference in essence between God the Father and God the Son. In his view God's essence (οὐσία) can fully be described by the notion of 'unbegotten' (ἀγέννητος), but this term cannot be applied to the Son (cf. *CE* 1.475). The Son is inferior and posterior to the Father (see the quotation from Eunomius in *CE* 1.151-154). This view, Gregory argues, implies that the divinity of the Son is denied, and so the Son turns out to be a creature (cf. *CE* 2.15). The consequence of the denial of the Son's divinity is that man's salvation is denied (*CE* 1.177-178). Gregory defends the Nicene creed that God the Father and God the Son have the same substance. Being can also be ascribed to the Son, and the Son is called the Existent. Eunomius' view that God's essence can be described implies that God essence is also comprehensible for human nature. This view is strongly rejected by Gregory, who makes a distinction between God's existence, which can be know, and God's essence, which is incomprehensible (*VM* II.163-169, *Cant.* 36.11-37.17, 357.3-359.4). God's unknowability is also an important theological issue in *VM*.

---

[6] For the controversy between Eunomius and the Cappadocians, see Diekamp (1896) 137-180, (1909), Abramowski (1966), Wiles (1989), Zachhuber (2000) 44-49.

[7] For Eunomius' *Apologia*, see Vaggione (1987) 3-75.

[8] For Eunomius' *Apologia apologiae*, see Vaggione (1987) 79-127.

[9] For the historical setting of Gregory's *CE* I, see Röder (1993) 64-73.

CHAPTER ONE

PHILO'S INFLUENCE ON GREGORY

1. *Contra Eunomium*

In his dogmatic work *Contra Eunomium*, in which Gregory employs every polemical and rhetorical means in order to refute Eunomius' doctrine, he names Philo twice by name.
In the first pasaage, *CE* 3.5.24, he attacks Eunomius' style:[1]

> For he (sc. Eunomius) continues with an 'encomium of significant arguments which elucidate the underlying subject', and in his usual style he compiles and glues together the rag-collection of terms tossed away at the cross-roads. Then once again the unfortunate Isocrates is nibbled at and depilated for words and figures that he can use for the composition of his subject. There are also places where even Philo the Hebrew suffers the same fate, supplying him with terms drawn from his own labours.[2]

Here Gregory accuses his opponent of plagiarism and he mentions, besides Isocrates, Philo as a source. Philo supplies Eunomius with terminology for his arguments. A few chapters later Gregory also associates Eunomius with Philo, claiming that Eunomius has taken over a sentence from Philo. He writes (3.7.8-9):

> For 'the most eminent God (of his), anterior, he says, to all other beings that are generated, has power over his own *dynamis*'. The statement in its actual wording has been transferred by our literary hack from Philo the Hebrew to his own text, and Eunomius' theft from the actual works compiled by Philo will become as clear as day (...). But I have indicated this in the present context not so much because I reproach our literary hack for the poverty of his own words and thoughts, but rather because I wish to demonstrate to my readers the affinity between Eunomius' doctrines and the texts of the Jews. [9] For the text of Philo in its very wording would not have been suited to his conceptions, if there was not a kinship of thought

---

[1] Daniélou (1967a), Runia (1992), (1993) 244-249. Daniélou misinterprets the first passage (3.5.23-24) and is corrected by Runia. See also Barnes (1998) 71-72.

[2] Translation Runia (1993) 245. *CE* 3.5.24 . . διὰ τῆς συνήθους ἑαυτοῦ λέξεως συντίθησι καὶ διακολλᾷ τὰ ἐν τριόδοις ἀπερριμμένα τῶν λεξειδίων ῥακώματα, καὶ πάλιν ὁ τλήμων Ἰσοκράτης περιεσθίεται ῥήματά τε καὶ σχήματα πρὸς τὴν σύνθεσιν τοῦ προκειμένου παρατιλλόμενος, ἔστι δὲ ὅπου καὶ ὁ Ἑβραῖος Φίλων τὰ ἴσα πάσχει, ἐκ τῶν ἰδίων πόνων συνερανίζων αὐτῷ τὰ λεξείδια.

between the two. Thus it is possible to find in Philo the text 'God is anterior to all other beings that are generated', while the following phrase 'has power over his own *dynamis*' has been thrown in from the Neo-Judaic sect. Examination of the text will clearly demonstrate its absurdity...[3]

Gregory claims that the phrase ὁ ἐξοχώτατος αὐτοῦ θεὸς πρὸ τῶν ἄλλων ὅσα γεννητά is literally taken over from Philo by Eunomius. This phrase, however, is not found in the Philonic corpus we possess. Therefore Runia suggests that 'Gregory remembered phrases of a similar kind from his reading of Philo and exaggerated the relationship into one of direct dependence.'[4] Perhaps Gregory also recalls that Philo frequently speaks about the δύναμις or δυνάμεις of God. It should be noticed that Gregory's attitude to Philo is rather negative, because he sees a relationship between the doctrine of Philo and the heresy of the Neo-Arian Eunomius.[5] This negative approach to Philo may be caused by the polemical context of *CE*.[6] Despite the negative attitude towards Philo here, Gregory does take over Philonic interpretations in other treatises.

2. *Other Writings*

The first work that Gregory wrote was *De Virginitate*, which is to be dated to about 371 and in which he shows that the state of virginity is a preparation for the vision of God. In his analysis of Gregory's sources its editor Aubineau also discusses Philo, concluding that Gregory had made a lengthy study of Philo's treatises.[7] He signals especially similarities with Philo's *De vita contemplativa*. To give only two examples:

---

[3] Translation Runia (1993) 245-246. *CE* 3.7.8. "Ὁ γὰρ ἐξοχώτατος αὐτοῦ θεὸς πρὸ τῶν ἄλλων, φησίν, ὅσα γεννητά, τῆς αὐτοῦ κρατεῖ δυνάμεως." ὁ μὲν λόγος ἐπ' αὐτῆς τῆς λέξεως ἀπὸ τοῦ Φίλωνος τοῦ Ἑβραίου μετενήνεκται παρὰ τοῦ λογογράφου ἐπὶ τὸν ἴδιον λόγον, καὶ ὅτῳ φίλον, ἐξ αὐτῶν τῶν πεπονημένων τῷ Φίλωνι κατάφωρος ἡ κλοπὴ τοῦ Εὐνομίου γενήσεται. ἐγὼ δὲ τοῦτο παρεσημηνάμην ἐπὶ τοῦ παρόντος οὐ τοσοῦτον τὴν πτωχείαν τῶν ἰδίων λόγων τε καὶ νοημάτων τῷ λογογράφῳ ἐπονειδίζων, ὅσον δεῖξαι τοῖς ἐντυγχάνουσι θέλων τὴν οἰκειότητα πρὸς τοὺς Ἰουδαίων λόγους τῶν Εὐνομίου δογμάτων. [9] οὐ γὰρ ἂν ἐπ' αὐτῆς τῆς λέξεως τοῖς τούτου νοήμασιν ὁ τοῦ Φίλωνος ἐνηρμόσθη λόγος, εἰ μὴ τις ἦν καὶ τῆς διανοίας τούτου πρὸς τὴν ἐκείνου συγγένεια. οὕτω γὰρ ἔστιν εὑρεῖν κείμενον παρὰ τῷ Ἑβραίῳ τὸν λόγον τὸ "ὁ θεὸς πρὸ τῶν ἄλλων ὅσα γεννητά", τὸ δὲ ἐφεξῆς ἐκ τῆς νέας Ἰουδαϊκῆς προσερρίφη τὸ "τῆς ἰδίας κατακρατεῖ δυνάμεως".
[4] Runia (1993) 246. He refers to *Leg.* 3.4 πρὸ γὰρ παντὸς γενητοῦ ὁ θεός ἐστι. Jaeger refers in his edition to a similar phrase in *Migr.* 183 πρὸ παντὸς τοῦ γενητοῦ (sc. ἐστιν ὁ θεός) and *Leg.* 3.175 ὁ λόγος τοῦ θεοῦ. . πρεσβύτατος . . τῶν ὅσα γέγονε.
[5] Cf. *CE* 1.117, see further Runia (1993) 246-249.
[6] Barnes (1998) 72.
[7] Aubineau (1966) 105-116, see also Runia (1993) 24-251. Aubineau's conclusion at 106.

— the idea of spiritual marriage, *Virg.* 308.14-19, 305.11-15, cf. Philo *Contempl.* 68, and *Cher.* 40-52.[8]

— the interpretation of Israel crossing the Red Sea. Gregory offers the Philonic exegesis of the crossing as the exodus of the soul from the sensible world and the passions to the intelligible realm, although an interpretation in terms of baptism was common among the Church fathers, *Virg.* 274.8 ff, 320.24-322.20, cf. Philo *Contempl.* 83-88.[9]

Gregory wrote two treatises dealing with the creation account in Genesis, namely *De opificio hominis* and *Apologia in Hexaemeron.* They were meant as a sequel to Basil's homilies on the same subject. Elements taken over from Philo's treatise *Opif.* are found in these works:[10]

— the idea that the creation has a logical sequence, expressed by the words εἱρμός and ἀκολουθία, *Hex.* 72C, 76B etc.; cf. Philo *Opif.* 28, 65, 131.

— the question why man is created last of all creatures and the answer that God, like a good host, invites his guests when everything is in readiness, *Opif. hom.* 132D-133B; cf. Philo *Opif.* 77-78.

— the idea of a double creation of man, *Opif. hom.* 181A-D; cf. Philo *Opif.* 69-71.

---

[8] Aubineau (1966) 112-113.
[9] Aubineau (1966) 113-114.
[10] Daniélou (1967a) 335-339, Alexandre (1971), Runia (1993) 251-256.

CHAPTER TWO

GREGORY AND PHILO'S JUDAISM

1. *General Remarks*

In the foregoing we have seen that in several writings Gregory makes use of Philo's exegesis and interpretations, but at the same time he speaks about Philo and the Jews in a rather negative way. In *CE* 3.7.8-9 he states that his adversary Eunomius has derived a sentence from Philo, and he sees an affinity between Eunomius' doctrine and the texts of the Jews, arguing that there is a kinship of thought between Philo and Eunomius. He refers to the Neo-Arians as the Neo-Judaic sect.[1] This leads to the question how Gregory on the one hand can exploit Philonic exegesis and theology, but on the other can display a negative attitude towards Philo and Judaism, e.g. by seeing an affinity between Philo and his adversary Eunomius. How, in fact, does Gregory assess Philo's Judaism?

To answer this question we need to investigate some passages in which Gregory speaks about Judaism. In the text from *CE* referred to above Gregory associates the doctrine of the Neo-Arians with Judaism.[2] He does so on more occasions. In *CE* 1.177-179 he states that Eunomius and his followers teach the doctrine of the Jews, namely that only the being of the Father exists, and that the beings of the Son and the Spirit are reckoned among the non-beings. 'Therefore, if the Father's being only is said properly to exist, and the Son's and Spirit's not so, what is this but the clear denial of the message of salvation? Let them therefore leave the Church and return to the synagogues of the Jews for, in refusing to attribute real being to the Son, they are actually denying his existence. What is not fully real is in effect non-existent.'[3] At another place he remarks that his opponents support the error of the Jews, who abolish the godhead of the Lord, and conceive of him as a created being (*CE* 2.14-15).

Gregory, in contrast, defends the view that the Son has real being and that being can also be ascribed to the Son. In *CE* 3.9.22-41 he discusses

---

[1] See I § 1.
[2] See for Arianism and Judaism, Lorenz (1979) 141-179.
[3] Translation Meredith (1999) 34.

Eunomius' statement that the Son does not appropriate the dignity of being (22). Gregory infers from this statement that Eunomius considers God the Word as not having the title 'Being' (23-25). In order to reject Eunomius' view that Christ is an angel, Gregory refers to the first chapter of the Epistle to the Hebrews, in which it is written that Christ is mightier than the angels (28; Hebr. 1:6, 8, 12). In Gregory's eyes Eunomius degrades the Lord of the angels to the rank of an angel (29). Because the only opposite of being is non-being, Gregory concludes that he who contrasts the Son with being Judaizes, robbing the Christian doctrine of the person of the Only-Begotten (31).

Eunomius presents Moses as a witness to his doctrine, writing that he who sent Moses was the Existent himself, but he by whom he was sent and spoken to was the angel of the Existent (32-34). To reject this statement Gregory quotes a few scriptural verses from Exodus in which God is conceived of as leading the people (Ex. 32:34, 33:2, 34:9, 33:15, 33:17; 34-35). He concludes that, if he who spoke with Moses becomes his fellow-traveller and the guide of the army, it is clearly shown that he who made himself known by the title of 'Being' is the Only-Begotten God (35). Again, Gregory refers to the Jewish faith, remarking that one who does not associate the Son with the deliverance of the people is a supporter of the Jewish conviction. He charges Eunomius with bringing the doctrine of the synagogue to the Church of Christ (36).[4]

Next Gregory points to the story of the burning bush, in which first an angel is mentioned as appearing (Ex. 3:2), and later on God makes himself known as He-who-is (Ex. 3:14). Gregory states that the prophet, wishing to make manifest to men the mystery concerning Christ, called Being 'angel', in order that the meaning of the words might not be referred to the Father, as it would have been if the title of 'Being' alone had been found throughout the dialogue (37).[5] The Son is called angel because he is the messenger of his Father's will; he is called Being because he does not have any name that gives knowledge of his essence, transcending every designation by name. For this reason his name is testified to as being above every name (41; Phil. 2:9, cf. *Cant.* 37.12-14).

From the discussion of these texts from *CE*, it becomes manifest that for Gregory an important aspect of the Jewish faith by which he distinguishes himself from Philo and the Jews is the view on the position of the Logos in

---

[4] Other passages in which Gregory refers to Judaism within the same context are *CE* 1.258, 261-269, 3.2.73, 156, 3.8.23, *Maced.* 110.21-23, *Ref. Eun.* 27-30, 48-49, 109, *Simpl.* 62.8-9.

[5] Same interpretation of Ex 3:14 in *VM* II.20-25, see Part III. II § 6.a.

relation to God. For this reason we now discuss Philo's view on God's Logos.

2. *The Doctrine of the Logos*

Philo's doctrine on God's Logos is complex and difficult to present systematically, but in general terms we can state that the Logos is that aspect of God that is directed towards and is present in created reality.[6] On some occasions Philo emphasizes the immanence of the Logos so that the Logos appears to be a hypostasis, that is, a being that exists outside God himself. God has contact with his creation through his Logos and his powers. Appearances of angels recorded in Scripture are explained as appearances of God's Logos, for instance the angel whom Hagar meets (Gen. 16:7; *Cher.* 3, *Fug.* 5), or the angel who appears to Balaam (Num. 22:31; *Cher.* 35, *Deus* 182).[7] In *Conf.* 146 Philo reflects on the expression 'Sons of God' (Deut. 14:1). He remarks that, if one is not yet fit to be called Son of God, one should take his place under God's First-born, the Logos, the eldest of the angels, the archangel. He has many names, like beginning, name of God, word, man after his image, and he that sees, that is, Israel.

The Logos seems to be subordinated to God. The subordinate position of the Logos comes to the fore in *Fug.* 94-101, where Philo discusses the six cities of refuge (Num. 25). He interprets them as God's Logos and God's powers. The mother-city is the divine Logos, while the other cities, as it were colonies, are the powers of him who speaks. Philo lists five powers: the creative, the royal, the gracious, the power that prescribes, and the power that prohibits (94-95). These five powers are also depicted in the Holy of Holies (cf. *QE* 2.68). The laws in the ark represent the powers of prescription and prohibition. The cover of the ark, called mercy seat, symbolizes the power of mercy, and the two Cherubim are symbols of the creative and royal powers.[8] The divine Logos, being above the powers, does not have a visible image because he is not like any of the sensible things. He is God's image, the eldest of all intelligible things, and is placed nearest to the only one who truly is.[9] For this reason God says: 'I shall speak to you

---

[6] For Philo's doctrine of God's Logos, see Wolfson (1947) 1.226-289, Pfeifer (1967) 48-51, Winston (1985) 9-25, Runia (1986) 446-451, Williamson (1989) 103-143, Downing (1990), Tobin (1992) 250-251.

[7] For God's Logos as angel, cf. *Leg.* 3.177, *Mut.* 87, *Somn.* 1.239.

[8] See Part III. II § 18.c.2.

[9] For God's Logos as God's image, cf. *Conf.* 97, *Fug.* 101, *Somn.* 1.239, *Spec.* 1.81.

above from the mercy seat, between the two Cherubim' (Ex. 25:22; cf. *Her.* 166, *QE* 2.68). The Logos is the charioteer of the powers, but he who speaks is seated in the chariot, giving directions to the charioteer (100-101). From this text it emerges that God, the speaker of the Word, stays above his Word. Therefore, the Logos can be called God's work (*Sacr.* 65, *Mos.* 1.283). The Logos is placed at a lower level than God, who is superior to his Logos. God himself is called ὁ ὤν or τὸ ὄν.[10] The subordinate position of the Logos appears also from the fact that God is called the source of the Logos (*Det.* 82, *Post.* 69).

The Logos, as we saw, is God's aspect that is related to created reality, and some passages suggest that the Logos belongs even to what has come into being. In *Leg.* 3.175 Philo explains the manna as God's Logos.[11] He remarks that the Logos is above the whole universe and is the eldest and most generic of all created things.[12] This passage from *Leg.* is, perhaps, one of the texts that Gregory has in mind when he refers to a statement by Philo in *CE* 3.7.8-9.[13] In *Migr.* 6 Philo interprets 'the house of God' (Gen. 28:17) as God's Logos. It is the eldest of all things that are created. When God created the universe, he used the Logos as an instrument.[14] In both texts the Logos is presented as belonging to the things that have a coming into being (γένεσις). God himself is uncreated (ἀγένητος; *Leg.* 1.51, *Cher.* 44, 48 etc.). In *Her.* 205-206 Philo writes that the Father of all has given to the Logos a special gift in order that the Logos, standing on the borderline, may separate the creature from the creator. He pleads as a suppliant with the immortal for afflicted mortality. The Logos is proud of this gift, saying: 'and I stood between the Lord and you' (Deut. 5:5), that is, he is neither uncreated like God, nor created like you, but midway between two extremes. In this passage the ambiguous and not fully coherent position of the Logos is clearly indicated. On the one hand, it is an aspect of God, belonging to the divine realm. The Logos is presented as God's angel and as the eldest of intelligible things. On the other hand, he is the eldest of all things that are created.

As already said it is the doctrine of the Logos in which Gregory differs most from Philo. As we have seen in the Philonic texts discussed, the Logos

---

[10] For ὁ ὤν and τὸ ὄν indicating God, see Starobinski-Safran (1978), and the list in Leisegang PCW 7.226-227.

[11] See Part III. II § 16.

[12] Cf. the explanation of manna in *Leg.* 2.86, where God is called the supremely generic, and at the second place is God's Logos.

[13] See I § 1.

[14] For the Logos as God's instrument, cf. *Leg.* 3.96, *Sacr.* 8, *Deus* 57, *Fug.* 12, 95, *Somn.* 2.45, *Spec.* 1.81.

seems to be subordinated to God in one way or another. Philo places the Logos at a lower level of being than God himself in his essence. For this reason, he can never refer to the Logos as ὁ ὤν. Being is only ascribed to God himself, and the Logos has a less real existence than God. The Logos is also presented as a angel. Some passages suggest that the Logos belongs to what has come into being. Both Philo and Gregory believe in the existence of God and the Logos, but they differ regarding the position of the Logos in relation to God. For Gregory this is a crucial issue because the salvation of man depends on it. If the Son does not have real being, then salvation is at risk, as he himself remarks at *CE* 1.178. Gregory sees Philo's view reflected in the thought of the Neo-Arians, for whom God's Logos is inferior to God and therefore Gregory associates their doctrine with Judaism. He defends the Nicene belief that God's Logos, the Son, should be placed on the same level of being as God the Father. Being should be ascribed to all the persons of the divine Trinity, God the Father, God the Son, and the Holy Spirit. Gregory draws a line between the divine nature and created reality, to which the angels also belong.

Gregory can display a negative attitude towards Philo and Judaism, because in his view an important aspect of Judaism is the doctrine that the Logos is inferior to God. He does, however, uses Philonic material in which the Logos does not play a key role. As we shall see, he uses much allegorical exegesis derived from Philo in *VM*. At many places in *Virg.* he is also indebted to Philo.[15]

3. *Negative Theology*

A prominent theological issue in which Gregory does concur with Philo is the doctrine of God's unknowability. Both Philo and Gregory show a negative approach to the divine nature, which they describe in negative terms as invisible and incomprehensible. The tradition of negative or apophatic theology is also met with in other patristic writers, like Clement of Alexandria, Origen and the Cappadocians.[16] John Chrysostomus, Gregory's younger contemporary, wrote twelve homilies *On the Incomprehensible Nature of God.*[17] Gregory finds biblical support for God's incomprehensibility in Ex. 20:21, where it is said that Moses enters the

---

[15] See Aubineau (1966) 105-116.

[16] See Part III.II § 18.b.3.

[17] The first five were delivered in Antioch about 386-387; the other series was delivered in Constantinople in 397; for the incomprehensibility in John, see Daniélou-Malingrey-Flacelière (1970) 15-29, where similarities to Gregory are also signalled.

darkness where God is. Gregory interprets the darkness as referring to God's unknowability (*Bas.* 129.5-9, *Cant.* 181.4-8, 322.11-323.9, *Inscr. Psal.* 44.18-19, *Thaum.* 10.10-14, *VM* II. 163).[18] This interpretation was already given by Philo (*Post.* 14, *Mut.* 7),[19] and was taken over by Clement of Alexandria (*Strom.* 2.6.1, 5.78.3).

In *CE* Gregory defends God's incomprehensibility against Eunomius, who claims that God's essence is comprehensible to the human intellect and can be expressed by the term 'unbegotten'. As an example of Gregory's argumentation we discuss two passages from *CE*, starting with *CE* 2.85-105. Gregory begins this passage by exclaiming that Eunomius and his followers have removed themselves very far from Abraham, the father of the faith. The migration of Abraham from his country denotes in allegorical terms the quest for the knowledge of God (85-86).[20] Passing over sensible objects, Abraham is eager to see the archetype of all beauty. All things that he grasps on his journey, whether God's power, or his goodness, or his being without beginning, or his being bounded by no boundary, or whatever idea can be found about the divine nature — Abraham uses all these notions as supplies for his upward journey. He always makes one discovery a stepping stone to another, ever stretching himself out to things that lie before him (Phil. 3:13). Finally, he arrives at the faith that this is the clear feature of the knowledge of God, namely to believe that God is better and higher than every knowable mark (89). Abraham then falls back from his high thoughts to his human weakness and says: 'I am earth and ashes' (Gen. 18:27), that is, he is without voice and power to interpret the good that he has perceived (90). The history of Abraham shows that it is impossible to draw near to God, unless faith mediates and joins the seeking soul to the incomprehensible nature of God (91).

In order to emphasize the important role of faith, Gregory refers to Gen. 15:6 'Abraham believed God and it was counted to him for righteousness'. It is not written, Paul says, for his sake, but for our sake (Rom. 4:2-24) that God counts to men for righteousness their faith, not their knowledge (92). Knowledge deals with what is known, but faith makes ours that which escapes our knowledge. Vain is he who says that it is possible to know the divine essence (93).

---

[18] See Part III. II § 18.b.1.
[19] See Part III. II § 18.b.2.
[20] The allegorical interpretation of Abraham's journey has a Philonic background, cf., for instance, *Migr.* 194-195.

In what follows Gregory makes the distinction between knowledge of God's existence and knowledge of what God is in his essence. Gregory explains that the disciple of the gospels and of prophecy believes that He-who-is exists. He believes it on the basis of the harmony of the things that appear, and of the works of providence. But this disciple does not research what and how God is (98). Gregory charges Eunomius with deifying the idea of ungeneracy as being itself God or God's essence (100). We do have names for making clear God's knowledge, but they are related to human characteristics (104). All voices in Holy Scripture denote something about God. By these expressions we learn God's power, or that he does not admit of worse, or that he is without cause, or that he is not circumscribed by any end or that his might is above all things. But we leave aside his very essence without further research as not to be conceived by the intellect or expressed in words (105).[21]

Gregory begins the second passage (*CE* 3.1.103-110) by stating that the infinite cannot be grasped by any conception of words. To confirm God's infinity he appeals to Ps. 144:3-5, where it is written that there is no limit in God's splendour, glory, and holiness. And if what is around God has no limit, so much more God himself in his essence cannot be circumscribed by any boundary. Since God is infinite, he cannot be comprehended, and the incomprehensible cannot be described by any name. By which name, Gregory asks rhetorically, shall I grasp the incomprehensible? Next he deals with the reproach of his adversary that, if Gregory and his followers do not know God's essence, 'they worship what they do not know' (cf. Joh. 4:22).[22] Responding to this reproof, Gregory refers to Paul, who calls God's judgements 'unsearchable' and his ways 'unscrutable' (Rom. 11:33), and who writes that the things promised to those that love God are above comprehension (1 Cor. 2:9). Gregory understands Paul to mean that knowledge of God is unattainable by human calculations. He ends with a positive statement: we really worship what we know, for we know the loftiness of God's glory. In this passage Gregory bases God's incomprehensibility on his infinity: what is infinite cannot be circumscribed and comprehended (cf. *VM* II.238). He also links Gods incomprehensibility with unnameabilitiy.

---

[21] This text shows a great resemblance to *VM*. Like Moses, Abraham searches for knowledge of God. In this quest both sensible and intelligible things are passed over. Knowledge of God's essence is, however, never reached. In both *CE* and *VM* Phil. 3:13 is quoted as referring to the endless ascent of the soul.

[22] For this reproof of Eunomius, cf. Basil *Ep.* 234.

As already said, the doctrine of God's incomprehensibility occurs also in Philo, who, like Gregory, interprets the darkness from Ex. 20:21 as referring to God's unknowability. In other texts Philo emphasizes the unknowability of God's essence without referring to Ex. 20:21. To illustrate Philo's view we discuss two texts, namely *Fug.* 161-165 and *Post.* 167-169. In the first text Philo presents Moses as searching for God, discussing Moses' quest as an example of seeking and not finding. Moses searches for the causes of the phenomena in the creation, and he says: 'Why is it that the bush burns, and is not burnt?' (161; Ex. 3:2-3). Philo explains that Moses inquires curiously about the inaccessible place, and that he is about to engage in an endless labour. His task is made easier by God who says: 'Do not draw near.' (Ex. 3:5), that is, 'Do not conduct such an inquiry.' This work requires a curiosity too great for human power. One should marvel at the created things, but not inquire about the causes by which they come into being and pass away (162).

Philo continues by saying that Moses, having surpassed the whole universe, searches for its maker. Moses asks what he is who is so difficult to see and to fathom. Is he a body or incorporeal, or something beyond these? Is he a simple nature or a composite one? Seeing that this is difficult to catch and to grasp, Moses prays to learn from God himself what God is (164; cf. Ex. 33:13). But he does not succeed in finding anything by searching, respecting the essence of Him-who-is because God answers: 'You will see what is behind me, but you will not see my face.' (Ex. 33:23). Philo ends the passage by explaining that it suffices the wise man to know all that is after God, but one who wishes to see the supreme essence will be blind before seeing it (165).[23]

In his exegesis of Ex. 33:23 Philo alludes to the distinction between God's existence and his essence. This distinction is more elaborately discussed in *Post.* 167-169. Speaking about the calf made by the Israelites from earrings (Ex. 32:2), Philo states that no god made with hands is a God for seeing and a true God, but is a God for hearing (166). The truly Existent, however, cannot be known through the ears, but only through the eyes of the understanding[24] from the powers in the universe and from the ceaseless motion of his works. Therefore God says: 'See, see that I am' (167; Deut. 32:39). That God is visible is not said with a proper use of words, but with an improper use, referring to each of his powers. He does not say 'See me' — because it is entirely impossible that God's essence is

---

[23] For Philo's interpretation of Ex. 33, see Part III. II § 19a.

[24] I follow Cohn's conjeture, PCW 2.37. For the expression 'eyes of the understanding', cf. *Opif.* 71, *Post.* 118, *Ios.* 106, *Spec.* 3.2.

perceived by created being —, but 'See, that I am', that is 'See my existence.' It is enough for man's reasoning faculty to learn that the cause of the universe is and exists, but to go further and to search for his essence or quality is a folly (168). God does not even permit it to Moses, for he says: 'You will see what is behind me, but you will not see my face' (Ex. 33:23). This saying means that all that is behind God is comprehensible for the wise man, but he himself alone is incomprehensible.[25] He is incomprehensible through direct contact, but comprehensible from the powers that follow and attend to him. They make evident not his essence, but his existence from the works accomplished by him (169).[26]

4. *Conclusion*

The texts of Philo and Gregory dealing with knowledge of God show a great resemblance. Both insist strongly on the incomprehensibility of God's essence for the human intellect, showing a negative approach to the divine principle, which is expressed with alpha-privatives. Both Philo and Gregory interpret the darkness from Ex. 20:21 as denoting God's invisibility and incomprehensibility. Both present Moses as an example of one who longs for knowledge of God but does not succeed. Speaking about God they make a distinction between God's existence, which can be known from God's works in the cosmos, and his unknowable essence. A difference is that Gregory bases God's incomprehensibility on his infinity, giving ample argumentation for the divine infinity. We can draw the conclusion that regarding the knowledge of God Gregory follows largely Philo's line of thought, defending the incomprehensibility of God's essence. This negative approach to the divine principle was also part of the Christian tradition before Gregory. Concerning the position of the Logos Gregory strongly rejects Philo's view, in which the Logos seems to be subordinated to God. For Gregory, this is the position of the Neo-Arians and therefore he associates the Neo-Arians with Judaism. Our research about Gregory and Philo's Judaism has to end with a paradox: on the one hand Gregory accuses Eunomius of Judaism and associates him with Philo, but at the other he defends against Eunomius theological positions that are also held by Philo.

---

[25] Cf. *Mut.* 9, *Fug.* 165.
[26] For the distinction between God's existence and God's essence, cf. *Det.* 89, *Deus* 62, *Spec.* 1.32, 39-41, *Virt.* 215, *Praem.* 40.

CHAPTER THREE

GREGORY'S *DE VITA MOYSIS*

Gregory wrote *De vita Moysis* in the last period of his life, between 390 and 392.[1] The treatises *De perfectione* and *De professione,* and the homilies on the Song of Songs, *In canticum canticorum,* date from the same period.[2] There are a large number of similarities between *Cant.* and *VM.* Both have as theme the unending quest of the soul for God. In *VM* Moses is taken as an example of the soul which ascends to God, while in *Cant.* the bride is the example of the ascending soul. The saying of Paul in Phil. 3:13, indicating the unending desire of the soul for God, plays a key role.[3] Negative theology occupies a prominent place in both treatises.[4]

1. *The Title of the Treatise*

In scholarly tradition both Philo's and Gregory's treatises bear the same Latin title *De vita Moysis.*[5] It would appear that this is the only case that a patristic work has the same title as a Philonic treatise. But in reality a closer look at the manuscripts shows that the matter is more complicated. Several manuscripts of Gregory's work confer different titles on the treatise, as can be seen from the following list:[6]

1. περὶ τοῦ βίου Μωϋσέως (ms. B)
2. τοῦ αὐτοῦ λόγοι περὶ ἀρετῆς δύο (ms. Λ)
3. περὶ ἀρετῆς ἤτοι εἰς τὸν βίον Μωϋσέως (ms. K)[7]
4. πρὸς Ὀλύμπιον ἀσκητὴν τοῦ αὐτοῦ εἰς τὸν βίον Μωϋσέως περὶ ἀρετῆς (ms. O)
5. περὶ ἀρετῆς ἤτοι βίου τελειότητος (ms. H)

---

[1] Daniélou (1966) 168-69, (1968) 14-15, May (1971) 63-4. Heine (1975) 15 supports an earlier date (in the mid 380s), arguing that the treatise belongs to the Eunomian controversy.
[2] For the date of *Cant.,* see Dünzl (1990), (1993) 30-33.
[3] *Cant.* 39.13-14, 119.16-17, 174.14-16, 245.15-17, 352.10, 366.15.
[4] See Dünzl (1993) 291-328.
[5] On the Latin titles of Philo's works, see Alexandre (1997).
[6] Musurillo (1964) 1. We follow Musurillo's indications for the manuscripts.
[7] Printed by Musurillo.

6. πρὸς Πέτρον τὸν ἴδιον ἀδελφὸν περὶ τοῦ βίου Μωϋσέως τοῦ νομοθέτου ἢ περὶ τῆς κατ' ἀρετὴν τελειότητος (mss. S)

7. πρὸς Καισάριον μόναχον περὶ τελειότητος ἐν ᾧ ἱστορεῖται καὶ ὁ τοῦ Μωϋσέως βίος (ms. Vat 444)

We can observe that four manuscripts offer a double title, having a reference both to Moses' life and to the subject of the treatise, namely virtue. This corresponds well with the structure of the treatise in two books. Such a double title is also found for Plato's dialogues, whose titles consist in a person's name and a descriptive subtitle.[8] The oldest manuscript, B, offers the most simple title: On the Life of Moses, which became the current one in its Latin translation. A reference to Moses' life is absent in two manuscripts. It is further remarkable that three different persons are mentioned as addressees: the monk Olympios, Gregory's brother Peter, and the monk Kaisarios. The manuscript that mentions Peter refers to Moses as legislator, though Moses' role as lawgiver is not especially discussed in VM. Two manuscripts (K, O) add the following subtitle at the end of the first book: τοῦ ἁγίου Γρηγορίου Νύσης λόγος α' εἰς τὸν βίον Μωϋσέως περὶ ἀρετῆς.[9] Although we have to remain in uncertainty about what was precisely the original title of Gregory's work, it seems that its title was not exactly the same as Philo's work on Moses. The majority of manuscripts of Philo gives the title περὶ τοῦ βίου Μωϋσέως,[10] and Philo himself points to it using the same title (Virt. 52, Praem. 53). Clement of Alexandria refers to Philo's treatise by this title as well (Strom. 1.153.2). It is also attested by John of Damascus in the Sacris Parallelis.

Comparing the titles of Gregory and Philo, we can state that in the titles given to Gregory's treatise the emphasis is more on its subject, namely virtue, whereas in Philo it is laid fully on the person of Moses. This reflects the difference in approach between the two treatises.

2. The Theme of the Treatise

De vita Moysis begins with an introduction (I.1-15), in which Gregory indicates the theme of the treatise.[11] The rest of book I, called historia, contains a historical sketch of Moses' life. In book II, called theoria,[12]

---

[8] Cf. Diogenes Laertius 3.58-59.

[9] Musurillo (1964) 33.

[10] See PCW 4.xxix, 119, 200.

[11] A short introduction to the treatise is given by Meredith (1995) 67-78. See further Malherbe-Ferguson (1979) 1-23.

[12] For Gregory's use of θεωρία, see Daniélou (1972).

Gregory shows by means of allegorical exegesis how the life of Moses can be an example for a virtuous life (cf. I.15). The treatise ends with an epilogue, in which Gregory makes concluding remarks on perfection in the virtuous life (II.319-321). Nearly every episode described in book one is explained allegorically in book two, so that there exists a close parallel between the two books.[13]

The theme of the treatise is explained in the introduction. Gregory has received a letter, perhaps from a monk, with a question about the perfect life (I.2). Answering this question Gregory states that perfection of all things that are measured by sense-perception is marked off by definite limits. Every quantitative measure is surrounded by its proper boundaries. Perfection of the number ten, for instance, consists in having both a beginning and an end. By contrast, the limit of perfection in virtue is the fact that it has no limit; this is taught by the apostle Paul, who ran the course of virtue but never stopped. Gregory refers here to Phil. 3:13, where Paul says that he is always stretching himself to things that lie before him. This verse, in Gregory's interpretation indicating the unending longing of the soul for God, plays a key role in the treatise (cf. II.225, 242). Answering the question why Paul never stopped in the course of virtue, Gregory assumes that no good has any limit in its own nature but is limited by its opposite: life is limited by death and light by darkness (I.5). Just as the end of life is the beginning of death, so also stopping in the course of virtue becomes the beginning of the course of evil (I.6). The Cappadocian father continues by stating that the divine nature is goodness, and is also limitless because there is no boundary to virtue, and the divine does not admit of its opposite (cf. II.237-239).[14] He who pursues true virtue participates in nothing other than God, who is himself absolute virtue. The participant's longing for God never stops because the good has no limit (I.7). Gregory concludes that perfection of human nature consists in wishing to grow in the good (I.10).[15]

From the Introduction it appears that the doctrine of the unending quest of the soul for God is the most important theological issue in the treatise. Gregory bases this idea logically on God's infinity: because God is without end, the ascent of the soul to God is also without end (II.238). The soul longs for God, but its desire is never satiated, as Gregory explains:

> this truly is the vision of God: never to be satisfied in the desire to see him. But one must always, by looking at what he can see, rekindle his desire to

---

[13] I am indebted to J.C.M. van Winden for this observation.
[14] See Part III. II § 19.a.
[15] Same conclusion is drawn at the end of *Perf.* 214.1-6.

see more. Thus, no limit would interrupt growth in the ascent to God, since no limit to the Good can be found nor is the increasing of desire for the Good brought to an end because it is satisfied (II.239, tr. Malherbe-Ferguson).

He sees the endless desire expressed by Paul in Phil. 3:13. This is the core of Gregory's spiritual theology and mysticism.[16] Jean Daniélou, who wrote much about Gregory's mysticism, refers to it with the term *epektasis*, stretching out, which refers to Phil. 3:13.[17]

3. *Moses as Example*

The ascent to God is illustrated by Moses, who is an example of one who never stops in his longing for God. 'Once having set foot on the ladder which God set up (as Jacob says), he continually climbed to the step above and never ceased to rise higher, because he always found a step higher than the one he has attained.' (II.227, tr. Malherbe-Ferguson). To illustrate Moses' unending ascent, Gregory gives a summary of Moses' life from his denying of the specious kinship with the Egyptian queen until he asks God to appear to him (II.228-230, cf. 308-313). In other treatises as well Gregory gives summaries of Moses' life and presents him as an example for the virtuous life (*Bas.* 125.23-130.6, *Cant.* 354.8-356.16, *Inscr. Psal.* 43.21-45.17).[18] He compares Gregory Thaumaturgus and Basil with Moses (*Bas.* 110.7, 126.2-4, *Thaum.* 10.8-9). In *CE* 2.85-92 he describes Abraham along the same lines as he presents Moses in *VM*. The exodus of Abraham is the spiritual journey of the soul, which seeks God. In his quest for God, Abraham surpasses all sense-perception and gains the insight that God is unknowable. Gregory applies also to him the saying of Paul from Phil. 3:13.

In addition to Moses, Gregory uses the apostle Paul as an important example. Paul was in the third heaven, in paradise, and heard the ineffable words (*VM* II.178; 2 Cor. 12:2-4, cf. *Cant.* 40.11-3, 85.20-86.1, 245.17-20, 326.11-15). Like Moses, Paul never stops in the course of virtue, but

---

[16] The fundamental work on Gregory's mysticism is Daniélou (1954a); see also Id. (1953b). His interpretation is criticized by Crouzel (1957) and Völker (1955) v-vi, 283-295. An overview of the scholarly debate is given by Mühlenberg (1966) 147-151, Von Strizky (1973) 67-70. See further Horn (1927), Louth (1981) 80-97, Dünzl (1993) 329-352, Daley (1996).

[17] Daniélou (1954a) 198, (1968) 26.

[18] See Daniélou (1954b) 387-390.

forgetting what is behind he stretches himself to things that lie before (*VM* I.5, II.225, 242; Phil. 3:13, cf. *Cant.* 245.20-22, *Theoph.* 123.20-124.3).

The figure of Moses occupies an important place in early Christianity as a predecessor and forerunner of Christ. Clement of Alexandria gives an overview of his life, mainly based on Philo's *Mos.* (*Strom.* 1.151-166).[19] He claims that Moses is the truly wise man and the truly divine legislator: the law was divinely given by him (1.167.1, 170.2). The Greek philosopher Plato based his legislation on the laws of Moses (1.165). Justin Martyr (*Dial.* 131-132) offers also summaries of Moses's life and of the events told in Exodus, but he does not allegorize Moses' life.[20] The notion of Moses and other biblical figures as examples recurs in the Cappadocian fathers. In a letter written to Gregory of Nazianzus in about 358, Basil names some Old Testament figures as models that should be imitated. After referring to the examples of Joseph, Job, David, and Moses, he remarks that one who is eager to make himself perfect in all kinds of virtue should look to the lives of the saints as upon statues and make their excellence his own by imitation (*Ep.* 2).[21] Gregory of Nazianzus compares Basil with Moses in his funeral oration about him (*Or.* 43.74).

The presentation of Moses' life as a model (ὑπόδειγμα) for a virtuous life to be imitated (I.15, cf. II.319) has been prepared by Philo, as rightly remarked by Andia.[22] In a digression on Moses' leadership in *Mos.* 1.148-162, Philo writes that Moses entered into the darkness where God was (Ex. 20:21), that is, into the unformed, invisible, incorporeal, and archetypal essence of the existing things (τῶν ὄντων παραδειγματικὴν οὐσίαν), and saw what is hidden from the sight of mortal nature. Moses has set, like a well made picture, himself and his life as a model (παράδειγμα) for those who wish to imitate it (158).[23] Obviously, Philo interprets Moses' stay on the mountain in Platonic terms, and his depiction of Moses' life as a model is linked to this Platonic interpretation.[24] But he refers to Moses' life as a 'form of virtue in perfection' (159),[25] and it is particularly striking that

---

[19] See Van den Hoek (1988) 48-68.

[20] Moses' life is also recorded in the Pseudo-Clementines (*Recognitationes* 34-38).

[21] The comparison with a statue occurs also in *VM* II.313.

[22] Andia (1996) 312-313.

[23] For Moses as παράδειγμα, cf. *Virt.* 51. See Mack (1972), who argues that Moses' life was a model for the cosmic ascent of the soul, whose goal is vision of God. This corresponds with the cosmic destiny of the Israelite people. Cf. *Ios.* 87, where Joseph's life is called ἀρχέτυπος.

[24] For Philo's use of the Platonic notion of model, see Billings (1919) 98-99, Runia (1986) 113-114. The idea of imitation of good examples occurs also in *Praem.* 114-115.

[25] For Moses as perfect, cf. *Mos.* 1.1, *Leg.* 3.134; Moses as νοῦς τελεῖος *Agr.* 80.

virtue in perfection is just the theme of Gregory's *VM*. It is highly probable that Gregory is inspired by Philo to present Moses' life as a model.

4. *Allegorical and Typological Interpretations*

In the presentation of the virtuous life Gregory frequently emphasizes the need for fighting against the passions. A virtuous life consists mostly in a struggle against the passions, and many interpretations reflect this concern. Gregory interprets, for instance, the Israelites' labour in Egypt as being engaged in pleasures and leading a material life according to the passions (II.60-61). Hence the exodus of the Israelites from Egypt is a symbol of the liberation of the soul from the tyranny of the passions (II.26). The ruin of the Egyptian army in the Red Sea symbolizes the destruction of the passions (II.122-125), and the bitter water at Marah shows that a life without pleasures is at first very hard for those who have left behind the Egyptian pleasures (II.132). Gregory explains the serpents that arise in the wilderness as beastly desires (II.276). As we shall see, all these interpretations, which concern passions and the struggle against them, have a Philonic background.

In *VM* Gregory gives many typological interpretations, which are mostly part of the Christian tradition before him. The stretching of Moses' arms refer to Jesus on the cross (II.78, 151; Justin *Dial.* 90-91, Irenaeus *Dem.* 46). The interpretation of the lamb, slaughtered at Passover, as a prefiguration of Christ is based on Joh. 1:29 (II.95; Justin *Dial* 40, 106). The wood at Marah that makes the bitter water sweet points also to Jesus' cross (II.132; Justin *Dial.* 86, Origen *Ex.hom.* 7.1, *Ios. hom.* 10.2). The twelve springs and the seventy palms at Elim represent the apostles (II.134; Origen *Ex. hom.* 7.3). Referring to 1 Cor. 10:4, Gregory interprets the flinty rock which gives water as pointing to Christ (II.135; Justin *Dial.* 86, Irenaeus *Dem.* 46). The bunch of grapes hanging on the wood is a reference to the passion of Christ (II.267-68; Clement *Paed.* 2.19.3). Quoting John 3:14, Gregory explains the brazen serpent made by Moses in the desert as a symbol of the mystery of the cross (II.277; Justin *Dial.* 94).

The incarnation plays an important role in *VM*, which reflects the theological debate on this issue in the time of writing.[26] A great number of interpretations refer to the incarnation: the burning bush (II.20); the changing of Moses' rod into a serpent (II.26-27, 31-34) and the alteration of the colour of Moses' hand (II.26-30); the manna (II.139), the building

---

[26] See Daniélou (1954b) 398.

of the tabernacle (II.174); the tablets of stone (II.216). These interpretations seem to have originated with Gregory.

5. *Previous Research on Gregory and Philo*

It has often been observed that influence of Philo's writings and thought is present in Gregory's *VM*. The French cardinal Jean Daniélou (1905-1974), who did much research on Gregory,[27] discusses Philonic influence on Gregory's treatise in the introduction of his edition of *VM*,[28] remarking that Gregory borrowed much from Philo in the *historia*, mainly the amplification of the Bible story, which is also found in Philo's *Mos*. Further, the French scholar detects some nearly literal parallels between Philo's *Mos*. and Gregory's work.[29] In the *theoria* there is resemblance to Philo's *Quaestiones in Exodum*. Daniélou concludes that the dependence of Gregory on Philo is evident. A striking point of Philo's influence on Gregory's exegesis is the interpretation of the darkness into which Moses enters on Mount Sinai (Ex. 20:21) as a symbol of God's unknowability (II.162-169). Philo gives the same exegesis in *Post*. 5, 14.[30]

In the critical edition of Gregory's works, the *Gregorii Nysseni Opera*,[31] *VM* was edited in 1964 as volume 7.1 by H. Musurillo, who studied a few more manuscripts than Daniélou. He, too, made many references to Philo in his *apparatus testimoniorum*. An English translation was made by A.J. Malherbe and E. Ferguson in 1978. They remark that 'Gregory draws its format from Philo's *Life of Moses* and its allegorical method from other Philonic works as this method had been transformed by Christian doctrinal interests.'[32] The most recent edition is by M. Simonetti (1984) and consists of an introduction, the Greek text and a commentary, in which he gives many

---

[27] See his bibliography in Fontaine - Kannengiesser (1972) 675-689.

[28] 1st ed. 1942, only French translation (SC 1), 2nd ed. 1955 with Greek text (SC 1bis); 3rd revisited and augmented ed. 1968; 4th unchanged reprint 1984. Review of the 2nd ed. Petit (1958).

[29] Daniélou (1968) 17-18.

[30] Daniélou (1968) 20-21.

[31] The critical edition of all Gregory's works was begun in 1908 under the leadership of U. von Wilamowitz-Moellendorf and later of W. Jaeger, but is not yet finished, cf. Hörner (1972). The most recent volume to appear is 3.4 (*Or. cat.* 1996). It is unfortunate that Musurillo uses other sigla than Daniélou for the manuscripts and that he does not take over the division in paragraphs which the French scholar has. Review of Musurillo's edition by Daniélou (1965). The 4th ed. contains a table of correspondence between the sigla of Daniélou and Musurillo/Simonetti.

[32] Malherbe - Ferguson (1978) 5-6.

references to the works of Philo. For the most part these scholars give the same references, but they neglect to examine these references further.[33]

In her review of Musurillo's edition Marguerite Harl remarks that many of these references have little value, because they are vague. Many parallels can be explained through the fact that Philo and Gregory comment on the same biblical text. Certainly, some themes are Philonic — Egypt as symbol of the passions, for instance — but the interpretation Gregory gives often differs from the one Philo gives in his allegorical treatises. She concludes that the relationship between Philo's and Gregory's exegesis must be studied further.[34]

After Harl's review two Italian scholars did some further research on this subject. In an article from 1974 C. Peri mentions a few nearly verbal parallels, but he also sees great differences between the two works, for instance, regarding the audience.[35] P. Mirri discusses the allegorical method of Philo and Gregory in *De vita Moysis*, concluding that for both writers allegory is the way to truth. Gregory as a Christian sees in the life of Moses images of the coming of Christ. The actual allegorical method used, however, is derived from the allegorical treatises of Philo.[36] In his monograph on Philo's influence in early Christian literature D.T. Runia, partly basing his conclusion on the above-mentioned tradition of research, summarizes the differences between the two works in five main points, among which a difference in the writer's aim, the public and the use of the allegorical method.[37] Finally, we mention the study by Ysabel de Andia about the mystical union in Ps. Denys. In one of its chapters she compares Philo, Gregory, and Ps. Denys with each other on four different points. Among other things she concludes that the interpretation of the darkness as God's incomprehensibility occurs in all three authors.[38] How and to what extent Gregory makes use of Philo is examined in the next part of our study.

---

[33] A German translation was made by W. Blum in 1963; a Spanish translation by L. F. Mateo-Seco in 1993.

[34] Harl (1966) 556-557.

[35] Peri (1974).

[36] Mirri (1982).

[37] Runia (1993) 257.

[38] Andia (1999).

PART THREE

THE PHILONIC BACKGROUND OF GREGORY'S
DE VITA MOYSIS

CHAPTER ONE

METHOD OF RESEARCH

We have already mentioned in the Introduction that Gregory's *De vita Moysis* consists of two books, between which a close parallel is discernible: nearly all 30 episodes into which the *historia* can be divided have their allegorical counterpart in the *theoria*.[1] The analysis of *VM* is based on these episodes so that books one and two are dealt with together. This has the advantage that the same biblical issue is discussed at the same time both in its literal exposition and in its allegorical exegesis.

The treatment of each episode consists mainly of three points of attention, of which the first is formed by a presentation of Gregory's description and exegesis. Owing to the subject of our research, this presentation is focused on those aspects that reflect Philo's influence. In the analysis we are indebted in some places to the fine English translation made by Malherbe and Ferguson. We have used the critical text edition by Musurillo, combined with the paragraph numbering made by Daniélou.

The next point to be addressed is the question how Philo treats the same episode, not only in *De vita Moysis*, but also in other treatises, since events from Moses' life are also related in the Allegorical Commentary and in the works belonging to the Exposition of the Law. It is obvious that a very important work in this respect is *Quaestiones et solutiones in Exodum*, of which only two books have been preserved in an Armenian translation made in Constantinople in the 6th century.[2] In his list of Philo's writings the Church historian Eusebius mentions five books, of which three must have been lost soon after Eusebius' death (*HE* 2.18.5).[3] The two books preserved are the original books ii and v, dealing with Ex. 12 and 22 - 28. Useful instruments for detecting passages dealing with Moses' life are the *Biblia Patristica*, an index of all references to the Bible in Philo and the Church fathers,[4] and *La bible d'Alexandrie*, a French translation of the LXX,

---

[1] See Part II. III § 2.
[2] For the *QE*, see Morris (1987) 826-830, Hilgert (1991) 8-9. An overview of the contents of *QE* is given by Royse (1976-77).
[3] For this list, see Part I. I § 1.
[4] (1975- 91) 5 vols. and supplement, containing Philo.

which gives a valuable survey of the exegesis of Philo and the Christian authors.[5] All the references to Philo in the modern editions of and commentaries to Gregory's *VM* have also been checked.

The final point that we address is the Christian tradition up to Gregory. In our treatment of this tradition we concentrate on the exegetical themes that are related to Moses' life. The first Christian author with whom we are concerned is the apologist Justin (died ca. 160), of whom three works have been preserved, viz. two *Apologies* and the *Dialogue with the Jew Trypho*. His exegesis of the Old Testament falls for the most part under the category of typology. Typology means that figures in the New Testament are foreshadowed in the Old Testament. In this kind of interpretation Moses is conceived of as a type of Christ (e.g., *Dial.* 111).[6] Another second-century theologian whom we research is Irenaeus of Lyon. In his main work, *Adversus Haereses*, he gives, like Justin, typological interpretations. Some sections of his *Demonstratio* are devoted to an exposition of the exodus from Egypt and the wanderings of the Israelite people in the desert (25-28). Because both Justin and Irenaeus do not offer elaborated allegorical interpretations of Moses' life, they are of relatively little relevance to our research.

Allegorical exegesis on a large scale is encountered for the first time in theologians connected with the catechetical school in Alexandria, Clement (ca. 145 - ca. 220) and Origen (185-253). The former, as we have already seen, makes extensive use of Philo's writings in the *Stromateis*;[7] the latter, a major transmitter of Philo's thought, is of great relevance to our subject, because he offers an allegorical interpretation of the events in Moses' life in the *Homilies on Exodus* and *Homilies on Numbers*. These homilies, delivered in about 239-242 in Caesarea,[8] have been preserved only in a Latin translation made by Rufinus of Aquileia at the beginning of the fifth century. Some Greek fragments commenting on Exodus and Numbers have survived in the *Catenae* (PG 12.281-297, 576-584, 17.16-17, 21-24) and in the *Philocalia*, an anthology of Origen's writings made by Basil and Gregory of Nazianzus. With regard to the homilies the question can rightly be raised whether Rufinus' translation is trustworthy. This issue is discussed by R.E. Heine in the introduction to his translation of Origen's homilies

---

[5] For our research vol. 2 (Exodus) by Le Boulluec and P. Sandevoir (1989) and vol. 4 (Numbers) by Dorival (1994) are the most important. For the exegesis of Exodus in Judaism and early Christianity, see Daniélou (1969); for the interpretation of Moses' life in the Church fathers, see Daniélou (1950) 131-200.

[6] For typological exegesis of Moses and the exodus, see Daniélou (1950) 144-151.

[7] See Part I. I § 1.

[8] Nautin (1977) 401-405, 411

on Genesis and Exodus. He reaches the following conclusions: first, it is impossible from the translation to gain knowledge of the exact words of Origen. Secondly, Origen's homiletic style may have been altered. Finally, Rufinus gives answers to questions that Origen left unsolved. 'Nevertheless, one may say that, on the whole, the substance can be regarded as representing Origen's thought.'[9] The Greek fragments of the homilies on Exodus, preserved in the *Catenae,* confirm Heine's conclusion.[10] So, despite the loss of the original Greek text of Origen's writings, it is possible to gain a reliable knowledge of his exegesis of Moses' life.

Origen spent the last two decades of his life in Caesarea in Palestine, the birthplace of the later bishop Eusebius (ca. 263 - ca. 340), whose important role in the transmission of the Philonic corpus has already been mentioned.[11] He is best known as historian, but besides historical and apologetic works he composed two large commentaries, namely *On The Psalms* and *On Isaiah.* Both writings contain little allegorical exegesis concerning Moses' life. The feast of Passover is discussed in *De solemnitate Paschali,* dedicated to Emperor Constantine. The figure of Moses does have appeal to Eusebius because he sees in Constantine, who freed the Christian people, the new Moses.[12] The Church historian compares the fall of Maxentius, Constantine's adversary, together with his army in the Tiber to the destruction of Pharaoh's army in the Red Sea, and after the victory Constantine, like Moses, sang a hymn of triumph (*HE* 9.9.5-8).

Gregory Thaumaturgus (ca. 213 - ca. 270) was an important figure for the Church in Cappadocia. Originating from Neocaesarea in Pontus, he attended Origen's lectures in Caesarea for a period of five years (233-238). In his *Address to Origen* he describes his master's teaching. Having become bishop of his birthplace, he was very active in spreading the gospel in Cappadocia, and therefore he was regarded as the father of the Church in this country. He played a key role in the transmission of Origen's thought to Cappadocia, and he was the teacher of Gregory's and Basil's grandmother, Macrina. Gregory of Nyssa composed an encomium on him, *De vita Gregorii Thaumaturgi.*

It goes without saying that the writings of the Cappadocians, Gregory's elder brother Basil (ca. 330 - 379) and his friend Gregory of Nazianzus (ca. 330 - 390), have also to be included in our research on patristic exegesis. The three Cappadocians had close contacts with each other, and, without

---

[9] Heine (1982) 37-38.
[10] Heine (1982) 40.
[11] See Part I. I § 1.
[12] Chesnut (1986) 162-163.

doubt, influenced each other's thought. Basil, mainly known for his leading role in the organisation of monasticism, wrote a few exegetical works.
One of them, namely *In Hexaemeron*, which comments on the creation
account, displays knowledge of Philo's *De opificio mundi*. In his *Homilies on
the Psalms* and *Commentary on Isaiah* he relies strongly on Eusebius'
commentaries on the same biblical books. His authorship of the commentary on Isaiah is disputed, but its authenticity is defended by N.A. Lipatov,
who points to similarities with *In Hexaemeron*.[13] Gregory of Nazianzus did
not write specifically exegetical works. His literary activity consists for the
most part of orations, of which the five so-called *Theological Orations* (27-
31), delivered in Constantinople in 380 in defence of the Nicene
confession, are the most important. Although both Basil and Gregory of
Nazianzus do not give much allegorical exegesis, they do refer to events in
Moses' life. Gregory, for instance, discusses the Passover in his 45th speech.
Basil and his friend Gregory are the last writers involved in our research.
Dealing with patristic exegesis, we have to bear in mind that much of
patristic literature has not survived, but the Christian writers mentioned
above seem to be representative of patristic exegesis.

   Having thus discussed Gregory's interpretation of an episode, Philo's
treatment of the same event, and its patristic exegesis, we will be able to
determine whether and to what extent Gregory depends on Philo, and we
shall be in a position to offer answers to the questions posed in the
Introduction. An impediment may be formed by what H. Dörrie calls
'Gedanken-Zitate', that is, Gregory takes over an idea from a predecessor
but he rewords it so that similarity in expression disappears.[14] It is,
however, possible to trace such 'thought-citations' by comparing passages
from Philo and Gregory that deal with the same exegetical matter.

   In order to get a grip on Gregory's use of Philo, it is useful to make a
distinction between (A) borrowings on the level of phraseology and (B)
the use of Philo's material in the allegorical exegesis. It turns out that in a
great number of cases Gregory uses the same or nearly the same significant
words or expressions as Philo does in the same context, and these words or
phrases do not occur in the biblical text. Such cases can be labelled as
Philonic phraseology. We deal with imagery and metaphorical use of words
under the heading of phraseology as well. In the analysis of this kind of
borrowing the texts of Philo and Gregory are placed side by side in order
to make Philo's influence visible. Comparable words and expressions are

---

[13] Lipatov (1993).
[14] Dörrie (1983) 885.

marked in the same way (underlining, double underlining). Translations of longer citations are given in the footnotes. We do not wish to suggest that Gregory, having Philo's texts on his desk, was only copying Philo. He makes a creative use of the Philonic material. The proof for Gregory's use of Philo's expressions is cumulative: the more expressions in Gregory which run parallel to expressions in Philo, the more it is likely that Gregory borrows them from his Jewish predecessor. When we draw conclusions, we have to take into account two points: first, the loss of the Greek text of Origen's works may be a handicap to settle Gregory's use of Philo's writings. What we call a Philonic expression may also have occurred in Origen. Nevertheless, it is clear that Gregory was acquainted with the writings of Philo and employed them. Secondly, we should take into consideration the possibility of a *topos*: what seems to be a phrase derived from Philo may be a *topos* used by both Philo and Gregory. The lexical database of the Thesaurus Linguae Graecae is useful for identifying such *topoi*.

Besides Philo's influence on the level of phraseology, there is also Gregory's use of Philo in the allegorical interpretation. In this case there are the following possibilities:

(B1) Gregory has exactly the same interpretation of a biblical passage as Philo, and this interpretation does not recur in the Christian exegetes mentioned above. It is highly plausible that Gregory derives it from Philo.

(B2) Gregory gives an exegesis comparable to an interpretation in Philo but this exegesis is also encountered in the Christian tradition, and it is thus impossible to determine whether Gregory derives his interpretation from Philo.

(B3) The exegesis that Gregory offers occurs — to a smaller or greater extent — in Philo and cannot be found in the Christian writers involved in our research. Gregory, however, changes Philo's exegesis in some respects, giving it, for instance, a Christian turn; nevertheless, the Philonic background remains recognizable. In these cases the conclusion can be drawn that Gregory derives his interpretation from Philo. This conclusion can be strengthened if Gregory also uses Philonic phraseology. The final category is, of course, the most interesting. Here we are able to see in what exegetical themes Gregory is influenced by Philo, to what extent he relies on Philo, and in what way he alters Philonic exegesis. The classification system cannot be applied too rigorously, because the borders between categories are vague in some cases. It is only meant as a means to get insight into Gregory's use of Philo's exegesis, and it does not do full justice to Gregory as interpreter and writer.

A final remark must be made concerning our treatment of Gregory's *VM*. Its analysis is rather one-sided because it is made from a Philonic point of view. It concentrates on Philo's influences, which entails that other considerable points in the treatise are not examined. Only those aspects are dealt with that are relevant to the subject of our research: the influence of Philo's treatises in Gregory's *De vita Moysis*.

CHAPTER TWO

ANALYSIS OF GREGORY'S *DE VITA MOYSIS*

0. *Introduction* (I.1-15)

In the introduction of *De vita Moysis* Gregory expounds its central theme: perfection in the virtuous life.[1] He argues that perfection in virtue has no boundary and that the desire of the soul for God is unending, because God is without end. Gregory concludes that perfection of human nature consists in wishing to grow in the good (I.10).[2] Next he refers to a remark of Isaiah, who says: 'Look to Abraham, your father, and to Sarah, who gave birth to you' (Is. 51:2). By the example of Abraham and Sarah, Scripture may guide to the harbour of the divine will those adrift on the sea of life with pilotless minds (I.11). The memory of those distinguished in life shows how it is possible to anchor the soul in the calm harbour of virtue, where it no longer has to pass the winter amid the storms of life or be shipwrecked in the depth of evil by the waves of passion (I.13).

Gregory intends to set forth the life of Moses as an example for the virtuous life. First, he will outline Moses' life on the basis of divine Scripture; thereafter, he will seek out the spiritual meaning corresponding with the history in order to obtain suggestions for the virtuous life (I.15).

In the introduction Gregory employs the imagery of the sea of life with the waves of passions in contrast to the calm harbour of virtue, where the soul can be anchored safely. Although the expression 'sea of life' can be regarded as a commonplace in the Church fathers, having its origin in Plato, the whole image has a Philonic background because the phrase 'harbour of virtue' seems to be exclusive to the Jewish author.[3] The

---

[1] For the introduction, see Macleod (1982) and Böhm (1996) 27-66. The theme of perfection in the virtuous life is also dealt with in *Perf.* (cf. 173.1-3).

[2] Same conclusion is drawn at the end of *Perf.* 214.1-6.

[3] The expression 'sea of life' occurs in Origen (*Lev. hom.* 7.7, *Ios. hom.* 19.4, *Jer. hom.* 18.5, *Ps. fr.* PG 17.141A), Eusebius *Es. com.* 1.64 (p. 91.8). Comparable image in Clement *Prot.* 12.118.4. See further Rahner (1964) 272-303, 548-564. The commentators on Gregory refer to Philo *Sacr.* 90 (Daniélou (1968) 53 n. 3, Musurillo (1964) 5, Malherbe-Ferguson (1978) 150 n. 22). A search in the TLG learns that the phrase 'harbour of virtue' does not occur in Plato, Clement, the Greek works of Origen, Eusebius, Basil, or Gregory of Nazianzus.

Philonic background is strengthened by the occurrence of more reminiscences of Philo in II.6 and II.8, where Gregory projects the same imagery.[4] The resemblance between the two writers becomes clear by a juxtaposition of the texts:

Spec. 1.224	*VM* I.11
...καὶ τὸ μακρὸν <u>τοῦ βίου πέλαγος</u> εὐθύνων ἐν εὐδίᾳ καὶ γαλήνῃ πραγμάτων.[5]	... τοὺς ἀκυβερνήτῳ τῇ διανοίᾳ κατὰ <u>τὴν</u> <u>τοῦ βίου θάλασσαν</u> πλανωμένους[7]
Sacr. 90	*VM* I.13
...ὥσπερ εἰς ...ναυλοχώτατον <u>λιμένα τὴν</u> <u>ἀρετὴν</u> ἀφικόμενος βεβαίως ἱδρυθῇς.	...<u>τῷ ἀκλύστῳ τῆς ἀρετῆς λιμένι τὴν</u> ψυχὴν <u>καθορμίσαι</u>
Somn. 2.225	
... τοῖς <u>τῆς ἀρετῆς</u> εὐδίοις καὶ ναυλοχωτάτοις <u>ἐνορμίζεσθαι λιμέσιν.</u>[6]	

Despite slight variations in wording (πέλαγος becomes θάλαττα), the picture remains the same as in Philo, and we can label the image as Philonic phraseology (A).

1. *Moses' Birth and the Tyrant* (I.16, II.1-5)

Gregory begins his narrative of Moses' life by reporting that at the time of his birth the tyrant[8] had issued the decree that male offspring should be destroyed but female offspring should stay alive (I.16; Ex. 1:16, 22). Responding to the question how we can imitate Moses' birth by our own free will, Gregory offers a symbolic interpretation of male and female.[9] The female form of life is the material and passionate disposition, to which

---

[4] See § 2.1.

[5] Gregory uses πέλαγος τοῦ βίου in *Cant.* 81.13.

[6] Cf. *Fug.* 50: 'You will find the house of wisdom a calm and fair haven, which will welcome you, when you come to anchor.'

[7] Gregory employs the same image in *Eccl.* 290.20, *Mart.* Ia 142.12-13, *Melet.* 455.7-8, *Virg.* 274.9-275.16, 321.19-23, 322.5.

[8] Gregory often denotes Pharaoh as tyrant (I.16, 17, II.1, 2 etc.) even though this appellation does not occur in Exodus. The rule of Pharaoh symbolizes the tyranny of the passions, see Daniélou (1954a) 79. For Philo's and Gregory's interpretation of Pharaoh, see § 7.1.

[9] Later on, free will is emphasized in the discussion on the hardening of Pharaoh's heart, VM II.73-77, 80, 86. The doctrine of free will occupies an important place in Gregory's thought, see Muckle (1945), Gaïth (1953) 67-81, Völker (1955) 74-80; for free will in Philo, see Winston-Dillon (1983) 181-195.

human nature has fallen. The tyrant wishes this to stay alive. On the contrary, the male child signifies the hard and intensive life of virtue, which is hostile to the tyrant and suspected of rebellion against his rule (II.2). Man can imitate Moses' birth because he is able to generate himself by his own free will in accordance with whatever he wishes to be, whether male or female (II.3). The rational faculties are the parents of virtue (II.4),[10] and free will serves as a midwife in this kind of birth (II.5). Two issues from Gregory's exegesis of Moses' birth should be dealt with, namely the metaphor of giving birth to virtue (1.1), and the interpretation of male and female (1.2).

1.1. *The Metaphor of Giving Birth to Virtue*

In his interpretation of Moses' birth Gregory makes use of a biological metaphor, in which the rational faculties of men are compared to parents who generate a male offspring, namely virtue (II.4). According to Daniélou this is a Philonic theme, and he refers to *Leg.* 3.180 and *Cher.* 42-52.[11] In the latter text Philo discusses Gen. 4:2, which reads: 'Adam knew his wife and she conceived and bore Cain.' He explains that the lawgiver does not present virtuous persons, like Abraham, Isaac, Jacob, and Moses, as knowing women (40). Woman is, figuratively speaking, sense-perception, which is rejected by the lovers of wisdom because knowledge is brought about through estrangement from sense and body.[12] The wives of these men, Sarah, Rebecca, Leah, and Zipporah, are called women, but are in reality virtues (41). Virtues, however, that give birth to perfect offspring are not permitted to have contact with a mortal man (43). On the contrary, they receive seed from the Father of all, the unbegotten God and begetter of all things (44).

Philo treats the example of Rachel in *Leg.* 3.180 with reference to Gen. 30:1, where she says to Jacob 'Give me children.' Jacob answers that he does not take the place of God, who alone has power to open the wombs of souls, to sow virtues in them, to make them pregnant with beautiful things, and to give birth to them. Leah, too, does not receive seed and offspring

---

[10] *VM* II.4 λογισμοὶ δ' ἂν εἶεν οὗτοι οἱ τῆς ἀρετῆς γινόμενοι πατέρες. Cf. II.6 ... γεννῆσαι τὸ ἀνδρεῖον τοῦτο καὶ ἐνάρετον γέννημα . . II.7 οἱ δὲ σώφρονές τε καὶ προνοητικοὶ λογισμοί, οἱ τῆς ἀνδρείας γονῆς πατέρες. II.37 τεκνογονία ἀρετῆς. Cf. *Virg.* 308.16-17.

[11] Daniélou (1968) 108 n. 1; cf. Musurillo (1964) 34, Malherbe-Ferguson (1978) 157 n. 6.

[12] For the Philonic interpretation of woman as sense-perception, see Baer (1970) 38-39, Sly (1990) 91-110, and Mattila (1996) 112-120.

from a man but from God, for it is written: 'The Lord, when he saw that Leah was hated, opened her womb, but Rachel was barren' (Gen. 29:31; cf. *Leg.* 2.46-47).[13]

Although both Philo and Gregory employ a comparable metaphor of giving birth to virtue, they strongly differ regarding the content. Central in Philo is the idea that God, the begetter, sows seed in the virtues symbolized by women,[14] whereas Gregory underlines that men themselves bring forth virtue with free will as midwife. The notion of free will is absent in Philo's texts on the impregnation of the soul. A further discrepancy between Philo and Gregory is that in the former virtue is represented by the wives of the patriarchs, whereas in the latter the male child signifies virtue. Because of these considerable differences between the two authors in employing and elaborating the metaphor, it would be going too far to label Gregory's use as Philonic. Furthermore, the image is also found in Origen. In *Num. hom.* 20.2, commenting on the adultery of the Israelite men (Num. 25:1), he writes that a soul that leaves God's word commits adultery and gives birth to vices, but a soul that has intercourse with God's word gives birth to good children, like modesty and courage.[15]

1.2. *The Symbolic Explanation of Male and Female*

Like Gregory, Philo offers a symbolic interpretation of male and female, and the commentators on Gregory refer to *Leg.* 3.3, 3.243, and *QE* 1.8.[16] In the first two texts the Jewish exegete deals with the midwives who do not carry out Pharaoh's orders (Ex. 1:17). At *Leg.* 3.3 Philo discusses Ex. 1:21 'Because the midwives feared God, they made houses for themselves', linking it with verse 17 'The midwives saved male children alive.'[17] He

---

[13]   For a discussion of the theme of the divine impregnation of the soul, see Baer (1970) 55-64. Sly treats the marriages of the patriarchs (1990) 132-160. For God as begetter, cf. *Leg.* 1.49, 3.219, *Post.* 135, *Det.* 60, *Deus* 137, *Migr.* 34, 142, *Her.* 50-51, *Congr.* 138, *Mut.* 132, 137-138, *Praem.* 160. In *Abr.* 100-101 Philo speaks about the marriage made by wisdom, in which virtue (the wife) sows good counsels, whereas thought (the man) receives the holy seed. Festugière (1949) 547-551 names as Philo's sources, on the one hand, Diotima's speech in Plato's *Symp.* (208-209) about the generating of virtue as an immortal child. On the other hand, he points to the image in the OT of God's marriage with the Israelite people, who commit adultery. For the Platonic background, see Billings (1919) 96-98, who refers to *Theat.* 150B-151D, *Rep.* 490B, *Phaedr.* 256E, as well as to *Symp.*

[14]   Same conclusion by Baer (1970) 61.

[15]   The same notion is also met with in the *Corpus Hermeticum* 9.3-4. For the theme of the marriage of the soul in Origen, see Crouzel (1977).

[16]   Daniélou (1968) 107 n. 2, Musurillo (1964) 34, Malherbe-Ferguson (1978) 157 n. 3, Simonetti (1984) 274.

[17]   LXX Ex. 1:21 ἐπειδὴ ἐφοβοῦντο αἱ μαῖαι τὸν θεόν, ἐποίησαν ἑαυταῖς οἰκίας. The

explains the midwives as looking for God's hidden mysteries — that is 'saving the males alive' — and as building up the affairs of virtue, in which they chose to live. Further on in the treatise (243) Philo brings up the same midwives again. They disregard the commands of Pharaoh, the scatterer, and keep alive the male offspring of the soul, which he wishes to destroy, because he is a lover of female matter, not knowing the Cause and saying 'I do not know him' (Ex. 5:2). A concise explanation of male and female is given at *QE* 1.8, where Philo discusses the sheep that must be slaughtered on the Passover (Ex. 12:5). Symbolically, the sheep indicates progress towards perfection, and at the same time the male. 'For progress is indeed nothing else than giving up the female gender by changing into the male, since the female gender is material, passive, corporeal and sense-perceptible, while the male is active, rational, incorporeal and more akin to mind and thought' (tr. Marcus).[18]

Gregory's exegesis of male and female as virtue and passion is in line with Philo's interpretation, but it occurs in Christian writers as well. Origen, for instance, conceives of woman as flesh and affections of the flesh, whereas man is rational sense and intellectual spirit.[19] Pharaoh, interpreted as the devil and the prince of this world (Joh. 16:11),[20] wants to kill rational sense, which is able to understand heavenly things and to perceive God. He wishes to augment what belongs to flesh and bodily matter (*Ex. hom.* 2.1). Since the Egyptians save the girls and hate the boys, they hate virtues and nourish only vice and pleasure (*Ex. hom.* 2.3).[21] Because Philo's exegesis of male and female recurs in some Church fathers, we can conclude that Gregory's exegesis falls under category B2: a Philonic exegesis that is also found in other Christian writers.

2. *Moses' Basket in the River* (I.17, II.6-9)

After Moses' birth his parents lay the child in a basket, which they place in the marsh near the river (Ex. 2:3). Deviating from the biblical report,

---

translation of the Hebrew text runs: 'He (*sc. God*) made for them (*masc.*) houses'.

[18] Philo gives the same interpretation of man as virtue and woman as passion in *Sacr.* 102-103, *Det.* 28, *Gig.* 1-5, *Deus* 3, 111, *Ebr.* 211, *Mut.* 261, *Abr.* 102, *Mos.* 2.184, *QE* 2.3. For a discussion of Philo's interpretation of male and female, see Baer (1970) 35-54, Bitter (1992).

[19] Same interpretation in *Gen. hom.* 4.4, 5.2, see Borret (1985) 70 n. 2.

[20] For Origen's interpretation of Pharaoh, see § 7.1.

[21] Cf. Clement *Strom.* 3.63.2, where female is explained as desire. Methodius gives the same interpretation of Pharaoh, man and woman (*Symp.* 4.2).

Gregory writes that the basket[22] is placed in the river but, being guided
by some divine power, lands at the bank, where it is discovered by
Pharaoh's daughter (I.17).[23] In his allegorical exegesis the river stands for
life made turbulent by the waves of passions.[24] Some parents deliver their
children to the stream without forethought (II.6) but the parents of the
male child make their son safe in a basket so that he will not be immersed
when he is given to the stream.[25] The basket, constructed out of various
boards, is a symbol of education in the different disciplines, which holds
what it carries above the waves of life (II.7). Gregory here means by
education the regular school course, which consists of different subjects
such as grammar, arithmetic, geometry, etc., and which is usually called
ἐγκύκλιος παιδεία.[26] Two points in this passage deserve our attention,
namely the image of the stream of life (2.1), and the exegesis of Moses'
basket (2.2).

2.1. *The Stream of Life*

Following up on his allusion to 'the sea of life' in the introduction (I.11),
Gregory here employs the image of the stream of life tossed by passions, in
which the soul is immersed. The same imagery, which is ultimately derived
from Heraclitus (fr. B 12, 49DK) and Plato's *Timaeus* (43 A-D), is also
repeatedly used by Philo.[27] To give only a few examples, in *Fug.* 49 and

---

[22] The LXX translates the Hebrew word for basket by θῖβις. Gregory uses κιβωτός (I.17,
II.7,9), which is only used in the LXX for Noah's ark (Gen. 6:14) and for the ark of
covenant (Ex. 25:10) but he also employs λάρναξ (I.17, *Diem lum.* 233.1). Aquila renders
κιβωτός, see Harl (1987) 31-35, Le Boulluec-Sandevoir (1989) 80-81, Houtman (1986-96)
1.263-264.
[23] Philo (*Mos.* 1.12, 17, 19) and Josephus (*AJ* 2.223) also discern God's leading hand in
the events (cf. *CE* 2.285). In *Mos.* Philo does not mention the basket, but narrates only the
exposure at the bank of the river (*Mos.* 1.10). For Philo's treatment of Moses' birth and
exposure, see Cohen (1993) 40-46.
[24] The same imagery is found in I.11, 13.
[25] Gregory associates the word ἀσφαλτόπισσα (Ex. 2:3) with ἀσφαλής (=safe). Philo does
so in *Conf.* 106.
[26] See for ἐγκύκλιος παιδεία SVF 1.259, 349, 350, 3.294, 738, Origen *Ep. ad Greg.* 88A,
Eusebius *HE* 6.18.3. In *Diem lum.* 233.1 Moses in the basket represents the law. In Origen's
interpretation Pharaoh's daughter is the Church which comes to the waters of baptism
and accepts the law (=Moses) laid down in the basket. The pith and asphalt of the basket
signify the letter of the Jewish law (*Ex. hom.* 2.4). The interpretation of Moses as law is
found repeatedly in Origen's writings, see Borret (1985) 84 n. 3.
[27] See the list and discussion in Runia (1986) 260-262; see further Billings (1919) 69-70,
and Méasson (1987) 176-192. Methodius makes use of the image in *Symp.* 4.2-3.

Mut. 214 he explicitly speaks about the river of life.[28] In *Leg.* 3.18 he explains that the river which Jacob crosses is the river that drowns the soul under the flood of passions. When Jacob had crossed it, he sets feet on the high land, that is the principle of perfect virtue. Philo refers to the Egyptian river as the river of passions, explaining it as the body in *Somn.* 2.109. Though Gregory employs the same image as Philo, he does not interpret the river as the body. In the context of this image the Cappadocian father makes a metaphorical use of σάλος (swell), speaking about 'the swell of life'. As already stated by Billings the metaphorical use of σάλος and σαλεύω is typical of Philo, and a nearly verbal parallel with Gregory's text is found in *Sacr.* 13:[29]

Sacr. 13
τοῖς μὲν γὰρ εἰς τὸν τοῦ βίου σάλον καὶ
κλύδωνα παρεληλυθόσιν ἐπινηχομένοις
ἀνάγκη φορεῖσθαι...[30]

VM II.8
...ἔξω τοῦ βιωτικοῦ σάλου...

It is significant that in the same treatise Philo uses the figurative expression 'harbour of virtue' (*Sacr.* 90), which, as we saw above, occurs in Gregory as well (I.13). Although elements of the imagery of the stream of life moved by the passions as waves are encountered in other writers, it is very likely that Gregory's employment of the same image results from his reading of Philo because of the copious use that the Jewish exegete makes of it. Furthermore, we have observed some verbal parallels between the two authors in the phrases 'swell of life', 'sea of life', and 'harbour of virtue'.[31] For this reason it is appropriate to label Gregory's use of the image as Philonic (classification A).

2.2. *Exegesis of Moses' Basket*

Philo regards both Moses' basket and Noah's ark as a symbol of the body,[32] and this interpretation does not, to the best of my knowledge, occur in

---

[28] *Fug.* 49 ...εἰς μέσον τὸν χειμάρρουν ποταμὸν τοῦ βίου, καὶ μὴ ἐπικλυσθεὶς ἐγκαταποθῇς,... *Mut.* 214 ... εἴ τις ἐν μέσῳ τοῦ βίου ποταμῷ φορούμενος... Gregory uses the word ῥεῖθρον (II.6).

[29] Billings (1919) 92.

[30] Other examples in Philo are *Leg.* 2.90, *Cher.* 12-13, *Sacr.* 90, *Post.* 22, 32, *Deus* 26, *Congr.* 60, *Somn.* 2.225, *Decal.* 67. See also *Enar. Es.* 272A, ascribed to Basil: 'those who are tossed in the salt billow of this life.'

[31] See § 0.

[32] *Det.* 170, *Plant.* 43, *Conf.* 105-106, *QG* 2.1-8, 25.

Gregory's writings. Rather, it seems that he avoids an allegorical exegesis in terms of the body since he also does not explain the Egyptian river as the body, as Philo does (*Somn.* 2.109). However, his explanation of the basket as education, which I have not found in other Church fathers, may have a Philonic background. Marguerite Harl refers to Procopius of Gaza's commentary on Exodus, where the same interpretation of the basket is given, perhaps derived from Philo's *QE* (PG 87.518.22-28).[33] It may be questioned, however, whether Procopius here reports Philo's exegesis. James Royse has argued that Procopius' commentary does not contain any extracts from the lost books of Philo's *QE*, and that Philo does not treat Exodus 2 in *QE*.[34] Furthermore, it is not very likely that the Jewish exegete would have explained Moses' basket as education in *QE*, whereas he interprets it as the body in several places in his other writings. A suggestion made by Monique Alexandre is more justified. She proposes that Gregory's interpretation is a transposition of an exegesis found in *Somn.* 1.205, where Philo discusses the art of variety (ποικιλτικὴ τέχνη).[35] This art is practised by Bezaleel, who is able to bring together many different things into one and the same thing. Taking elements from various disciplines, namely grammar, arithmetic, geometry, music, rhetoric, philosophy, and all other things that constitute the whole life of men, he makes a single work.[36] It is indeed probable that Gregory makes use of this passage of Philo. In Gregory's exegesis the basket, consisting of various disciplines, takes the place of Bezaleel's work, made of elements from different disciplines. Bezaleel's work can be associated with Moses' basket because Bezaleel is said to be the maker of the ark (Ex. 38:1), and for Bezaleel's ark the same word is used in the LXX as Gregory employs for Moses' basket, namely κιβωτός.[37] The interpretation of the basket as education can thus be labelled as a Philonic exegesis which has been altered (B3). The alteration consists in the transposition of the exegesis from one biblical object (Bezaleel's work) to another (Moses' basket).

---

[33] Harl (1987) 34 n. 29. In PG 87 a Latin translation is printed.

[34] Royse (1976-77) esp. 56, 61.

[35] Alexandre (1967) 92.

[36] Cf. Ex. 36:36, where his work is called ἔργον ποικιλτοῦ, cf. in Gregory ἡ ποικίλων μαθημάτων πηγνυμένη παίδευσις (II.7).

[37] Cf. *Plant.* 144, where παίδευσις is presented as saving the soul from being hurt by the stream. This remark comes close to Gregory's interpretation of the basket as education, which is a means of salvation from the stream of life.

3. *Moses adopted by Pharaoh's Daughter* (I.17-18, II.10-12)

Having been found and adopted by Pharaoh's daughter, Moses receives an education at Pharaoh's court,[38] after which he returns to his natural mother, rejecting Pharaoh's daughter as mother (I.17-18; Ex. 2:5-10).[39] In Gregory's interpretation Pharaoh's childless and barren daughter[40] is a symbol of pagan education and philosophy[41] because pagan culture is really childless and always in labour but it never gives birth. Do not all, Gregory asks rhetorically, who are full of wind and who come never to fulfilment miscarry before they come to the light of the knowledge of God? (II.11).[42] We should address three aspects from this passage, viz. Moses' royal education (3.1), the interpretation of Pharaoh's daughter (3.2), and the image of the woman being in labour (3.3).

3.1. *Moses' Royal Education*

Both Philo and Gregory refer to the education Moses receives at Pharaoh's court as a royal education:

Mos. 1.8 τροφῆς δ' ἠξιώθη βασιλικῆς.   *VM* I.18
1.20 τροφῆς οὖν ἤδη βασιλικῆς καὶ   ἐκβὰς δὲ ἤδη τὴν ἡλικίαν τῶν παίδων ἐν
θεραπείας ἀξιούμενος...   βασιλικῇ τῇ τροφῇ καὶ παιδευθεὶς τὴν
1.25 ἤδη δὲ τοὺς ὅρους τῆς παιδικῆς ἔξωθεν παίδευσιν, .
ἡλικίας ὑπερβαίνων

Not only is there an exact verbal parallel in the phrase 'royal education', but also the expression for leaving childhood is nearly similar. Here we have for the first time a direct echo of Philo's *Mos.* in Gregory's *VM*.

---

[38] Cf. in Gregory *Bas.* 126.8-9. Moses' education is not explicitly mentioned in Exodus, but reported by Ezekiel Tragicus (*Exagoge* 37) and Philo (*Mos.* 1.20-24). Cf. further Act. 7:22 (for the Hellenistic background of Act. 7:22, see Runia (1993) 66), Clement *Strom.* 1.153.2-3 (see Van den Hoek (1988) 54) and Basil (*Hom. hex.* 1.1 (5A), *Libris* 3, *Enar. Es.* 433C). For the interpretation of Ex. 2:1-15 in Hellenistic Judaism and the NT, see Barclay (1992).

[39] For Moses' rejection of Pharaoh's daughter, cf. Hebr. 11:24. Moses' preference for his own people and natural parents is also mentioned by Philo (*Mos.* 1.32). For Moses in the Epistle to the Hebrews, see Williamson (1970) 449-491 and D'Angelo (1979).

[40] The notion that Pharaoh's daughter is barren is part of the Jewish tradition (Philo *Mos.* 1.13, Josephus *AJ* 2.232, Artapanus *ap.* Eusebius *PE* 9.27.2).

[41] Gregory uses the terms ἡ ἔξωθεν παίδευσις (*VM* I.18, II.11, 115, *Opif. hom.* 144D), and ἡ ἔξωθεν φιλοσοφία (*VM* II. 10, 40, 41) to denote pagan culture and philosophy. Later on Gregory interprets Moses' wife in the same way (II.37), see § 7.3.

[42] Origen sees in Pharaoh's daughter the Church, see further § 2.

Because I do not know of any examples of this phrase in other Church fathers in the same context, it is appropriate to label the phrase as Philonic (A).

3.2. *Interpretation of Pharaoh's Daughter*

Regarding the interpretation of Pharaoh's daughter, the commentators on Gregory refer to *Leg.* 3.244-45, where Philo discusses the intercourse between Abraham and the female servant Hagar (Gen. 16:2).[43] When Abraham had not yet become perfect he had intercourse with Hagar, that is the school education (ἐγκύκλιος παίδεια).[44] Her name means 'sojourning' because he who is studying for life in perfect virtue sojourns with the school education in order that he may be led by this to perfect virtue. Later on, having become perfect, Abraham has intercourse with Sarah, symbol of supreme virtue.[45]   Gregory's interpretation can be regarded as a transposition of Philo's exegesis: in Gregory's allegory Pharaoh's daughter, symbol of pagan education and philosophy, takes the place of Hagar, symbol of school education, whereas Moses' natural mother occupies Sarah's place. A distinction between the two authors is that Philo's translations of the names Hagar and Sarah, on which he partly bases his interpretation, are absent in Gregory. This is, of course, a result of his transposition but it is also characteristic of Gregory that he never translates biblical names, as Philo does. Despite these differences, it is essential in both Philo and Gregory that one should not permanently stay with the school education or pagan culture respectively. Finally, two remarks have to be made. First, Monique Alexandre has remarked that Gregory uses the same verb to denote Moses' return to his own mother (II.12) as Philo employs to indicate Abraham's return from Hagar to Sarah in *Congr.* 77, namely ἀνατρέχω (cf. *Ebr.* 51).[46] Second, in Philo's interpretation Abraham strives for perfect virtue, which is precisely the theme of Gregory's *VM*, and

---

[43]   Daniélou (1968) 113 n. 3, Malherbe-Ferguson (1978) 158 n. 16. Philo does not give an interpretation of Pharaoh's daughter.
[44]   Philo also employs the terms μέση παιδεία (*Congr.* 12, 14), and ἐγκύκλιος μουσική (*Cher.* 3, *Congr.* 9). Philosophy belongs to it as well (*Congr.* 21). See Alexandre (1967) 27-82.
[45]   Same interpretation in *Congr.* 1-24, see § 7.3. For Philo's interpretation of Hagar and Sarah, see Henrichs (1968).
[46]   Alexandre (1967) 92-93.
Gregory *VM* II.12 ἀναδραμέτω πρὸς τὴν κατὰ φύσιν μητέρα . . ἐντεῦθεν τῆς εἰς ὕψος ἀναδρομῆς τὰς ἀφορμὰς ποιουμένη. Cf. II.10, 22, *Cant.* 16.4-5 (ὁ . . πρὸς τὸ τέλειον ἀναδραμὼν τῇ ψυχῇ), 131.5-6.
Philo *Congr.* 77 . . οἱ δὲ ἄλλοις μυρίοις, οὐ δυνηθέντες ἐπὶ τὴν ἀστὴν ἀναδραμεῖν.

so there is an association between Philo's passage and Gregory's treatise. In general, we can say that Gregory takes over important elements from Philo's exegesis, and elaborates them in a different way, using the method of transposition. His exegesis of Pharaoh's daughter thus falls in the category of a Philonic exegesis that has been altered (B3).

3.3. *The image of the Woman being in Labour*

The Philonic character of the interpretation of Pharaoh's daughter is reinforced by the observation that Gregory combines this exegesis with the Philonic image of a woman being in labour but never giving birth.[47] It is found in *Leg.* 1.75-76, where Philo gives a symbolic interpretation of the river Pheison, which streams through the land Evilat (Gen. 2:11). The river symbolizes prudence, which surrounds Evilat, that is folly, which is in labour.[48] 'Being in labour' is a fitting name for folly because the foolish mind, loving unreachable things, like money, glory, and pleasure, is always in labour but never gives birth. The soul of the wicked man does not by nature have the power to bring forth any offspring: what it seems to produce turns out to be abortive children and miscarriages. The resemblance between Philo and Gregory can be seen by the juxtaposition of the texts:

Leg. 1.75

ἀφροσύνη δὲ κύριον ὄνομά ἐστιν ὠδίνουσα, ὅτι ὁ ἄφρων νοῦς ἀνεφίκτων ἐρῶν ἑκάστοτε ἐν ὠδῖσίν ἐστιν, ὅτε χρημάτων ἐρᾷ, [ὠδίνει,] ὅτε δόξης, ὅτε ἡδονῆς, ὅτε ἄλλου τινός. [76] ἐν ὠδῖσι δὲ ὢν οὐδέποτε τίκτει· οὐ γὰρ πέφυκε γόνιμον οὐδὲν τελεσφορεῖν ἡ τοῦ φαύλου ψυχή· ἃ δ' ἂν καὶ δοκῇ προφέρειν, ἀμβλωθρίδια εὑρίσκεται καὶ ἔκτρωμα.[49]

VM II.11

ἄγονος γάρ ὡς ἀληθῶς ἡ ἔξωθεν παίδευσις ἀεὶ ὠδίνουσα καὶ μηδέποτε ζῳογονοῦσα τῷ τόκῳ ... οὐ πάντες ὑπηνέμιοί τε καὶ ἀτελεσφόρητοι πρὶν εἰς τὸ φῶς τῆς θεογνωσίας ἀμβλίσκονται, δυνάμενοι ἴσως γενέσθαι ἄνθρωποι, εἰ μὴ διόλου τοῖς κόλποις τῆς ἀγόνου σοφίας[50] ἐνεκαλύπτοντο;[51]

---

[47] Daniélou (1968) 113 n. 2, Musurillo (1964) 36, Malherbe-Ferguson (1978) 158 n. 15, Simonetti (1984) 276, Alexandre (1967) 93.

[48] For the etymologies in this passage, see Grabbe (1988) 24-26, 159, 213.

[49] In *QE* 2.19 he uses the same figure. Metaphorical use of miscarriage also in *Congr.* 129.

[50] For ἡ ἄγονος σοφία, cf. Plato *Theat.* 150C and Philo *Ebr.* 212, *Ios.* 59 ἄγονος σοφίας.

[51] Same image in *Inscr. Psal.* 164.9-24, referring to Ps. 57:9.

Both authors employ the same image but in a different context. For Philo the foolish mind (symbolized by the river Evilat) is always in labour, never giving birth to any offspring, but having only miscarriages. Gregory transposes this image to Pharaoh's daughter, symbol of pagan education. This use of the image can be classified as Philonic (A), combined with a Philonic exegesis of Pharaoh's daughter (B3).

4. *Moses kills an Egyptian* (I.18, II.13-16)

When Moses returns to his own people and sees a fight between a Hebrew and an Egyptian, he kills the latter (I.18; Ex. 2:11-12). This fight, Gregory explains, is like the battle of idolatry against true religion, of licentiousness against self-control, of injustice against righteousness, of arrogance against humility, and of everything against what is perceived as its opposite (II.14).[52] The killing of the Egyptian man denotes the destroying of what is opposite to virtue (II.15).[53] Gregory's interpretation of the Egyptian man fits in well with his general exegesis of Egypt as land of the passions — an interpretation that has a Philonic background.[54] The exegesis of the killing of the Egyptian man can also be labelled as Philonic.

Philo allegorically interprets the murder committed by Moses in *Leg.* 3.37-38 and *Fug.* 148, to which the commentators on Gregory refer.[55] In Philo's view the Egyptian man is one who thinks that bodily things rule, counting things of the soul for nothing, considering pleasure the highest goal in life. This lover of pleasure is smitten and hidden by Moses (*Leg.* 3.37-38).[56] Both Philo and Gregory see in the Egyptian man a person who lives according to the passions, and therefore is killed. A slight difference is that Gregory associates the Egyptian with every vice, whereas Philo associates him only with pleasure and bodily things. Gregory's exegesis comes in category B3.

---

[52] Regarding these opposites Malherbe-Ferguson (1978) 158 n. 22 refer to Philo *QE* 2.17 (exegesis of Ex. 23:24c), where a list of virtues and vices is given. Such a list can, however, be regarded as a commonplace, cf. Diogenes Laertius 7.92-93.

[53] In *Bas.* 126.15-22 the Hebrew symbolizes the purified and undefiled thought, which kills the members of the earth (cf. Col. 3:5). Origen does not comment on this passage in his *Ex. hom.* or in the *Catenae*.

[54] See § 7 and 8.

[55] Daniélou (1968) 115 n. 1, Musurillo (1964) 37, Malherbe-Ferguson (1978) 158 n. 20.

[56] Interpretation along the same lines in *Fug.* 148. In *Mos.* 1.43-44 Philo recounts the story in a literal way.

5. *Moses in Midian* (I.19, II.17-18)

After he has killed an Egyptian man, Moses flees to Midian, where he, we are told by Gregory, practises a higher form of philosophy.[57] He marries a daughter of the foreigner whose daughters he protected against the attack of other shepherds (Ex. 2:15-21), and he lives alone in the desert, caring for his sheep (I.19; Ex. 3:1). Explaining this episode Gregory states that one should live in oneself without getting involved in others' fights. One should live amidst like-minded people, while all the movements of the soul are shepherded, like sheep, by the will of guiding reason (II.18).[58] From Gregory's passage two issues should be examined, namely the description of Moses' father-in-law (5.1), and the image of the shepherding of the movements of the soul (5.2).

5.1. *Description of Moses' Father-in-law*

According to Daniélou the passage in which Gregory speaks about Jethro, Moses' prospective father-in-law, is borrowed nearly literally from Philo's *Mos.*[59] To show the similarities the texts are placed side by side:

Mos. 1.59	*VM* I.19
ὁ δὲ πατὴρ τὴν μὲν ὄψιν εὐθὺς τὸ δὲ βούλημα ὀλίγον ὕστερον καταπλαγεὶς - ἀρίδηλοι γὰρ αἱ μεγάλαι φύσεις καὶ οὐ μήκει χρόνου γνωριζόμεναι - δίδωσι τὴν καλλιστεύουσαν αὐτῷ τῶν θυγατέρων γυναῖκα, δι᾽ ἑνὸς ἔργου πάνθ᾽ ὅσα τῶν εἰς καλοκἀγαθίαν μαρτυρήσας καὶ ὡς ἀξιέραστον μόνον τὸ καλόν ἐστι τῆς ἀφ᾽ ἑτέρου συστάσεως οὐ δεόμενον, ἀλλ᾽ ἐν ἑαυτῷ περιφέρον τὰ γνωρίσματα.[60]	κηδεύσας τινὶ τῶν ἀλλοφύλων, ἀνδρὶ διορατικῷ τοῦ βελτίονος καὶ κρίνειν ἤθη τε καὶ βίον ἀνθρώπων ἐπεσκεμμένῳ, ὃς διὰ μιᾶς πράξεως, λέγω δὴ τῆς κατὰ τῶν ποιμένων ὁρμῆς, ἐνιδὼν τοῦ νέου τὴν ἀρετήν, ὅπως οὐ πρὸς οἰκεῖον βλέπων κέρδος τοῦ δικαίου ὑπερεμάγησεν, ἀλλ᾽ αὐτὸ τὸ δίκαιον τίμιον τῇ ἰδίᾳ φύσει κρίνων.[61]

---

[57] Cf. *Inscr. Psal.* 43.26-44.3, *Thaum.* 14.18-23. The notion of the philosophical life of Moses in Midian is also found in Philo (*Mos.* 1.48), and Basil (*Hom. hex.* 1.1 (5B), *Enar. Es.* 129A, 437A, *Libris* 3); see Harl (1967).

[58] The phrase 'movements of the soul' is a Stoic expression denoting the passions, SVF 3.377, 391, 412, cf. Gregory *An. et res.* 61 A-C.

[59] Daniélou (1954b) 391, (1967a) 344, (1968) 59 n. 4, Musurillo (1964) 8, Peri (1974) 315, Malherbe-Ferguson (1978) 152 n. 38.

[60] 'Their father was at once struck with admiration of his face, and soon afterwards of his disposition, for great natures are transparent and need no length of time to be recognized. Accordingly, he gave him the fairest of his daughters in marriage, and, by that one action, attested all his noble qualities, and showed that excellence standing alone

Although no exact verbal parallels can be discerned, Daniélou's verdict on this passage, 'La dépendance est patente', is justified because of the resemblance.[62] According to the working method that is characteristic of Gregory, he rewords Philo's text by using synonyms. He replaces ἔργον by πρᾶξις; τὸ καλόν becomes τὸ δίκαιον; and τῆς ἀφ' ἑτέρου συστάσεως οὐ δεόμενον is substituted for τίμιον τῇ ἰδίᾳ φύσει, both phrases meaning the same. A difference regarding the content is that in Philo the ἔργον is done by Jethro, who gives Moses one of his daughters as wife, whereas in Gregory the πρᾶξις refers to Moses' defence of Jethro's daughters. We can, however, safely conclude that Gregory's description of Moses' father-in-law comes in the category of Philonic phraseology (A).

5.2. *The Image of the Shepherding of the Movements of the Soul*

The image of the shepherding of the movements of the soul by the logos as shepherd is Philonic,[63] and is derived from *Sacr.*; a treatise from which we already have seen influences in Gregory's *VM.*[64] In *Sacr.* 45-51 the Jewish exegete explains why Abel is called a shepherd (Gen. 4:2). When the mind turns away from pleasure and cleaves to virtue it becomes a shepherd of sheep, a chariot and helmsman of the irrational faculties of the soul. The mind does not permit them to move irregularly without a master or a guide (45). Philo illustrates this with the examples of Jacob (Gen. 30:36), his sons (Gen. 47:3), and Moses (46-51). Moses rules the conceptions of the superfluous Jethro, leading them into the desert lest they do injustice (50; Ex. 3:1, cf. *Agr.* 43).[65] Later on in the treatise the same image is used

---

deserves our love, and needs no commendation from aught else, but carries within itself the tokens by which it is known' (translation Colson).

[61] 'He became the son-in-law of one of the foreigners, a man with insight into what is noble, and perceptive in judging the habits and lives of men. This man saw in one act -the attack on the shepherds- the virtue of the young man, how he fought on behalf of the right without looking for personal gain. Considering the right valuable in itself. .' (translation Malherbe-Ferguson).

[62] Daniélou (1954b) 391.

[63] Daniélou (1954a) 64 n. 1, (1968) 117 n. 2, Malherbe-Ferguson (1978) 159 n. 24.

[64] See § 0, 1.2

[65] In *Mos.* 1.60-61 Philo explains Moses' shepherding differently. It is a preliminary exercise in kingship for one who is destined to command the herd of mankind. Therefore, kings are called 'shepherds of their people' (Homer *Ilias* 1.263, Philo *Agr.* 41, 50, *Ios.* 2-3, *Prob.* 31, *Legat.* 44, Clement *Strom.* 1.156.3). In *Mut.* 103-120 Philo interprets Jethro and his daughters allegorically. The name Jethro means 'superfluous' (περισσός), and his seven daughters represent the seven powers of the irrational soul. Traces of this allegory are not found in Gregory.

(104-106), in which Philo likens the senses to cattle (104). Senses are either wild or tame. They are wild when they rebel against their shepherd, the mind; tame, when they obey their guide, i.e., reasoning, and are guided by him (105).[66] To make clear Philo's influence on Gregory's imagery we place the texts of the two authors side by side:

Sacr. 45	II.18
τότε καὶ γίνεται ποιμὴν <u>προβάτων</u>, <u>τῶν</u> <u>κατὰ ψυχὴν ἀλόγων δυνάμεων</u> ἡνίοχός τε καὶ κυβερνήτης, οὐκ ἐῶν αὐτὰς ἀτάκτως φέρεσθαι καὶ πλημμελῶς δίχα <u>ἐπιστάτου</u> καὶ ἡγεμόνος, 105 ἀτίθασον μὲν ὅταν ἀφηνιάσαν ὥσπερ βουκόλου τοῦ νοῦ . . , ἥμερον δὲ ὅταν ὑπεῖξαν πειθηνίως τῷ...ἡγεμόνι <u>λογισμῷ</u>...	<u>πάντων</u> τῶν ἐν ἡμῖν τῆς <u>ψυχῆς</u> <u>κινημάτων</u> προβάτων δίκην τῷ βουλήματι τοῦ <u>ἐπιστατοῦντος λόγου</u> ποιμαινομένων.

It is clear that Gregory employs the same image of the shepherding of the irrational elements of the soul as Philo. A difference in wording is that the Jewish exegete writes about the irrational faculties of the soul, whereas Gregory speaks about the movements of the soul; but the meaning is the same. The image recurs in Origen. In *Ier. hom.* 5.6 he comments on the sheep in Jer. 3:24, associating them with Christ, the good shepherd, who shepherds the irrational movements of the soul. Because Origen, in all likelihood, depends on Philo for this image and Gregory adheres closely to Philo, Gregory's use of it can be classified as Philonic phraseology (A).[67]

6. *Moses' Encounter with God* (I.20-21, II.19-34)

6.a. *The Shining of the Truth* (I.20, II.19-25)

The next episode in Moses' life is the famous encounter with God in the burning bush. When we, Gregory relates, lead a quiet and peaceful life in the desert, like Moses, the truth will shine, illuminating the eyes of our soul[68] with its own rays. This truth, which manifested itself to Moses, is God

---

[66] Same image, less elaborated, in *Leg.* 2.9, *Cher.* 70, *Det.* 3, 9, 25, *Post.* 66, 69, *Agr.* 30-31.

[67] See Nautin (1976-77) 1.296 n. 1.

[68] 'Eyes of the soul' is a Platonic phrase (*Rep.* 533D, cf. *Symp.* 219A), which recurs in Philo (*Sacr.* 36, *Plant.* 22, *Deus* 181, *Migr.* 39, *Mut.* 3; see Billings (1919) 66) and in Gregory (*Cant.* 4.4, 143.17-144.1 etc., *Mort.* 47.11, *Virg.* 267.8, *VM* II.189). Used by other Church

(II.19).[69] Truth is also light, and 'truth' and 'light' are the names that indicate the God who made himself manifest in the flesh (Joh. 1:9, 8:12, 14:16). It is thus not God the Father who reveals himself in the burning bush, but God the Son, who is the light that has reached down to human nature (II.20).[70] The fact that the bush is not destroyed by being burned refers to the mystery of Mary's virginity, which is not corrupted by giving birth (II.21). When we take off our shoes (Ex. 3:5) knowledge of the truth (ἡ τῆς ἀληθείας γνῶσις)[71] will follow. Gregory makes a contrast between truth and falsehood. Falsehood is an impression that arises in the understanding about non-being. Truth is the sure apprehension of real Being (τὸ ὄντως ὄν), which possesses existence by its own nature (II.23). Real Being is described in Platonic terms: it is always the same, neither increasing nor diminishing, immune to every change whether for better or for worse, needing nothing else, alone desirable, participated in by all, but not lessened by their participation. Perception of the truly Being is knowledge of the truth (II.25).[72] Gregory finds biblical support for this Platonic interpretation in Ex. 3:14, where God makes himself known, saying 'I am He-who-is' (ἐγώ εἰμι ὁ ὤν).[73] Two points should be examined, viz. Gregory's description of the burning bush (6.a.1), and the interpretation of the appearance in the burning bush (6.a.2).

6.a.1. *The Description of the Burning Bush*

From the juxtaposition of the texts, it appears that Gregory's description of the burning bush recalls Philo's depiction in *Mos.* 1.65.[74]

---

fathers; cf., for instance, Basil *Eun.* 1.3, *Ps. 1 hom.* 5, Gregory of Nazianzus *Or.* 43.41.

[69] Comparable description of this episode in *Bas.* 127.6, *Cant.* 148.18-19, 355.2-4, *Inscr. Psal.* 44.3-4.

[70] Cf. *CE* 2.349, 3.6.3, 3.9.36-38.

[71] The phrase γνῶσις or ἐπίγνωσις τῆς ἀληθείας (cf. *Cant.* 15.16, *Ref. Eun.* 16, *VM* II.25, II.235) occurs in the NT (1 Tim. 2:4, 2 Tim. 2:25, Tit. 1:1, Hebr. 10:25). Cf. Justin *Dial.* 3; it is also used by Plato (*Rep.* 477A, 478C, 484C) and Philo (*Leg.* 3.48, 126, *Deus* 143).

[72] Balás (1966) 102-122 gives an analysis of this passage; see also Völker (1955) 31-35, Böhm (1993), (1996) 240-247.

[73] For Ex. 3:14 in Gregory, see Canévet (1983) 98-103; for the use of this verse by the Church fathers, see Harl (1978), Nautin (1978). A general discussion of this verse is found in Houtman (1986-96) 1.102-104.

[74] Daniélou (1968) 61 n.1, Musurillo (1964) 39, Malherbe-Ferguson (1978) 152 n. 40, 41.

Mos. 1.65

βάτος ἦν, ἀκανθῶδές τι φυτὸν καὶ
ἀσθενέστατον· οὗτος, οὐδενὸς πῦρ
προσενεγκόντος, ἐξαίφνης ἀνακαίεται
καὶ περισχεθεὶς ὅλος ἐκ ῥίζης εἰς
ἀκρέμονα πολλῇ φλογὶ καθάπερ ἀπό
τινος πηγῆς ἀνομβρούσης διέμενε
σῷος,⁷⁵

VM I.20

...ἐν σταθερᾷ μεσημβρίᾳ φωτὸς ἑτέρου
ὑπὲρ τὸ ἡλιακὸν φῶς τὰς ὄψεις
περιαστράψαντος.⁷⁶ τὸν δὲ ξενισθέντα
τῷ ἀήθει τῆς θέας ἀναβλέψαι πρὸς τὸ
ὄρος καὶ ἰδεῖν θάμνον⁷ ⁷ ἀφ' οὗ
πυροειδῶς τὸ φέγγος ἐξήπτετο, τῶν δὲ
κλάδων τοῦ θάμνου καθάπερ ἐν δρόσῳ
τῇ φλογὶ συναναθαλλόντων,...⁷⁸

VM II.20

εἰ δὲ καὶ θάμνου τινὸς ἀκανθώδους τὸ
φέγγος ἐξάπτεται, ...

Both Philo and Gregory describe the burning bush more extensively than
the scriptural account does.⁷⁹ An element common to both is the
comparison in which water takes part: for Philo the flame is like a spring
gushing water; Gregory writes that the branches of the bush sprout up in
flame as in pure water. Though the common reference to the bush as
thorny occurs also in Clement (*Paed.* 2.8.75),⁸⁰ Gregory has, in all
likelihood, Philo's depiction in mind. His description can be labelled as
Philonic phraseology (A).

6.a.2. *The Exegetical Tradition of God's Appearance in the Burning Bush*

Gregory's interpretation of the appearance in the bush as God's Word has
a long tradition beginning with Ezekiel Tragicus and Philo. According to
Ezekiel it is God's Logos which shines in the bush (*Exagoge* 99). Philo
explains in *Mos.* 1.66-67 that in the middle of the flames God's image

---

⁷⁵ 'There was a bramble-bush, a thorny sort of plant, and of the most weakly kind, which,
without anyone's setting it alight, suddenly took fire; and, though enveloped from root to
twigs in a mass of fire, which looked as though it were spouted up from a fountain, yet
remained whole, ...' (translation Colson).

⁷⁶ Cf. the description of Saul's conversion in Act. 22:6 περὶ μεσημβρίαν ἐξαίφνης ἐκ τοῦ
οὐρανοῦ περιαστράψαι φῶς (cf. 9:3). See also Gen. 18:1, where God appears at noon. At
CE 2.349 Gregory refers to Ex. 3:2, Joh. 1:9, and Act. 9:3,5 in order to show that Christ is
called 'Light'.

⁷⁷ The LXX reads βάτος, which Gregory uses in II.26 and in *Diem nat.* 247.9.

⁷⁸ 'At high noon a light brighter than the sunlight dazzled his eyes. Astonished at the
strange sight, he looked up at the mountain and saw a bush from which this light was
flaming up like a fire. When he saw the branches of the bush sprouting up in flame as if
they were in pure water,' (translation Malherbe-Ferguson).

⁷⁹ Cf. Ex. 3:2 ὤφθη δὲ αὐτῷ ἄγγελος κυρίου ἐν φλογὶ πυρὸς ἐκ τοῦ βάτου.

⁸⁰ This element is also found in *Midrash Rabbah Exodus* 2.5.

appears, which is rightly named angel here (Ex. 3:2) because he forecasts the future (1.66). The burning bush is a symbol of those who suffer wrong, and the flame of the wrongdoers. The fact that the bush is not burned indicates that the sufferers will not be destroyed by their assailants.[81] The angel symbolizes God's providence (1.67). Further on, the Jewish exegete discusses God's disclosure in Ex. 3:14 as He-who-is (ὁ ὤν).[82] God says to Moses: Tell them that I am He-who-is, that they may learn the difference between being and non-being and further may learn that no name can properly be used of me, to whom alone existence belongs.' He is not only God, but also God of the three men who are named after their virtue, God of Abraham, of Isaac, and of Jacob (Ex. 3:15). Each of them is an example of the wisdom he has acquired: Abraham by teaching, Isaac by nature, and Jacob by practice (1.74-76).[83] According to Philo, it is an angel who appears in the bush and he identifies the angel with God's Logos.[84]

Following in Philo's footsteps, the Church fathers interpret the appearance in the bush as God's Logos, identifying him with Christ, God's Son and his Word (cf. the prologue of the gospel of John). According to the apologist Justin, for example, it is not the Father and maker who appears, but an angel (cf. Ex. 3:2), who is also called Son, wisdom, Lord and Logos (*Apo.* 1.62-63, *Dial.* 59-61, 127). Clement of Alexandria, conceiving of the appearance as the Logos, sees in the thorns a reference to Jesus, who was crowned with a crown of thorns (Mat. 27:29; *Paed.* 2.8.75, *Strom.* 1.164.4, 5.100.4).[85] From these examples it appears that Gregory's exegesis of the appearance in the burning bramble as God's Son is fully in accordance with the patristic tradition, which has been influenced by Philo's exegesis. When we compare Gregory's text with Philo's *Mos.* 1.75 we observe the striking parallel that both, in explaining Ex. 3:14, make a distinction between being and non-being. It is possible that Grgeory is inspired by Philo. A difference between Philo and Gregory is that Philo adds the statement that God has no proper name. Philo also focusses on the pronouncement of God in Ex. 3:15. Finally Gregory does not take over the symbolic explanation of the burning bush which Philo offers in *Mos.*

---

[81] Same symbolic interpretation in *Midrash Rabbah Exodus* 2.5.
[82] See Runia (1995a) 146-147.
[83] Interpretation of Ex. 3:14 and 15 along the same lines in *Mut.* 11, *Somn.* 1.230, and *Abr.* 51.
[84] Cf. *Cher.* 3, *Deus* 182, *Conf.* 146, *Mut.* 87, *Somn.* 1.239.
[85] Cf. further Iraeneus *Dem.* 46, *Adv. Haer.* 4.5.2, 4.10.1, Origen *Num. hom.* 27.11, Eusebius *DE* 5.13, Basil *Eun.* 2.18.

6.b. *The Covering of Skin* (II.22)

Referring to Ex. 3:5, God's command to Moses to take off his shoes, Gregory remarks that it is not possible to ascend with sandaled feet the height where the light of truth is seen. We should remove from the feet of the soul the dead and earthly covering of skins, which was placed around our nature at the beginning when we were found naked because of disobedience to the divine will.[86] When this has been done, knowledge of the truth will follow, because knowledge of the Existent comes about by purifying our opinion about non-being (II.22). The Cappadocian father alludes here to Gen. 3:21, where it is written that Adam and Eve are clothed with tunics of skins after the fall. These tunics are interpreted as man's irrational disposition, which is added to his original nature as a result of his tendency towards evil.[87] It has its essential features in 'sexual intercourse, conception, parturition, impurities, suckling, feeding, evacuation, gradual growth to full size, prime of life, old age, disease and death' (*An. et res.* 148C-149A).[88] This irrational constitution, resulting from the fall, is contrasted with man's original nature made after God's image (Gen. 1:26), which consists of virtue, immortality, purity, and ἀπάθεια (freedom from passion).[89] Man's true nature has been corrupted by the fall, but can be re-established by striving for ἀπάθεια and purity.[90] In the passage at hand, Gregory sees in the tunic of skin a symbol of a wrong opinion, which should be taken off.

Nowhere in his writings does Philo comment on God's command to Moses, but regarding Gregory's interpretation Daniélou does refer to Philo, remarking that the interpretation of a tunic as δόξα derives from *Leg.* 2.56.[91] Here the Jewish exegete deals with the command that the high

---

[86] Cf. *Cant.* 329.18-330.1, 355.5, *Inscr. Psal.* 44.4-5, *VM* II.201. Daniélou (1954a) 27-31 links this passage with the sacrament of baptism, at which it was customary to take off clothing and shoes, cf. *Cant.* 327-332.

[87] For the tunics of skin, cf. *An. et res.* 148C, *Beat.* 161.21-23, *Mort.* 55.11-23, *Or. cat.* 30.3-13. For Gregory's interpretation, see Daniélou (1954a) 56-60, (1967b), (1970) 154-164, Kees (1995) 231-236. Daniélou argues that Gregory, interpreting the tunics in terms of mortality, follows rather Methodius (cf. *Res.* 1.29, 39.5-6) than Philo, who sees in them a symbol of the body (*QG* 1.53). In *Leg.* 2.58 Philo interprets the tunics of Nadab and Abihu (Lev. 10:5) as the parts of the irrational by which the rational is hidden.

[88] Translation Moore-Wilson (1893) 465.

[89] Cf., for instance, *Beat.* 80.26-81.7, *Cant.* 458.6-8, *Eccl.* 386.5-387.1, *Opif. hom.* 136C-137B; for Gregory's doctrine on man as God's image, see Muckle (1945), Merki (1952) 138-175, Daniélou (1954a) 48-55, Völker (1955) 57-74.

[90] Cf., for instance, *Cant.* 25.7-9, 60.1-22, 272.17-19, *Mort.* 53.13-54.1, *Opif. hom.* 201A, *Virg.* 298-302, *VM* II.316; see Daniélou (1954a) 92-103.

[91] Daniélou (1954a) 27. In his SC edition he does not refer to Philo with regard to the

priest should not enter the holy of holies in his robe (Lev. 16:3-4), but should lay aside the tunic of opinion and impression of the soul (χιτὼν τῆς δόξης καὶ φαντασίας ψυχῆς) and leave it behind for those who love outward things and honour opinion (δόξα) more than truth (ἀλήθεια). He should enter naked without his robe. Apart from the fact that in both texts the notion of ἀλήθεια plays a role, the similarities are nebulous. The tunic, mentioned by Philo, does not explicitly occur in Gregory's text. It is only implicitly present via the allusion to Gen. 3:21. So, it seems that the question whether Gregory is here indebted to Philo must remain unsolved.

6.c. *Deliverance from Tyranny* (II.26-34)

In Exodus 3 it is recorded that God, speaking from the burning bush, gives Moses the command to return to Egypt and to lead the Hebrew people from Egypt to the land of the Canaanites. In his exegesis Gregory states that everyone who, like Moses, has taken off the earthly covering and looks to the light is able to free others and to destroy tyranny (II.26). The wonders that God performs — the change of Moses' rod into a serpent and the alteration of the colour of his hand (Ex. 4:1-7) — signify the manifestation of the Lord's divinity in the flesh.[92] His coming effects the destruction of the tyrant and the liberation of those under his power (II.27). This interpretation, too, has the notion of man as God's image as background. As was already noted above, man was made after God's image, of which freedom is also a major feature. This image, however, was corrupted by the fall. Man is subject to slavery and tyranny of the passions,[93] but he should strive for restoration of this image by trying to control the passions, to achieve *apatheia*, and to become free from the tyranny of the passions. Christ, having become God's image, came to restore God's image in man.[94] In the passage from *VM* the central notion is ἐλευθερία (freedom), historically denoting the exodus of the Hebrews

---

interpretation of the tunics of skin.

[92] Philo interprets Moses' hand as activity and his rod as education, while the serpent represents pleasure (*Leg.* 2.88-93; for staff as education, cf. *Sacr.* 63, *Post.* 97, *Congr.* 94, *Fug.* 150, *Mut.* 135). Origen gives an interpretation in terms of the letter and the spirit of the law (*Io. com.* 32.267-270).

[93] Cf., for instance, *An. et res.* 101C, *Beat.* 106.4-18, 132.17-133.4, *Opif. hom.* 136B, 148B. See Daniélou (1954a) 79-83, 107-109, Gaïth (1953) 118-134. The image of the slavery of the soul to the despotic tyranny of the passions already occurs in Plato (*Rep.* 329C, 577C-578A) and Philo (*Leg.* 2.91); cf. *VM* II.128-129.

[94] Cf. *Perf.* 194.14-195.5.

from Egypt, symbolically the liberation of the soul from slavery to the passions.[95]

Gregory's allegorical interpretation of the exodus from Egypt has a Philonic background, which is found in *Her.* 268-272, where Philo comments on Gen. 15:13. In this verse God says to Abraham: 'You will surely know that your seed will be a stranger in a land not his own.' This points to the slavery of the soul to the passions because the true passions of the body are bastards and strangers to understanding (268). The slavery will last 'four hundred years' (Gen. 15:13) according to the powers of the four passions: pleasure, desire, grief, and fear (269-270).[96] Philo refers here to Israel's labour and slavery in Egypt, which he explains as leading a life according to passions. God, the Jewish exegete continues, will liberate the slaves from the mastery of the passions, separating the sufferers from the wrongdoers (cf. Gen. 15:14). It is necessary that mortal man should be oppressed by the people of the passions, but it is God's will to lighten the evils inherent in the human race (272).[97]

Philo thus interprets the slavery of the Hebrews as the slavery of the soul to the passions and the body, from which it will be liberated by God. Egypt is figuratively the passions and the body, while the exodus from Egypt indicates the deliverance of the soul from its slavery to the tyranny of passions. It is plain that Gregory follows Philo's line of exegesis, although he places the liberation in a Christian framework by regarding Christ as the cause of the liberation. That the connection between passions and body made by Philo is absent in Gregory corresponds with the earlier observation that Gregory avoids an allegorical exegesis in terms of the body.[98] Because it seems that the interpretation of the exodus as liberation from the passions does not occur in other Church fathers,[99] Gregory's exegesis of the exodus falls under our category B3.

---

[95] In the LXX the word ἐλευθερία is not used with regard to the Exodus, see Nestle (1972) 286; the word slavery (δουλεία) does occur in Ex. 6:6. Egypt is called οἶκος δουλείας in Ex. 13:3; cf. 1:14 κατεδουλοῦντο.

[96] Stoic notion of the four passions, cf. SVF 3.378, 391, 394, 412; in Philo *Leg* 2.8, 99, 3.139, *Agr.* 83, *Conf.* 90, *Abr.* 236, *Mos.* 2.139, *Praem.* 71, *QE* 2.17.

[97] Same interpretation of the slave labour in Egypt in *Conf.* 92-93 and *Migr.* 14-15. The passage in *Conf.* is discussed in § 8.

[98] See § 2.1 and 2.2.

[99] Irenaeus sees in the exodus a type of the exodus of the Church from among the gentiles (*Adv. Haer.* 4.30.4). Origen interprets the exodus as the abandoning of this world (*Ex. hom.* 3.3).

7. *Moses' Return to Egypt* (I.22, II.35-53)

Having dealt with God's orders to Moses and the wonders, Gregory treats Moses' return to Egypt and Pharaoh (Ex. 4:18-20), omitting Moses' objections to his commission (Ex. 4:10-16). In his interpretation Pharaoh is one who resists the truth, and spurns listening to Him-who-exists as idle, saying 'Who is he, to whose voice I shall listen? I do not know the Lord' (Ex. 5:2). He only values material and fleshly things (II.35). Next Gregory compares Moses, who had been strengthened by the illumination and had received power over his enemies, to an athlete who has trained his athletic power. The rod in his hands is the word of faith, through which he will conquer the Egyptian serpents (II.36).[100] On his way back Moses is accompanied by his wife, who originates from an alien people. Gregory allegorizes her as pagan education and philosophy, arguing that moral and natural philosophy[101] is valuable for giving birth to virtue, if its fruits do not bear foreign defilement (II.37). If the impure elements are not cut off, the angel brings the fear of death. Moses' wife appeases him, showing her child purified of alien elements (II.38; Ex. 4:24-26).[102] The Cappadocian father sees in the circumcision a symbol of the removal of foreign philosophical ideas.[103] After the encounter with the angel Moses meets his brother Aaron (Ex. 4: 27-28), whom Gregory understands in figurative terms as the angel who is helping Moses in his struggle against Pharaoh and who is sent by God like Aaron (II.43, 47).[104] With regard to Philonic influence on Gregory here three issues should be examined, namely the interpretation of Pharaoh and Egypt (7.1), the comparison of Moses to an athlete (7.2), and finally the interpretation of Moses' wife (7.3).

---

[100] For the rod of faith, cf. II.34. Later on Gregory explains the rod as the staff of virtue (II.64, 73). For Justin the rod is a symbol of the cross of Jesus (*Dial.* 86).

[101] Theology belongs to natural philosophy as well (Stoic, cf. svf 2.35-44). Philo, too, distinguishes between physics and ethics (*Leg.* 1.39, 2.12, *Mos.* 2.96, *QG* 2.12), see Winston-Dillon (1983) 79-81.

[102] For this obscure episode in Exodus, see Houtman (1983), (1986-96) 1.408-423. Philo nowhere makes mention of the meeting with the angel. A survey of the patristic exegesis of the passage is given by Le Boulluec (1987).

[103] Philo symbolically interprets the circumcision as the cutting off of pleasure and of all passions and the destruction of impious opinion (*Migr.* 92, cf. *Spec.* 1.8-10, 305, *QE* 2.2).

[104] Gregory returns to this interpretation in II.119, 209-210. In Philo's interpretation of the meeting Moses is thought or understanding, while Aaron represents speech (*Det.* 38-40, *Migr.* 77-85, 169, *Mut.* 208, *QE* 2.27, 44). Malherbe-Ferguson (1978) 165 n. 71 refer to Philo *QE* 1.23, where Philo writes that two powers enter into every soul, namely the salutary and the destructive. For the helping angel in Gregory, see Völker (1955) 137.

7.1. *Interpretation of Pharaoh and Egypt*

An overview of Philo's exegesis of Pharaoh and Egypt shows that Gregory follows Philo's line of interpretation to a great extent. For the Jewish exegete Pharaoh is a leader of passions, lover of matter, pleasure, and the body,[105] while Egypt represents the body and passions.[106] Philo refers to several passions (among which the four cardinal ones) as real children and the firstborn of Egypt (*Somn.* 2.266). He sees in Pharaoh the figure of the godless mind, which sets itself up against God,[107] and as proof of his godless attitude Philo cites Ex. 5:2 'I do not know the Lord.' The leader of godlessness says: 'Who is he, to whom I shall obey?' and 'I do not know the Lord' (*Ebr.* 19).[108] Those who dare to say that they did not know the true God forget their humanity because of their excessive enjoyment of bodily and outward things (*Post.* 115). With regard to the knowledge of imperishable things, the lover of passion dwells in night and profound darkness, welcoming drunkenness, which gives birth to pleasure (*Ebr.* 209). Pharaoh does not know an intelligible God at all, outside of visible gods (*Mos.* 1.88). Philo translates the name Pharaoh as 'scatterer of beautiful things': he is one who scatters and throws away all thoughts concerning beautiful things. When he seems healthy, we welcome pleasure but drive self-restraint beyond limits. He is the cause of a disgusting and wanton life (*Det.* 95).[109]

It is important to observe that Origen gives an exegesis of Pharaoh and Egypt which differs from both Philo and Gregory. Origen, employing New Testament texts, regards Pharaoh as the devil,[110] the prince of this world (Joh. 16:11),[111] and the ruler of this darkness (Eph. 6:12).[112] He does take over Philo's translation of Pharaoh as 'scatterer', who scatters the works of virtue done in the light by means of his power.[113] The Alexandrian theologian conceives of Egypt as a symbol of the flesh, this world, and

---

[105] *Leg.* 3.13, 38, 212, 243, *Ebr.* 209, *Somn.* 2.277, *Abr.* 103; see also the references in Earp PLCL 10.399-401.
[106] *Leg.* 2.59, 77, 85, 3.175, *Det.* 95, *Sacr.* 48, *Post.* 62, 96, 155, *Agr.* 57, *Ebr.* 208, *Conf.* 81, 88, *Congr.* 20, 83, 163, *Migr.* 14, 159, *Fug.* 124, *Mut.* 90, 209, *QG* 3.16, 19 etc. See for Philo on Egypt and the Egyptians, Pearce (1998) 88-97.
[107] ἄθεος *Leg.* 3.12, 212, *Ebr.* 19; ἀντίθεος *Conf.* 88, *Congr.* 118, *Somn.* 2.183.
[108] *Leg.* 3.12, 243, *Ebr.* 77, *Somn.* 2.182, *QG* 4.87.
[109] *Leg.* 3.236, 243, *Sacr.* 48, 69, *Post.* 156, *Her.* 60, *Somn.* 2.211. See Grabbe (1988) 212-213.
[110] *Ex. hom.* 1.5, 2.1, 3.3, 6.1, *Ps. 36 hom.* 3.1. Methodius also sees the devil in the Pharaoh (*Symp.* 4.2.)
[111] *Ex. hom.* 2.1, 2.3.
[112] *Ex. hom.* 3.3.
[113] *Pasc.* 49.

darkness. In one of his *Homilies on Exodus* he writes: 'To love the world and what is in the world is an Egyptian disease.... To be a slave to luxury of flesh, to be eager for voluptuousness, to have time for sensuality is an Egyptian disease' (*Ex. hom.* 7.2).[114] In his interpretation the exodus from Egypt is thus the abandoning of this world by advancing in faith. The three days' journey (Ex. 3:18) denotes him who says 'I am the way, the truth and the life' (*Ex. hom.* 3.3; Joh. 14:6).[115]

We can draw the conclusion that Gregory generally follows Philo's exegesis, rather than Origen's line of thought. The latter's symbolic explanation of Pharaoh as devil and Egypt as this world has hardly left any traces in Gregory.[116] Even though the Cappadocian father follows Philo, two marked differences from his Jewish predecessor can be noticed. First, Gregory does not, like Philo, explain Pharaoh as a lover of bodily things and Egypt as the body, avoiding an interpretation in terms of the body. Second, he does not translate the name 'Pharaoh', as Philo does, and we have already observed that the absence of interpretation of biblical names is characteristic of Gregory.[117] The exegesis of Pharaoh thus comes in the category of a Philonic exegesis that has been altered (B3).

7.2. *The Comparison of Moses to an Athlete*

Gregory's comparison between Moses and an athlete is also encountered in Philo in the same context, namely before Moses' return to Egypt in order to fight against Pharaoh, i.e. the passions. In *Leg.* 3.12-14 Philo narrates that Moses withdraws to Midian from the godless opinion of Pharaoh, leader of passions (reference to Ex. 5:2). Moses does not flee, but withdraws, that is, he makes a break in the war like an athlete in order to get back his breath. Despite the use of the same image it would be going too far to see in Gregory direct influence of Philo, because the figure of an athlete fighting against the devil and the passions is a commonplace in Christian literature.[118]

---

[114] Cf. *Ex. hom.* 1.5, 2.1, 3.3, 5.2, 5.5, 7.2, 8.1.

[115] Cf. *Num. hom.* 26.4, 27.2. Gregory of Nazianzus sees in Egypt a symbol of persecuting sin (*Or.* 45.15). Irenaeus interprets the mastery of the Egyptians as the mastery of idolatry (*Dem.* 46).

[116] In II.59 Gregory refers to Pharaoh as demon; in *Diem lum.* 233.11 he calls Pharaoh διάβολος.

[117] See § 3.2.

[118] Cf. 1 Cor. 9:24-26; Gregory *Macr.* 380.15, *Mart.* Ib 152.5-9, *Steph.* I 76.1-11, *Thaum.* 19.21-20.7; Origen *Ex. hom.* 11.5; see Völker (1955) 237, Garrison (1997) 95-104.

7.3. *The Interpretation of Moses' Wife*

As we have already seen Gregory earlier interpreted Pharaoh's daughter in the same way as he now explains Moses' wife, viz. as a symbol of pagan education and philosophy.[119] His interpretation of Moses' wife differs from Philo's one; for the Jewish exegete she is a symbol of winged virtue, who is running upwards from earth to heaven, and contemplates the divine and blessed natures there. This is based on her name Zipporah, which is translated as 'bird'.[120] Moses found her pregnant through no mortal man (*Cher.* 41, 47,[121] cf. *Mut.* 120). It is plain that this interpretation is not taken over by Gregory, but his exegesis may have the same Philonic background as the interpretation of Pharaoh's daughter, namely the allegory of Hagar and Sarah.[122] Hagar, the female servant of Sarah, is a figure of education, which consists of grammar, music, rhetoric, and dialectic, including philosophy as well (*Leg.* 3.244-45, *Congr.* 15-18), and this education is a road leading to virtue (*Congr.* 10).

Seeing in a foreign wife (pagan) education and philosophy is thus a Philonic kind of exegesis. In Philo's interpretation Hagar represents the school education, consisting of several disciplines and philosophy, whereas in Gregory Moses' wife symbolizes pagan education and philosophy. The Cappadocian theologian stresses that pagan elements in philosophy should be removed, explaining the story of the circumcision in this way. It is, however, not possible to label Gregory's exegesis as exclusively Philonic, because an interpretation along the same lines is given by Origen, who derives it from Philo. In *Gen. hom.* 11.2 he understands a marriage with a wife from a foreign people as the use of pagan disciplines, such as literature, grammar, geometry, arithmetic, and dialectic. Origen refers also to Moses' marriage with the daughter of Midian's priest, explaining that Midian is a son of Abraham and Ketura (Gen. 25:2), so that Moses' wife is from Abraham's seed and not from a foreign people. This last point is not present in the exegesis of Gregory, who underscores that she originates from an alien people. This notion is suitable for his interpretation of Moses' wife as pagan education. From the above the conclusion can be drawn that Gregory's interpretation of Moses' wife as education and philosophy falls under the category of a Philonic exegesis which occurs also in other Christian writers (B2).

---

[119] See § 3.2.

[120] Zipporah as bird also in *Midrash Rabbah Exodus* 1.33.

[121] See § 1.1.

[122] Daniélou (1968) 127 n. 3, Malherbe-Ferguson (1978) 163 n. 56, Simonetti (1984) 283.

8. *The Israelites' Labour in Egypt* (I.23, II.54-62)

When Moses and Aaron arrive in Egypt, they announce the liberation from tyranny to the people. Reacting to their action, the tyrant increases the Israelites' slave labour, which consists in making bricks out of clay (I.23; Ex. 5:6-9). In his allegorical exegesis Gregory explains that the harmful demon wishes his subjects not to look to heaven, but to bend down to earth and to make bricks from clay within themselves (II.59). For what belongs to material enjoyment consists entirely of earth or water, and the mixture of these elements is clay. Those who pursue pleasures of clay fill themselves with clay, but they are never able to fill the receiving-space of pleasures.[123] As soon as it is filled it becomes empty. In the same way the brick-maker is always throwing clay into the mould, which is always being emptied. This figure, Gregory explains, relates to the desiring part of the soul (II.60). When one desire is satisfied another arises, and this process never stops, until one departs from the material life (II.61). This interpretation of the brick-making in terms of being involved in pleasures and as leading a material life coheres with the exegesis of Pharaoh as lover of the material life (II.35),[124] and like the explanation of Pharaoh the exegesis of the making of bricks has a Philonic background.

The Alexandrian exegete discusses the making of bricks in *Conf.* 83-100, where the building of the tower of Babel out of bricks is his point of departure. The wicked man, wishing to build a city or tower for vice as a citadel for a tyrant (83), says: 'Come let us make bricks and bake them with fire' (Gen. 11:3a). Philo interprets this verse as follows: all parts of the soul are confused so that no clear form of any particular kind can be seen (84). It is appropriate to take passion and vice, which are without form and quality, and to divide them into the fitting qualities and forms. So, one gets both a clearer apprehension of them, and that use and enjoyment that seem to bring forth more pleasures and delight (85). Next Philo introduces Pharaoh, who enjoys buildings made out of brick (88). When one mixes water and earth — the one liquid, the other solid — a third substance is produced on the borderline between the two, and this is called clay. Thereafter, it is divided into portions, and the proper shape is given to each of the sections in order that it may become firmer (89). The naturally bad men imitate this process when they mix the irrational impulses of passions with the gravest vices. Then they divide the mixture

---

[123] For clay of pleasure, cf. *Cant.* 332.2.
[124] See § 7.

into its kinds: sense-perception into the five senses; passion into pleasure, desire, fear, and grief (90). Some people go further and force others to make bricks (91). The Israelites, bound in the bodily nets of Egypt, are compelled to make bricks and every earthly substance (92). They cry aloud to God, the only saviour of their souls, that he may lighten their works and provide a ransom and a reward for the soul (cf. Ex. 30:12) and release it into liberty (93).[125] The most sure liberty is the service of the only wise Being[126] because it is said: 'Send away the people, in order to serve me' (94; Ex. 4:23). It is the mark of those who serve the Existent neither to do the works of bakers, nor cooks,[127] nor other earthly works, nor to make material forms like brick. On the contrary, it is characteristic of them to ascend the heavenly height in their thoughts with Moses as their leader (95).[128] At § 101 Philo returns to the word 'fire' from Gen. 11:3: the fact that the bricks are baked in fire denotes symbolically that the passions and vices are strengthened by the heat of argument.[129]

Although it is difficult to follow Philo's line of thought in this passage, it is easy to observe that he interprets the brick-making as being engaged in passions and vices, seeing in the making of bricks the laying of a foundation for the destruction of virtue (86). In his exegesis of the brick-making Gregory generally follows Philo's line of interpretation, although differences are discernible. The Jewish exegete primarily explains the building of the tower of Babel, associating it with the Israelites' labour in Egypt; Gregory's focus of attention is, of course, only the brick-making in Egypt. Whereas Philo speaks about passions, divided into the four cardinal ones, and vices, Gregory concentrates on one passion, namely pleasure. Further, Gregory brings in the notion of the continuously arousing of one desire after the other, which is absent in Philo.

---

[125] Cf. *Her.* 268-272, see § 6.c.

[126] For the service of God, cf. *Deus* 116, *Ebr.* 85, 87, *Somn.* 1.217, *Abr.* 125, 130, *Mos.* 2.5, 67, *Spec.* 1.20, 96, 263.

[127] Philo here recalls the chief baker, the chief butler and the chief cook from the Joseph story. They are the servants of the licentious soul. The king of Egypt, being a friend of passions and of drunkenness, which gives birth to pleasure, becomes reconciled with the chief butler (Gen. 40:21). All three are eunuchs (Gen. 39:1, 40:2), neither men, nor women because they are barren of wisdom and rejoice only in costly food and drink. (*Ebr.* 208, 212, cf. *Ios.* 151-156; for 'barren of wisdom', cf. Plato *Theat.* 150C, Gregory of Nyssa *VM* II.11, see § 3.3).

[128] Cf. *Her.* 274: the mind, having come down from heaven, is bound in the constraints of the body.

[129] Cf. *Her.* 255, where the task-drivers (Ex. 5:6) are presented as urging others to the enjoyment of pleasures.

Besides the resemblance in the exegesis there is a verbal parallel between Gregory and Philo in the definition of clay.

Conf. 89
ἐπειδὰν γάρ τις τὴν ὕδατος καὶ γῆς τὴν μὲν ὑγράν, τὴν δ' αὖ στερεὰν οὐσίαν, διαλυομένας καὶ φθειρομένας, ἀνακερασάμενος τρίτον μεθόριον ἀμφοῖν ἀπεργάσηται, ὃ καλεῖται πηλός.

VM II.59
ὅ τι γὰρ ἂν ᾖ τῆς ὑλικῆς ἀπολαύσεως ὡς ἐκ γῆς ἐστι πάντως ἢ ὕδατος παντί που δῆλον . . . [60] ἡ δὲ τῶν στοιχείων τούτων μίξις πηλὸς γίνεται καὶ ὀνομάζεται.

Because a similar definition occurs also in Plato *Theatetus* 147C, it is not possible to designate it right away as Philonic.[130] We can, however, argue for a link between the passages of Philo and Gregory because they have the same context, viz. an exegesis of the brick-making of the Israelites. Furthermore, it is important to note that the notion of clay, which is important in Gregory's exegesis, is absent in Exodus 5, the text he explains. Clay is only referred to in Ex. 1:14, and it is likely that Gregory brings in the notion of clay as a result of his reading of Philo's text. Finally, in both authors the same contrast between heaven and earth can be discerned: Philo opposes the doing of earthly works, like brick-making, to the ascent of the soul to the heavenly height (*Conf.* 95), while Gregory explains that it is the wish of the demon that his subjects do not look to heaven but bend to earth and make bricks from clay (II.59). In general, it seems very likely that Gregory is indebted to Philo in the interpretation of the brick-making, in which a verbal parallel with Philo is also recognizable (category A + B3).[131]

9. *The Miracle at Pharaoh's Court* (I.24, II.63-64)

This episode depicts Moses and Aaron performing the miracle with the staff at Pharaoh's court. The rod, thrown on the ground, becomes a serpent. The Egyptian sorcerers react to this by doing the same with their staffs but their serpents are swallowed up by Aaron's one (Ex. 7:8-12). Gregory, retelling this story, narrates that Pharaoh attempts to use devices against the divine wonders when Moses does the marvel with the rod.[132]

---

[130] *Theat.* 147C ...ὅτι γῆ ὑγρῷ φυραθεῖσα πηλὸς ἂν εἴη...
[131] Origen refers shortly to the labour as works of the flesh and earthly works (*Ex. Hom.* 1.5). In Basil's *Enar. Es.* the labour is denoted as material and bodily works (620C).
[132] In the scriptural account Aaron performs the wonder (Ex. 7:11). Gregory wishes to stress Moses' role.

The Egyptians magicians do the same but their device is exposed by the facts (I.24). In the *theoria* the Cappadocian exegete explains that the Egyptian serpents are the sophistical tricks of deceit that are invented by the adversary against the divine law. They are overcome by Moses' rod, that is the staff of virtue (II.63-64). Regarding Gregory's treatment of the story, Malherbe and Ferguson have remarked that Philo uses similar language; so we have to take a closer look at Philo's texts.[133]

The Jewish exegete retells the story in *Mos.* 1.91-94, where he refers to the sorcerers as sophists and magicians (92). After the Egyptian serpents have been swallowed up by Aaron's serpent, it is thought that the events are not devices and skills of men in order to deceive, but that their cause is some diviner power (94).

An allegorical interpretation is found in *Migr.* 82-85. In the foregoing (76-81) Philo deals with Moses' meeting with Aaron, explaining that Moses symbolizes thought and his brother speech.[134] Now Moses, we are told by Philo, is about to face a contest with sophists (82). The enchanters and sorcerers use devices against the divine word (83), and in order to counter these men Moses is in need of Aaron, i.e. speech, the interpreter of thought (84). Aaron's rod eats up the Egyptian rods because the sophistical arguments are done away with by the many-sided skill of nature (85). In *Det.* 38 Philo uses similar words in his description of the Egyptian sorcerers: 'Moses avoids the sophists, whom he calls 'magicians', because good morals are done away with by the skills and tricks of sophistry acting on them like the enchantments of magic.'

In order to see the similarities between Philo and Gregory the texts are placed side by side:

Mos. 1.

[92] σοφισταὶ δ᾿ ὅσοι καὶ <u>μάγοι</u> παρέτυγχανον.

[94] ὡς μηκέτι νομίζειν ἀνθρώπων <u>σοφίσματα</u> καὶ τέχνας εἶναι τὰ γινόμενα πεπλασμένας <u>πρὸς ἀπάτην</u>, ἀλλὰ δύναμιν θειοτέραν τὴν τούτων αἰτίαν.

VM I.24

Τοῦ δὲ Φαραὼ . .τοῖς . .σημείοις <u>ἀντισοφιστεύειν</u> . . ἐπιχειροῦντος, ὅτε . . τὸ ἴσον ἐνομίσθη θαυματοποιεῖν ἡ γοητεία ἐν ταῖς <u>μάγων</u> ῥάβδοις. καὶ ἠλέγχθη διὰ τῆς ἐνεργείας <u>τὸ σόφισμα.</u>

---

133 Malherbe-Ferguson (1978) 152 n. 47.
134 See § 7.

Migr.
[83] ἢ οὐχ ὁρᾷς τοὺς ἐπαοιδοὺς καὶ φαρμακευτὰς ἀντισοφιστεύοντας τῷ θείῳ λόγῳ.
[85] ἐγκαταπίνονται γὰρ καὶ ἀφανίζονται πάντες οἱ σοφιστικοὶ λόγοι τῇ τῆς φύσεως ἐντέχνῳ ποικιλίᾳ, ὡς ὁμολογεῖν ὅτι "δάκτυλος θεοῦ" τὰ γινόμενά ἐστιν,

Det. 38
οὐχ ὁρᾷς ὅτι Μωυσῆς τοὺς ἐν Αἰγύπτῳ τῷ σώματι σοφιστάς, οὓς φαρμακέας ὀνομάζει, παραιτεῖται — σοφισμάτων γὰρ τέχναις καὶ ἀπάταις ἤθη χρηστὰ τρόπον τινὰ φαρμακεύεται καὶ διαφθείρεται —...

I.26 ...ἔσχε καὶ ἡ μαγγανεία καιρὸν .....παρασοφίσασθαι

II.63
.. οἶδεν ὁ ταῖς ποικίλαις ... μεθοδείαις κατὰ τῶν ψυχῶν ἡμῶν σοφιστεύων ἀντιπαρεισάγειν τῷ θείῳ νόμῳ τὰ τῆς ἀπάτης σοφίσματα. ταῦτα δὲ λέγω πρὸς τοὺς Αἰγυπτίους δράκοντας βλέπων τῷ λόγῳ, τουτέστι πρὸς τὰς ποικίλας τῆς ἀπάτης κακίας, ὧν τὸν ἀφανισμὸν ἡ τοῦ Μωϋσέως ῥάβδος ἐργάζεται

II. 64
.. ῥάβδον τὴν τὰς σεσοφισμένας ἐξαφανίζουσαν[135]

The reference to the sorcerers as σοφισταί in the LXX (Ex. 7:11) may be a source of inspiration for both Philo and Gregory, enabling them to see in the practises of the sorcerers sophistical tricks. Nevertheless, Gregory, referring to the tricks as τὰ τῆς ἀπάτης σοφίσματα, clearly recalls the phraseology and exegesis of Philo, who calls the activities of the sorcerers σοφίσματα καὶ τέχνας .. πρὸς ἀπάτην. In Philo they are performed against the divine word (τῷ θείῳ λόγῳ), in Gregory against the divine law (τῷ θείῳ νόμῳ). Both refer to the sorcerers as μάγοι, and use the verb ἀντισοφιστεύω with regard to the activities of the Egyptian sorcerers and Pharaoh.[136] Gregory does not place the interpretation in the context of a symbolic explanation of Moses and Aaron as thought and speech, as Philo does in Migr. and Det.

It is remarkable that Gregory does not give a Christological explanation of Moses' staff in this passage, as he did earlier (II.31-34).[137] This kind of interpretation occurs in Origen (Ex. hom. 4.6), who explains that Moses' rod is Christ's cross, by which this world is overcome, and by which the prince of this world (Joh. 16:11) is defeated together with his principalities

---

[135] Cf. VM II.67 ὁ παρασοφισμὸς τῆς ἀπάτης
[136] According to the TLG this verb does not occur in Clement, the Greek works of Origen, Eusebius, Basil, or Gregory of Nazianzus.
[137] See § 6.c.

and powers (Col. 2:15). The serpent is a symbol of wisdom or prudence, because the Gospel says 'Be prudent like serpents' (Matt. 10:16). When Moses' staff is thrown on the ground, that is after the coming of Christ for the belief of men, it is changed into wisdom, and swallows up the large wisdom of the Egyptians. God has made the wisdom of this world foolish, after he had made manifest Christ, who is crucified, and who is God's power and wisdom (1 Cor. 1:20, 23, 24). Like Philo and Gregory, Origen refers to the sorcerers as magicians.[138] His interpretation, however, differs clearly from Philo's and Gregory's treatment. It is thus appropriate to label Gregory's interpretation of the story as a Philonic exegesis combined with Philonic phraseology (A + B3).

10. *The Ten Plagues* (I.25-28, II.65-111)

After the performance of the miracle with the staff at Pharaoh's court, the Egyptian people are hit with ten plagues because Pharaoh does not let the people go. In his retelling of the plagues in the *historia*, Gregory relates that Moses strikes the whole nation of the Egyptians with a common plague because he sees that the Egyptians agree with their leader in his evil. The elements of the universe — earth, water, wind, and fire, which are found in everything — cooperate with him in the attack on the Egyptians. They are like an army under orders, and they change their activities according to the dispositions of men (I.25).

Gregory begins his allegorical interpretation by remarking that only the Egyptians are beaten, whereas the Hebrews remain unhurt. This denotes the opposition between, on the one hand, those who accept the word and have their minds in the light and, on the other, those who do not look to the beams of the truth and remain in the darkness of ignorance (II.65).[139] Thereafter the Cappadocian father treats the first and second plague allegorically: the stream of faith becomes corrupted blood for those who live like the Egyptians (II.66; Ex. 7:14-25); the frogs are the harmful offspring of vice, arising from the dirty heart of men as from mud. They live in the houses of those who choose to live the Egyptian life (II.69). Gregory sees in those who lead a licentious life, sprung from clay and

---

[138] *Ex. hom.* 4.4, 13.4, *Ex. fr.* 281C. Justin also refers to the Egyptian sorcerers as magicians (*Dial.* 69, 79). In Irenaeus (*Adv. Haer.* 3.21.8) Moses' staff is a symbol of Christ.

[139] Probably Gregory has in mind the ninth plague: the Egyptians are struck with darkness, whereas the Hebrews live in the light (Ex. 10:21-23). Philo connects this darkness with ignorance in *Somn.* 1.114. Cf. Origen *Pascha* 43, where darkness signifies ignorance.

mud,[140] amphibians: being human by nature, they have become beasts by passion (II.70; Ex. 7:26-8:11).[141] Referring to the biblical remark that God hardens Pharaoh's heart (Ex. 7:22 etc.), Gregory makes a digression on free will and providence, underscoring that free will is the cause of the hardening of the tyrant's heart (II.73-77; cf. 80, 86). After explaining the stretching out of Moses' hands as pointing to Jesus' hands on the cross, he deals shortly with the darkness from the ninth plague and the ashes from the sixth, connecting them with the darkness and the fire in hell (II.80-84; Ex. 10:21-29, 9:8-12). The other plagues — except for the tenth — are only mentioned, without an explicit interpretation (II.85).[142]

The final plague — the death of the Egyptian firstborn — indicates that one should destroy the first beginnings of evil because it is impossible to flee the Egyptian life in any other way (II.90; Ex. 11:4-10, 12:29-36).[143] Security against the entrance of the destroyer who brings the firstborn's death is the pouring out of the blood of the lamb on the upper doorpost and the side doorposts (Ex. 12:7, 22-23). According to the Christian tradition Gregory regards the lamb as a symbol of Christ (II.95).[144] Next he connects the upper doorpost and the side posts with the pagan teaching on the tripartition of the soul into the rational, appetitive, and spirited parts.[145] The spirited and the appetite parts are placed below, while the

---

[140] The notion of mud is derived from the Platonic tradition (Plato *Rep.* 533D, Plotinus *Enn.* 1.6.5, 1.8.13, 6.7.31). See further Aubineau (1959); in Gregory *Virg.* 299.25-29, *VM* II.302; in Philo *Spec.* 1.148; for pleasure of clay, see *VM* II.60.

[141] The idea of man having become beast also in *Inscr. Psal.* 156.23-25, *Prof.* 137.17-19, 178.20-179.22, *VM* II.316.

[142] Gregory's exegesis differs from Philo's and Origen's interpretations. Philo refers shortly to the first plague in *Somn.* 2.259-260, explaining that the Egyptian river, which is changed into blood, is soulless speech. The fish that died in it symbolize thought, for thoughts die in undisciplined speech. In *Sacr.* 69 the frogs are soulless opinions. Origen explains all ten plagues allegorically in *Ex. hom.* 4. For the treatment of the plagues by Philo and the Church fathers, see Brottier (1989).

[143] Cf. Origen *Ex. hom.* 4.8, where the Egyptian firstborn represent the first movements of the soul made according to the flesh, which should be destroyed, if the conversion leads the better course for the rest of life. Philo explains the Egyptian firstborn as the most dominant elements of blind passion. When they are destroyed, the offspring of the one that sees God become holy (Num. 3:13). The destruction of evil brings about the entrance of virtue (*Sacr.* 134).

[144] For the lamb as a symbol of Christ, cf. Joh. 1:29, 1 Cor. 5:7, Justin *Dial* 40, 106, Origen *Pasc.* 13, 17, *Gen. hom.* 10.3, *Io. com.* 10.92-93. Irenaeus explains that the slaughter of the lamb is a reference to the passion of Christ (*Dem.* 25).

[145] The tripartition of the soul is Platonic *Rep.* 434E-444D, *Phdr.* 246B-249D, *Tim.* 69C-71A. Philo refers to it in *Leg.* 1.70-73, 3.114-116, *Conf.* 21, *Migr.* 66-67, *Her.* 64, *Spec.* 1.146-148, 4.92-94, *Virt.* 13, *QG* 1.13, 4.195, *QE* 1.12. See Billings (1919) 51, Daniélou (1954a) 67-69, Völker (1955) 61-62, Méasson (1986) 150-160, Runia (1986) 301-305.

rational one keeps them together and is held up by them (II.96). As long as the soul is safeguarded in this manner, all the parts work together for good (II.97) but when this arrangement is upset and the upper part becomes the lower the destroyer enters (II.98). Thereafter Gregory offers an allegorical exegesis of the prescriptions for the Passover (Ex. 12:8-11), which he does not mention in the *historia*. We can detect Philo's influence in two issues, namely Gregory's description of the plagues (10.1), and in the exegesis of the doorposts (10.2).

10.1. *Description of the Plagues*

The Italian scholar Manlio Simonetti detects Philo's influence in Gregory's remark that the Egyptians agree with their leader in his evil (I.25).[146] He refers to *Mos.* 1.95, where the Jewish exegete says that the Egyptians cling to their inhumanity and impiety, neither showing mercy to those who are enslaved nor carrying out God's orders.[147] In the biblical account nothing is said about the Egyptians' attitude. Both Philo and Gregory wish to explain why the whole Egyptian nation is struck and not only Pharaoh. Common to both authors is that they notice a wicked attitude of the Egyptian people, but because the correspondences between the two authors are very vague it is unlikely that Gregory is here indebted to Philo.

A clearer resemblance between Gregory and Philo can be seen in the notion that the four elements perform the plagues:[148]

Mos. 1.96	*VM* I.25
τὰ γὰρ στοιχεῖα τοῦ παντός, γῆ καὶ ὕδωρ	συνεκινεῖτο δὲ αὐτῷ πρὸς τὴν τοιαύτην
καὶ ἀὴρ καὶ πῦρ, ἐπιτίθενται,	κατὰ τῶν Αἰγυπτίων πληγὴν οἷόν τις
δικαιώσαντος θεοῦ, οἷς ἀπετελέσθη ὁ	στρατὸς ὑποχείριος αὐτὰ τὰ στοιχεῖα
κόσμος, τὴν ἀσεβῶν χώραν φθαρῆναι,	τῶν ὄντων τὰ ἐν τῷ παντὶ θεωρούμενα,
πρὸς ἔνδειξιν κράτους ἀρχῆς ᾗ κέχρηται,	γῆ τε καὶ πῦρ καὶ ἀὴρ καὶ ὕδωρ,[150]
[149]	

Although he makes some slight variations in wording (ὄντα τὰ ἐν τῷ παντί replaces τὸ πᾶν), Gregory uses the same expressions as Philo in the same context. The Jewish exegete adds an elucidation for the cooperation of the elements, arguing that God considers it right that the land of the impious

---

[146] Simonetti (1984) 268.
[147] For the interpretation of τῶν λόγων in this sentence, see Colson PLCL 6.324 n. a.
[148] Daniélou (1968) 65 n. 1, Malherbe-Ferguson (1978) 152 n. 49.
[149] Cf. *Mos.* 1.143, 156, 202, *QE* 1.4.
[150] Ms. Λ reads γῆ .. ὕδωρ .. ἀὴρ .. πῦρ.

should be destroyed by the same elements by which the world has been framed; this explication is absent in Gregory.

The commentators on Gregory's passage refer also to a text from the LXX (Sap. 19:18-20), which runs:[151] 'The elements alter by themselves ....
Land animals changed to aquatic animals, and aquatic animals went to earth, fire was strong in water, and water forgot its extinguishing power.'
This text in the Wisdom of Solomon can hardly explain Gregory's statements because it is about alteration of the elements and not about their cooperation in the production of the plagues.[152] Because we have detected in Gregory several expressions derived from Philo's *Mos.*, we can classify Gregory's mention of the cooperation of the elements as Philonic phraseology (A).

10.2. *The Exegesis of the Doorposts*

Like Gregory, Philo connects the upper doorpost and the side posts with the three elements of the soul in *QE* 1.12, but Gregory's exegesis differs from Philo's in details.[153] Marcus' translation runs as follows: 'Since our soul is threefold, the heart is likened to the lintel, desire to the house, and reason to the two doorposts.'[154] Exactly the same exegesis as Gregory gives is encountered in Origen, who ascribes it to one of his predecessors (*Ex. fr.* PG 12.285A);[155] By this expression he refers usually to Philo[156] but his interpretation differs from Philo's one in *QE* 1.12. An interpretation comparable to Gregory is found in an anonymous Easter homily, dating from the fourth century and written in the Alexandrian tradition.[157] In this homily the upper doorpost represents λογισμός, because it is guiding and higher; passion has an analogy with the sideposts, for it is placed beneath reasoning (2.8). Eusebius and Gregory of Nazianzus, too, relate the doorposts to the mind. The former speaks about the doorposts of the mind, which are daubed with blood in order to avert the destroyer (*Pas.*

---

[151] Daniélou (1968) 65 n. 1, Musurillo (1964) 11, Malherbe-Ferguson (1978) 152 n. 49, Simonetti (1984) 294-295.

[152] The production of the plagues by the four elements is also found in the Jewish tradition, cf. Ginzberg (1909-38) 2.341.

[153] Daniélou (1968) 164 n. 1, Musurillo (1964) 62, Malherbe-Ferguson (1978) 169 n. 116, Runia (1993) 258.

[154] In *Leg.* 2.34 Philo explains the entrance of the destroyer in the houses as the entrance in the soul.

[155] *Ex. fr.* PG 12.285A φλιᾶς μὲν, ὡς ἀποδέδωκέ τις τῶν πρὸ ἡμῶν, τοῦ λογικοῦ· ἀμφοτέρων δὲ σταθμῶν θυμικοῦ καὶ ἐπιθυμητικοῦ. See Nautin (1953) 40 n. 1.

[156] Runia (1993) 161-162.

[157] Edited by Nautin (1953).

11, 705B). The latter explains that after the slaughter of the lamb deed and word are sealed with blood; deed and word are habit and action, the side posts of our doors, that is of the movements of mind and opinion (*Or.* 45.15).[158] It can be concluded that Gregory's line of interpretation of the doorposts is part of the patristic tradition, and thus falls under category B2. It is plausible that the exegetical tradition which combines the doorposts with the three parts of the soul is inspired by Philo.

10.a. *The Passover Regulations* (II.102-111)

After the allegorical treatment of the ten plagues Gregory discusses the prescriptions for the way in which the sheep should be eaten at Passover. The meat should be eaten while one has a girdle round the loins, shoes under the feet, and a staff in the hand (Ex. 12:11).[159] Gregory explains that this equipment indicates that present life is transient, and man has to prepare for his departure with his hands and feet. The shoes symbolize the self-restrained and austere life, being a protection for the feet in order that the thorns of life may not hurt them (II.107). The traveller's belt represents self-control, which draws in the tunic, that is, the enjoyments of life. That the belt is placed around the loins confirms this interpretation (1 Pet. 1:13, Eph. 6:14, cf. *Cant.* 317. 11). The staff is the word of hope (II.108).

With regard to this symbolic interpretation the commentators on Gregory refer to Philo's *QE* 1.19, where the Jewish exegete discusses Ex. 12:11.[160] In allegorical terms 'the girdles represent drawing together and the coming together of the sensual pleasures and other passions, which, being, as it were, released and let go, overtake all souls. Wherefore not ineptly does He add that one must have a girdle about the middle, for this place is considered as the manger of the many-headed beast of desire within us.[161].... The rod is a symbol of kingship and an instrument of discipline for those who are unable to act prudently without being scolded. And it is a figure of unmoving and stable souls which abandon whatever inclines to either side and in two (directions). And the shoes indicate the

---

[158] Gregory of Nazianzus *Or.* 45.15 ...καὶ σφραγίζονται ...αἵμασι πρᾶξις καὶ λόγος, εἴτουν ἕξις καὶ ἐνέργεια, αἱ τῶν ἡμετέρων θυρῶν παραστάτιδες, λέγω δὴ τῶν τοῦ νοῦ κινημάτων τε καὶ δογμάτων, ... Cf. *Or.* 16.11.

[159] For Gregory's interpretation of the Passover regulations, see Drobner (1990).

[160] Daniélou (1968) 171 n. 1, Musurillo (1964) 66, Malherbe-Ferguson (1978) 170 n. 121, Simonetti (1984) 296.

[161] Comparable interpretation of the girdle in *Leg* 2.27-28 (with reference to the girdle in Deut. 23:13) and 3.154.

covering and protection of one who is engaged in hurrying not on a trackless way but on a well-travelled and worn path which leads to virtue' (tr. Marcus).[162]

The same kind of interpretation is also found in several Christian writers. In his treatise on the Passover, *De Pascha*, Origen explains that the loins girdled show that one should abstain from sexual intercourse during the eating of the flesh of Christ (35-36). Referring to 1 Cor. 9:25, Origen then presents an athlete who exercises self-restraint.[163] The shoes on the feet indicate preparedness (37, cf. Eph. 6:15), while the staff is a symbol of education (39).[164] In the same line Eusebius (*Pas.* 4, 697C) and Gregory of Nazianzus (*Or.* 45.18) interpret the belt as self-control.

From this short sketch of the exegetical tradition it emerges that both Philo and Gregory see in the girdle an instrument for controlling and restraining the passions, pointing to the place around the middle as a confirmation. Gregory, although he follows Philo's line of thought, is more in accordance with Eusebius and Gregory of Nazianzus, because he explicitly interprets the girdle as a symbol of self-control. His interpretation comes in category B2.

11. *The Spoiling of the Egyptians* (I.29, II.112-116)

After the ten plagues Pharaoh lets the Israelite people go, who then proceed to take the Egyptians' wealth with them at God's order (Ex. 11:2-3, 12:36). In his discussion on this so-called spoiling of the Egyptians, Gregory makes an indirect reference to predecessors.[165] He remarks that the lawgiver cannot issue this order because his laws forbid wrongdoing to one's neighbour, although it seems reasonable *to some* that the Israelites should have exacted wages from the Egyptians for their works (II.113).[166] It seems that Gregory refers here to Philo, who explains that the Jews took away the spoil as a wage for all the time of service (*Mos.* 1.141).[167] Gregory's reference, however, cannot be only to Philo because the same

---

[162] Philo interprets the girdling of the loins as being ready for service (*Sacr.* 63, cf. *Mos.* 2.144).

[163] For the image of an athlete, see § 7.2.

[164] Philonic interpretation, see § 6.c.

[165] Runia (1993) 258-259.

[166] *VM* II.113 κἄν τισι δοκῇ εὔλογον εἶναι τῶν ἔργων τὰ μισθώματα παρὰ τῶν Αἰγυπτίων τοὺς Ἰσραηλίτας διὰ ἐπινοίας ταύτης εἰσπράττεσθαι.

[167] *Mos.* 1.141 ἀλλὰ πρῶτον μὲν ὧν παρὰ πάντα τὸν χρόνον ὑπηρέτησαν ἀναγκαῖον μισθὸν κομιζόμενοι.

elucidation occurs in Ezekiel Tragicus (*Exagoge* 166), Clement (*Strom.* 1.157), Irenaeus (*Adv. haer.* 4.30.2), Eusebius (*Ps. com.* 1309B), and Gregory of Nazianzus (*Or.* 45.20, *Poem. mor.* 10.499), and so it belongs to the Jewish-Christian tradition.[168] For this reason the explanation falls under category B2.

It is noteworthy that Gregory does not agree with this interpretation because Moses' command does contain falsehood and deceit. For this reason, he explains the spoiling symbolically: those who live according to virtue should use the richness of pagan education in order to beautify the divine sanctuary of mystery (II.115). In the same way the Israelites use the Egyptian riches for the construction of the tabernacle (II.116; Ex. 35:4-29).[169]

12. *Crossing the Red Sea* (I.29-32, II.117-130)

When the Israelites depart from Egypt, the Egyptian army pursues them until they arrive at the Red Sea, where there seems no way out. The Israelite people become afraid but Moses strengthens their minds with the hope of divine help (II.117). While he exhorts them to be of good courage, he cries out, as God himself bears witness, even though he does not make any outward sound to God (Ex. 14:15). Gregory explains that Moses' cry is a meditation sent up from a pure conscience (II.118). God, answering Moses' call, provides a way through the sea for the Israelites but their persecutors are immersed in the Red Sea. The Cappadocian theologian allegorizes the Egyptian army as various passions of the soul to which man is enslaved, such as thoughts of anger, pleasure, grief, and avarice. Reproach is a stone from the sling and the impulse of anger is the quivering spear point; the passion for pleasures is seen in the horses (II.122). Gregory links the horsemen, called *tristatai* (Ex. 14:7), with the three parts of the soul, the rational, the appetitive and the spirited (II.123, cf. II.96).[170] In accordance with the patristic tradition the crossing is conceived of as a symbol of baptism,[171] and it shows that one who passes

---

[168] Runia (1993) 258-259 concludes that the reference specifically points to Philo but Winston (1994) 109 calls attention to the wider Jewish-Christian tradition. Josephus remarks that the Egyptians honoured the Jews with gifts (*AJ* 2.314). See also Kugel (1997) 324-326.

[169] Same exegesis of the spoiling in Origen (*Ep. ad Greg.* 1-2 (88B-89B)).

[170] See § 10.

[171] Based on 1 Cor. 10:2, cf. Origen *Ex. hom.* 5.5, *Ps. 36 hom.* 4.1, Basil *Spir. sanc.* 14.31, Gregory of Nazianzus *Or.* 39.17. See further Lundberg (1942) 116-135, Wessel 1959.

through the mystical water of baptism should put to death the whole army of evil (II.125). Gregory interprets the mystery of the Passover, at which unleavened bread should be eaten (Ex. 13:5-7), in the same way: it indicates that no remnant of evil should be mixed with the subsequent life (II.126).[172] There are, however, many who having accepted the mystical baptism mix the leaven of vice with their further life (II.127), being bowed under the yoke of bad despots (II.128).[173] Four issues in Gregory's treatment of the crossing of the Red Sea merit our attention, namely the description of Moses' cry to God (12.1), the recount of the crossing (12.2), the depiction of the Egyptian army (12.3), and, finally, its allegorical interpretation (12.4).

12.1. *The Description of Moses' Cry*

In his account in the *historia* Gregory, describing Moses' cry to God, writes that Moses does two things at once: with voice and word he encourages the people to have good hopes but inwardly, in his thought, he pleads with God on behalf of those who cower in fear. Philo, narrating this event in *Mos.*, makes a comparable distinction between νοῦς and λόγος.[174]

Mos. 1.173	*VM* I. 29
καὶ διανείμας τὸν νοῦν καὶ τὸν λόγον κατὰ τὸν αὐτὸν χρόνον τῷ μὲν ἐνετύγχανεν ἀφανῶς τῷ θεῷ, ἵν' ἐξ ἀμηχάνων ῥύσηται συμφορῶν, δι' οὗ δ' ἐθάρσυνε καὶ παρηγόρει τοὺς καταβοῶντας "μὴ ἀναπίπτετε" λέγων.[175]	διχῇ ταῖς ἐνεργείας τεμνόμενον, τῇ μὲν φωνῇ καὶ τῷ λόγῳ παραθαρρύνειν τε τοὺς Ἰσραηλίτας καὶ τὰς ἀγαθὰς ἔχειν ἐλπίδας παρακελεύεσθαι, ἔνδοθεν δὲ τῇ διανοίᾳ τῷ θεῷ προσάγειν τὴν ὑπὲρ τῶν κατεπτηχότων ἱκετηρίαν .

This distinction between word and thought with reference to Ex. 14:15 does not occur in Origen, Eusebius, Basil, or Gregory of Nazianzus. Because Gregory derives expressions from Philo's *Mos.* at more places in *VM*, it is possible to label Gregory's distinction as Philonic.

---

[172] Cf. 1 Cor. 5:8, Justin *Dial.* 14, Eusebius *Pas.* 2, 696C. Philo explains the baking of the unleavened bread as the kneading of the untamed and cruel passion (*Sacr.* 62). Leaven is generally seen as something evil, cf. Mat. 16:6. See Jacobson (1983) 129.

[173] For the image of despotic passions, see § 6.c.

[174] Simonetti (1984) 268-269.

[175] Cf. *Her.* 14, where the cry is said to be made by the organ of the soul or understanding.

12.2. *The Description of the Crossing of the Red Sea*

It is often remarked that Gregory's depiction of the march through the sea shows influence from Philo's *Mos.*[176] In order to examine this observation further the texts in question are placed side by side:

Mos. 1.177

προσταχθεὶς δὲ Μωυσῆς τῇ βακτηρίᾳ παίει τὴν θάλασσαν· ἡ δὲ ῥαγεῖσα διίσταται καὶ τῶν τμημάτων τὰ μὲν πρὸς τῷ ῥαγέντι μέρει μετέωρα πρὸς ὕψος ἐξαίρεται καὶ παγέντα τρόπον τείχους κραταιῶς ἠρέμει καὶ ἡσύχαζε, τὰ δ' ὀπίσω σταλέντα καὶ χαλινωθέντα τὴν εἰς τὸ πρόσω φορὰν καθάπερ ἡνίαις ἀφανέσιν ἀνεχαίτιζε, τὸ δὲ μεσαίτατον, καθ' ὃ ἐγένετο ἡ ῥῆξις, ἀναξηρανθὲν ὁδὸς εὐρεῖα καὶ λεωφόρος γίνεται.[177]

2.253

ῥῆξις θαλάττης, ἀναχώρησις ἑκατέρου τμήματος, πῆξις τῶν κατὰ τὸ ῥαγὲν μέρος διὰ παντὸς τοῦ βάθους κυμάτων, ἵν' ἀντὶ τειχῶν ᾖ κραταιοτάτων, εὐθυτενὴς ἀνατομὴ τῆς μεγαλουργηθείσης ὁδοῦ, ἢ τῶν κρυσταλλωθέντων μεθόριος ἦν.[178]

VM I.31

προσεγγίσας γὰρ κατὰ τὴν ἠϊόνα, πλήσσει τῇ ῥάβδῳ τὸ πέλαγος· τὸ δὲ περὶ τὴν πληγὴν ὑπεσχίζετο.[179] καὶ καθάπερ ἐπὶ τῆς ὑέλου γίνεσθαι πέφυκεν, εἰ κατά τι μέρος αὐτῆς ἀρχὴν ἡ ῥῆξις λάβοι, κατ' εὐθεῖαν πρὸς τὸ ἕτερον διεξέρχεται πέρας. οὕτω παντὸς τοῦ πελάγους ἐκείνου κατὰ τὸ ἄκρον ὑπορραγέντος τῇ ῥάβδῳ ἐπὶ τὴν ἀντικειμένην ὄχθην καὶ ἡ τῶν κυμάτων ῥῆξις ἐπέρασε. καὶ καταβὰς ἐπὶ τὸ βάθος ὁ Μωϋσῆς, καθὸ διετμήθη τὸ πέλαγος, σὺν παντὶ τῷ λαῷ βύθιος ἦν ἐν ἀβρόχῳ καὶ ἡλιουμένῳ τῷ σώματι. πεζῇ δὲ τὰς ἀβύσσους ἐν ξηρῷ πυθμένι τῆς θαλάσσης διεξερχόμενος οὐκ ἐδεδοίκει τὴν αὐτοσχέδιον ἐκείνην ἐκ κυμάτων τειχοποιίαν ἔνθεν καὶ ἔνθεν τείχους δίκην[180] παραπεπηγυίας αὐτοῖς ἐκ πλαγίων τῆς ἅλμης.[181]

---

176 Daniélou (1968) 71 n. 3, Musurillo (1964) 15, Peri (1974) 316, Malherbe-Ferguson (1978) 153 n. 65.

177 *Mos.* 1.177 'Moses now, at God's command, smote the sea with his staff, and as he did so it broke and parted into two. Of the waters thus divided, one part rose up to a vast height, where the break was made, and stood quite firmly, motionless and still like a wall; those behind were held back and bridled in their forward course, and reared as though pulled back by invisible reins; while the intervening part, which was the scene of the breaking, dried up and became a broad highway.' (translation Colson).

178 *Mos.* 2.253 'The sea breaks in two, and each section retires. The parts around the break, through the whole depth of their waters, congeal to serve as walls of vast strength: a path is drawn straight, a road of miracle between the frozen walls on either side.' (translation Colson).

179 Cf. Ex. 14:21 καὶ ἐσχίσθη τὸ ὕδωρ.

180 Cf. Ex. 14:22 καὶ τὸ ὕδωρ αὐτοῖς τεῖχος ἐκ δεξιῶν καὶ τεῖχος ἐξ εὐωνύμων.

181 *VM* I.31 'He approached the bank and struck the sea with his rod. The sea split at the blow, just as a crack in glass runs straight across to the edge when a break occurs at any point. The whole sea was split like that from the top by the rod, and the break in the waters reached to the opposite bank. At the place where the sea parted, Moses went down into the deep with all the people and they were in the deep without getting wet and their bodies were still in the sunlight. As they crossed the depths by foot on dry bottom, they

The Exodus account depicts the events less elaborately. It runs as follows:

ἐξέτεινεν δὲ Μωυσῆς τὴν χεῖρα ἐπὶ θάλασσαν, καὶ ὑπήγαγεν κύριος τὴν θάλασσαν ἐν ἀνέμῳ νότῳ βιαίῳ ὅλην τὴν νύκτα καὶ ἐποίησεν τὴν θάλασσαν ξηράν, καὶ ἐσχίσθη τὸ ὕδωρ (14:21).

Philo and Gregory have the following common notions that are not explicitly found in the biblical story: the striking of the sea with Moses' rod, the breaking (ῥήγνυμι), the parting (τέμνω), and the fixing (πήγνυμι) of the waters. The first element — Moses striking the sea with his staff — is, however, narrated by the Jewish writers Ezekiel (*Exagoge* 224-228) and Josephus (*AJ* 2.338).[182] The breaking of the sea is mentioned in God's order to Moses at Ex. 14:16, and recurs in Origen (*Ex. hom.* 5.5) and Gregory of Nazianzus (*Or.* 32.16), while the parting of the waters is also reported by other Christian writers, Justin (*Dial.* 86) and Gregory of Nazianzus (*Or.* 45.21). The only assertion common to Philo and Gregory which I have not found in other Jewish or Christian writers is that regarding the fixing of the sea. Although this basis seems to be too small to settle the question of Gregory's dependence on Philo, it is highly probable that he is primarily inspired by the Jewish exegete because of the many other references to Philo's *Mos.* in Gregory.

Influence of Philo can also be observed later on in Gregory, where he refers to the victory over the Egyptians as 'bloodless':

Mos. 1.180	*VM.* I. 32
τὸ μέγα τοῦτο καὶ θαυμαστὸν ἔργον	ἦσαν ᾠδὴν τῷ θεῷ τῷ τὸ <u>ἀναίμακτον</u>
Ἑβραῖοι καταπλαγέντες <u>ἀναιμωτὶ</u> νίκην	ὑπὲρ αὐτῶν ἐγείραντι τρόπαιον πάντων
οὐκ ἐλπισθεῦσαν ἤραντο	

The use of this word in this context can be classified as Philonic phraseology (A).

12.3. *The Description of the Egyptian Army*

Gregory's description of the Egyptian army in the *theoria* is probably also borrowed from Philo's *Mos.* and is thus an example of Philonic phraseology.

---

were not alarmed at the water piled up so close to them on both sides, for the sea had been fixed like a wall on each side of them.' (translation Malherbe-Ferguson). Cf. the description in *Or. cat.* 59.4-6, *Diem lum.* 226.19-20, *Thaum.* 32.2-7.

[182] Cf., however, God's command to Moses at Ex 14:16 καὶ σὺ ἔπαρον τῇ ῥάβδῳ σου καὶ ἔκτεινον τὴν χεῖρά σου ἐπὶ τὴν θάλασσαν καὶ ῥῆξον αὐτήν. See Jacobson (1983) 141-142.

Mos. 1.168

εἶθ' ἅπασαν τὴν ἱππικὴν δύναμιν
παραλαβὼν ἀκοντιστάς τε καὶ
σφενδονήτας καὶ ἱπποτοξότας καὶ τοὺς
ἄλλους ὅσοι τῆς κούφης ὁπλίσεως καὶ τὰ
κάλλιστα τῶν δρεπανηφόρων ἁρμάτων
ἑξακόσια τοῖς ἐν τέλει δούς.

VM. II.122

ἐκεῖνοι οἱ ἵπποι, ἐκεῖνα τὰ ἅρματα καὶ οἱ
ἐπ' αὐτῶν ἀναβάται, τοξόται καὶ
σφενδονῆται καὶ ὁπλομάχοι καὶ ὁ λοιπὸς
ὅμιλος τῆς τῶν ἐχθρῶν παρατάξεως.

In both descriptions archers and slingers, who are not mentioned in the biblical account, are part of the army, the horses and the chariots having a scriptural precedent (Ex. 14:9, 17, 23). As in other cases of Philonic phraseology Gregory shows a slight alteration in wording (οἱ ἵπποι instead of ἡ ἱππικὴ δύναμις).

12.4. *The Allegorical Interpretation of the Egyptian Army*

Not only does Gregory's description of Pharaoh's army seem to be Philonic, but also his allegorical exegesis has traces of Philo, as remarked by the commentators.[183] The Alexandrian exegete discusses the downfall of the Egyptians at *Ebr.* 111, conceiving of the king of Egypt as representing the boastful mind; his six hundred chariots (Ex. 14:7) symbolize the six movements of the organic body, fitting the *tristatai,* who think that created reality stands firmly, admitting no alteration. The boastful mind suffers the penalty due to its impiety. After Pharaoh's destruction Moses sings a hymn to God: 'The horse and his rider he has thrown into the sea' (Ex. 15:1), that is to say: he destroyed the mind which rode upon the irrational impulses of the four-footed and unbridled passions, and this hymn is sung at the triumph over the passions.[184]

This allegorical exegesis is also found in Clement of Alexandria, who explains the horses as the many-limbed, beastly, and impulsive passion, that is desire. It is thrown into the sea, together with the charioteer, who gives the reins to pleasures. Next Clement refers to Plato, who says that the charioteer and the horse that ran off — that is the irrational part, divided in spirit and desire — fall down (*Strom.* 5.52.5-53.1, Plato *Phdr.* 247B). Origen follows in the footsteps of Clement and Philo, dealing with Moses' song after the victory over the Egyptian army (Ex. 15:1-19) in his sixth homily on Exodus. He writes that the horses (Ex. 15:1) are in a figurative

---

[183] Daniélou (1968) 181 n. 2, Musurillo (1964) 71, Malherbe-Ferguson (1978) 171 n. 137.

[184] Same interpretation in *Leg.* 2.99-102 and *Agr.* 82-83. Philo links the four cardinal passions with the four-footed horses, see § 6.c.

sense all who have been born in the flesh. There are horses which are ridden by the Lord, but there are also horses which have the devil and his angels as riders. All who persecute the saints are neighing horses, and they have evil angels as riders that drive them on (6.2). Explaining Ex.15:4, Origen writes: 'Know that all whom you see who are most disgraceful in luxury, most fierce in cruelty, most offensive in avarice, most shameful in impiety, are from the four-horse chariots of Pharaoh' (tr. Heine). The *tristatai* (Ex. 14:7) indicate the threefold way of sin: in deed, word, or in thought (3). At *Ios. hom.* 15.3 Origen considers the horses and chariots those who have been fallen down from the heavens through licentiousness and pride. He also interprets them as the passions of the body, such as libido, licentiousness, pride or levity, which should be hamstrung (cf. Ios. 11:6).[185]

In his interpretation of the destruction of the Egyptian army, Gregory joins in clearly with the Philonic and patristic tradition, although differences are observable in the details. Gregory does not, like Philo, interpret the four-footed horses as the four cardinal passions. The devil and his angels, mentioned by Origen, are absent in Gregory. It is, however, plain that Gregory's interpretation falls under category B2.

13. *Marah* (I.33, II.131-132)

After a three days' journey from the Red Sea the Israelites arrive at Marah, where the water is undrinkable and bitter but becomes sweet when Moses throws a piece of wood into the water (I.33, II.131; Ex. 15:22-26). This incident, Gregory explains, means that a life without pleasures is at first difficult and disagreeable for one who has left behind the Egyptian pleasures but the virtuous life becomes sweeter and more pleasant, when the wood is cast into the water. The wood points to the mystery of the resurrection, which has its beginning with the wood (II.132).[186] Two issues should be examined further, viz. the description of the wood (13.1), and the allegorical interpretation of the bitterness at Marah (13.2).

---

[185] Cf. *Cant. com.* 2.6. Irenaeus sees in the salvation from the Red Sea the salvation from the deadly confusion of the pagans (*Dem.* 46).
[186] For several symbolic interpretations of Marah and Elim, see Robinson (1987). Christological interpretation also in Justin *Dial.* 86, Origen *Ex. hom.* 7.1, *Ier. hom.* 10.2. For Origen the bitterness of the water is the literal interpretation of the law (*Ex. hom.* 7.1).

13.1. *Description of the Wood*

Philo describes the events at Marah in *Mos.* 1.181-187, where he, like Gregory, attributes power to the piece of wood:

Mos. 1.185
κατασκευασμένον ἐκ φύσεως ποιοῦν δύναμιν.

VM I.33
τὸ δὲ παραχρῆμα πότιμον ἦν, τοῦ ξύλου τῇ οἰκείᾳ δυνάμει τὴν τοῦ ὕδατος φύσιν εἰς ἡδονὴν ἐκ πικρίας μετακεράσαντος.

It is impossible to determine whether Gregory is here influenced by Philo's description because the notion of the change of the water by the wood may have independently led both authors to the attribution of power to the wood.

13.2. *Allegorical Interpretation of the Bitterness at Marah*

With regard to Gregory's interpretation the commentators refer to Philo's *Migr.* 36-37,[187] where he explains that the wood promises not only nourishment but also immortality because the tree of life is said to have been planted in the middle of paradise (Gen. 2:9).[188] The tree of life is goodness, having the particular virtues and the corresponding actions as its bodyguard (cf. *Leg.* 1.59). Simonetti assumes that Gregory substitutes the wood of the cross for the tree of life, maintaining the eschatological interpretation, in which the wood is a symbol of the resurrection, beginning with the cross.[189] It is, however, more likely that Gregory is inspired by the exegesis that is found in *Post.* 154-157 because Philo there interprets the bitterness of Marah as the bitter toil of the virtuous life. There are, Philo writes, some ascetics who at first consider the road to virtue rough and difficult but God makes it a highway, changing the bitterness of toil into sweetness (154). When God leads us out of Egypt, that is the bodily passions, we go a road without pleasures and camp at Marah, a place without drinkable water, but wholly bitter, because the pleasures of the eyes and the stomach are still strong and attractive to us (155). When we want ourselves to be entirely separated from them, they would fight against us so that we may become alienated from toil because it is very bitter and want to return to Egypt, the refuge of a wanton and licentious life, unless

---

[187] Daniélou (1968) 189 n. 1, Malherbe-Ferguson (1978) 172 n. 151, Simonetti (1984) 301 n. 131.

[188] Cf. Origen *Ex. hom.* 7.1, Gregory of Nazianzus *Or.* 36.4.

[189] Simonetti (1984) 301.

the saviour throws a sweetening piece of wood into our soul, creating love of toil rather than hatred of it (156).[190]

It seems highly probable that Gregory's interpretation comes in category B3: a Philonic exegesis which has been altered. Generally speaking, for both authors the bitterness indicates the difficulty of the beginning of a virtuous life without the Egyptian pleasures. The life becomes sweet through the throwing of a piece of wood. Gregory Christianizes Philo's interpretation, explaining the wood as a reference to Christ's cross and a symbol of the resurrection.

14. *Elim* (I.34, II.133-134)

The next halting place is Elim, where twelve springs rise and seventy palms grow (Ex. 15:27), which are described by Gregory more vividly and in more beautiful terms than in the biblical account. The springs are filled with pure and very sweet water, while the palms are very large and towering, making a deep impression on those who see them (I.34, II.133). In allegorical terms the twelve springs are the apostles, whom the Lord chooses for service and through whom he causes his word to spring (Mar. 3:14, Luc. 6:13). The seventy palms represent the seventy apostles sent out besides the twelve (II.134; Luc. 10:1).[191] In this passage there are no traces of Philo, who regards the springs and the palms as referring to the Israelite nation: the twelve springs stand for the twelve tribes, and the elders of the nation (cf. Ex. 24:1, 9, Num. 11:16) are likened to the palm tree, the best of trees (*Mos.* 1.189).[192]

15. *Water from the Rock* (I.35, II.135-136)

Having treated the stay in Marah and Elim, Gregory goes on to discuss the miracle of the rock, passing over other camp-sites, which are virtues. The resistant and hard nature of the rock becomes drink to those who are thirsty (II.135; Ex. 17:2-7).[193] The rock, Gregory explains with a reference

---

[190] For the notion of toil in the virtuous life, cf. *Mos.* 2.182-183, see § 26.

[191] Same exegesis in Origen (*Ex. hom.* 7.3, *Num. hom.* 27.11).

[192] This interpretation is according to the Jewish tradition, see Ginzberg 3 (1909-38) 14. Philo explains the springs as springs of education in *Fug.* 183.

[193] In Exodus the scene with the wonder of the rock follows the falling of the manna. Gregory discusses first the water from the rock (II.135-136) and thereafter the manna (II.137-146). Same sequence in I.35-38.

to Paul (1 Cor. 10:4), is Christ,[194] who is moistureless and resistant to unbelievers but if one employs the rod of faith he becomes drink to those who are thirsty and flows into those who receive him (II.136). Paul's interpretation of the rock as Christ may have a connection with Philonic exegesis,[195] because the Jewish exegete, commenting on Deut. 32:13, which speaks about honey out of the rock and oil out of the flinty rock, explains the rock as wisdom (*Det.* 115); later on he writes that the rock is also called 'manna', which is God's Logos (118).[196] Whatever the relationship between Paul and Philo may be, it is clear that in the passage at hand Gregory, appealing to Paul, is fully in accord with the Christian exegetical tradition without necessarily making any use of Philo.

16. *The Manna* (I.36-38, II.137-146)

After the marvel of the rock Gregory deals with the story of the food that falls down from heaven and is called manna (I.36-38; Ex. 16).[197] In the *theoria* he elucidates that this food, i.e. the bread that has come down from heaven (Joh. 6:33, 35, 51), is not incorporeal, because how, he asks rhetorically, can something bodiless be nourishment for the body? Neither ploughing nor sowing produces this bread but the earth, remaining unchanged, is found full of this food. This marvel points to the mystery of the virgin (II.139).[198] The bread, not produced by earth, is the Word, changing its power according to the capacities of the eaters.[199] Not only is it bread, but also milk, meat or vegetable (II.140; cf. Rom. 14:2, 1 Petr. 2:2, Hebr. 5:12-14).[200]

---

[194] Same interpretation of the rock occurs in Justin *Dial.* 86, Irenaeus *Dem.* 46, Origen *Gen. hom.* 10.3, *Ex. hom.* 11.2, *Rom. com.* 10.6.

[195] This subject is dealt with by Ellis (1993), who argues that Philo and Paul draw on a common Jewish tradition.

[196] Cf. *Leg.* 2.86, where Philo interprets the flinty rock (Deut. 8:15-16) as the wisdom of God. For Philo on manna, see § 16.

[197] In Ex. 16 quails are also shortly mentioned. They are not discussed here by Gregory but in I.63, II.264 (cf. Num. 11:31-35).

[198] Mary's virginity is also seen in the burning bush not being burned (II.21).

[199] The interpretation of manna as the word of Christ is also found in Origen *Ex. hom.* 7.8, *Num. hom.* 3.1.

[200] The idea that the manna changes its quality is a Jewish tradition, cf. *Midrash Rabbah Exodus* 5.9, Sap. 16.20-21, Origen *Ex. hom.* 7.8. This notion is ascribed to Philo by Basil, who states that Philo was taught by a Jewish tradition (*Ep.* 190). This idea is, however, not found in the existing works of Philo, see Runia (1993) 236; see also Beauchamp (1967), who discusses correspondences between Sap. and Philo. Kamesar (1995) argues that in *Ep.* 190 Basil refers to Sap., regarding it as a work of Philo.

Concerning Gregory's interpretation of the manna as God's Word, the commentators refer to the exegesis of Philo, who deals extensively with the manna in *Leg.* 3.162-175.[201] With a reference to God's promise 'I rain upon you bread from heaven' (Ex. 16:4) he explains that the soul is fed by the words that God pours like rain (*Leg.* 3.162). Pointing to the Israelites' question 'What it is?' (τί ἐστιν τοῦτο; Ex. 16:15), he makes clear that 'manna' means 'something' (τι) and this is the most generic of the existing things.[202] It is God's Word, which is above the world and is the eldest and most generic of all that is created (3.175).[203]

There is, indeed, a continuity between Philo's interpretation of the manna as God's Logos and the Christian exegetical tradition, but the patristic interpretation is clearly based on Jesus' sayings about himself as bread from heaven in the gospel of John, and Gregory, also being led by other New Testament texts, is fully in accord with his Christian predecessors. Runia argues that Gregory, remarking that the manna is not τι ἀσώματον, refers to Philo's interpretation of the manna. With his remark Gregory underscores a considerable difference from Philo, namely that the Word has become corporeal. Gregory was acquainted with Philo's interpretation because in *CE* 3.7.8-9 he probably refers to *Leg.* 3.175.[204] It remains, however, unclear whether Gregory is especially thinking of Philo, because Philo does not explicitly call manna incorporeal. In Philo the emphasis is on τι, which refers to the Logos. It is also possible that Gregory emphasizes the corporeality of the Logos for dogmatic reasons.

17. *The Victory over the Amalekites* (I.39-41, II.147-151)

The next episode depicts the victory of the Israelites over the Amalekites. During the battle, which is led by Joshua, Moses stands on a hill, and whenever he holds up his arms the Israelites win; but whenever he lets them down the enemies become victorious (I.39-41; Ex. 17:8-15). In the *theoria* Gregory says that the soldiers of virtue, having received the mystical provision-money, go to fight against the enemy with Joshua, Moses'

---

[201] Daniélou (1968) 192 n. 1, Malherbe-Ferguson (1978) 173 n. 161, Runia (1993) 259. Borgen (1965) analyses *Leg.* 3.162-168 and *Mut.* 253-263, arguing that these passages are separate sermons made according to a homiletic pattern, in which Philo uses haggadic material.

[202] Cf. Origen *Ex. hom.* 7.5. This notion of τι is Stoic, SVF 2.333.

[203] Cf. *Leg.* 2.86, *Det.* 118, *Her.* 79, *Fug.* 137. Manna is interpreted as heavenly wisdom in *Her.* 191 and *Mut.* 259. The interpretation is based on the occurrence of ῥῆμα in Ex. 16:16.

[204] Runia (1993) 259. See Part II.I § 1.

successor, as leader of the battle (II.147). According to the patristic tradition Gregory sees in Joshua a *typos* of Christ (II.148).[205] The elevation of Moses' hands denotes the spiritual meaning of the law, whereas his hands keeping down indicate the literal and low exegesis and observation of the law (II.149).[206] Following common patristic exegesis, Gregory interprets the stretching out of Moses' hands as a reference to Jesus' cross (II.151).[207]

Influence of Philo is not discernible in this passage. His interpretation of the lifting up and falling down of Moses' hands is one of the few symbolic interpretations in *Mos.* Philo explains that the earth and the lowest parts of the universe are allotted to one party as its own, and the ether, the holiest region, is allotted to the other. Just as in the universe heaven rules over earth, so the Israelite nation will be victorious over the enemies (*Mos.* 1.217). In *Leg.* 3.186 the fight is interpreted as the war between mind and passion. When the mind lifts itself up from mortal things, that which sees God, Israel, is strong; but when it lowers its special powers and becomes weak, passion, named Amalek, is strong. Amalek means 'a people licking out', because passion eats up the whole soul and licks it out, leaving behind in it no seed or spark of virtue.[208]

18. *Moses on the Mountain* (I.42-55, II.152-201)

The scene of Moses on Mount Sinai, where he encounters God, receives the Ten Commandments, and sees the example of the tabernacle and of the priestly vestments, occupies an important place in Gregory's exposition of Moses' life. The passage can be regarded as essential in Gregory's thought because in it he discusses God's incomprehensibility, referring to Ex. 20:21. The biblical basis for Moses' ascent of Sinai is found in Ex. 19:1-25, 20:18-21;[209] the model of the tabernacle and its furnishings is related in

---

[205] Cf. Justin *Dial.* 75, 90, 106, 113, Irenaeus *Dem.* 27, 46, Clement *Paed.* 1.60.3, Origen *Ex. hom.* 11.3, *Ios. hom.* 1.1-4, 2.1, *Io. com.* 6.229, Eusebius *HE* 1.3.3-5.

[206] This exegesis is along the same lines as Origen's exegesis of the bosom of Moses (*Io. com.* 32.267-270) and of the bitter water at Marah (*Ex. hom.* 7.1).

[207] Cf. Justin *Dial.* 90-91, 106, 111-112, 131, Origen *Ios. hom.* 1.3, *Reg. hom.* 1.9, Gregory of Nazianzus *Or.* 2.88, 12.2, 18.14, 32.16, 45.12, Gregory of Nyssa *Trid.* 275.14-18.
Origen interprets the elevation of Moses' hands as the elevation of works and actions to God, and the avoidance of actions that fall (*Ex. hom.* 11.4, cf. *Reg. hom.* 1.9).

[208] Cf. *Migr.* 143-144, *Congr.* 55. For Philo's translation of Amalek, see Grabbe (1988) 131-132.

[209] The narrative of the theophany at Ex. 19, consisting of different levels, has a complex structure, see Houtman (1986-96) 2.382-394.

Ex. 25-27; Exodus 28 covers the description of the priestly vestments. Gregory's interpretation of the scriptural account is said to have been influenced by Philo, especially the exegesis of the darkness where Moses sees God (Ex. 20:21). Gregory's discussion can be divided into the following parts: Moses' ascent of the mountain (18.a); the exegesis of the darkness (18.b); the discussion of the tabernacle and its furnishings (18.c); and, finally, the treatment of the priestly vestments (18.d).

18.a. *Moses' Ascent of the Mountain* (I.42-45, II.152-161)

Gregory regards the mountain which Moses ascends as the mount of divine knowledge (ὄρος τῆς θεογνωσίας (II.152, cf. 158)[210] to which Moses is led in order to contemplate the transcendent Being (II.152-153). The Cappadocian theologian explains that the road to knowledge of God consists in purification (II.154): one who is about to know God should be purified of every sensible and irrational movement and be separated from sense-perception, upon which he usually relies (II.157). Gregory, offering this interpretation, has clearly in mind the command in Ex. 19:15: 'Come not to your wives.' Referring to the sound of the trumpets, which becomes louder and louder (Ex. 19:19), he sets out that the trumpet is the preaching of the divine nature, which becomes louder at the end (II.158). The law and the prophets had trumpeted the divine mystery of the incarnation but their sound was too weak to reach the disobedient ear. The later voices of the evangelists did strike the ears since the spirit was making the sound stronger through its instruments. These instruments, ringing out the sound of the spirit, are the prophets and apostles (II.159).[211] Two Philonic aspects from this passage should be discussed, namely the presentation of Moses as mystagogue (18.a.1), and the description of the divine voice (18.a.2).

18.a.1. *Moses as Mystagogue*

Gregory depicts Moses' ascent of the mountain as an initiation into a mystery, writing that Moses guides the people in a most secret initiation,

---

[210] For θεογνωσία, see Daniélou (1954a) 189-190.

[211] At *CE* 3.6.4 the prophet Isaiah is compared to an instrument, cf. *Cant.* 425.11-12. Malherbe-Ferguson (1978) 176 n. 186 refer to Philo (*Spec.* 1.65), Plutarch (*De defectu oraculorum* 436F) and Athenagoras (*Legatio* 9.1), see Völker (1955) 156-157, cf. Clement *Strom.* 6.168.3, Eusebius *DE* 5.13.3, Basil *Ps. 29 hom.* 7. Burdach (1912) 397-403 suggests that motives from Gregory's interpretation of Moses' ascent are found in Goethe's *Faust II.*

while the divine power itself initiates all the people and the leader himself into the mystery (I.42).[212] As remarked by the commentators on Gregory, Philo also presents Moses as being initiated into the mysteries, employing the same verb as Gregory, namely μυσταγωγέω (*Mos.* 2.71).[213] It is, however, not justified to label Gregory's depiction as exclusively Philonic because Christian writers commonly used mystery-terminology, and Gregory's portrayal of Moses may be a result of this employment.[214] Furthermore, Gregory of Nazianzus calls Moses a μυσταγωγός (*Or.* 11.2).[215]

18.a.2. *Description of the Articulated Voice*

Philonic phraseology is encountered in Gregory's reference to the sound of the trumpet as an articulated voice made by divine power. The same description is used by Philo in *Decal.* 33-35:[216]

Decal. 33	*VM.* I.44
ἥ . . ψυχὴ λογικὴ . . φωνὴν τοσαύτην ἔναρθρον ἐξήχησεν [35]τὴν δὲ κεκαινουργημένην φωνὴν ἐπιπνέουσα θεοῦ δύναμις[217]	ἡ δὲ φωνὴ αὕτη ἔναρθρος ἦν, θείᾳ δυνάμει δίχα τῶν προφητικῶν ὀργάνων τοῦ ἀέρος διαρθροῦντος τὸν λόγον.

Unlike other cases, this example of Philonic phraseology (A) does not derive from Philo's *Mos.*, in which the events from Ex. 19 are not narrated.

---

[212] *VM* I.42 ἐν τούτῳ δὲ καί τινος αὐτοῖς ἀπορρητοτέρας μυήσεως ὁ Μωϋσῆς καθηγεῖτο, αὐτῆς δυνάμεως διὰ τῶν ὑπὲρ λόγον θαυμάτων τὸν τε λαὸν πάντα καὶ αὐτὸν τὸν καθηγεμόνα μυσταγωγούσης. Gregory refers to God's disclosure in the bramble as ἡ πρώτη μυσταγωγία (II.201, cf. II.19 ἄρρητος φωταγωγία). Cf. *Bas.* 129.7, *Cant.* 25.19, *Or. dom.* 20.3, *Steph.* I.86.18, *Thaum.* 19.13-14. Other mystical terms in *VM*: ἀπορρητοτέρα μύησις (I.42), μυέω (I.42, II.160, 164), μυσταγωγία (I.42, 46, 49, 58, II.201), μυστικός (I.56). Gregory uses μυστήριον to denote (central aspects of) the Christian faith, cf. *VM* II.21, 27, 132 etc. For Gregory's use of mystical terms, see Daniélou (1954a) 178-189, Dünzl (1993) 330-336.

[213] Daniélou (1968) 79 n.1, Musurillo (1964) 19, Malherbe-Ferguson (1978) 153 n. 74, Andia (1996) 311, 323.

Mos. 2.71 ἔτι δ' ἄνω διατρίβων ἐμυσταγωγεῖτο παιδευόμενος τὰ κατὰ τὴν ἱερωσύνην πάντα. Cf. *Leg.* 3.100, *Gig.* 54. For Philo's use of mystical terms, see Riedweg (1987) 104-112.

[214] See Bornkamm (1942) 831-834. A discussion of mystical terms in Clement is given by Riedweg (1987) 116-161.

[215] *Or.* 11.2 (Moses) καὶ θείων μυστηρίων ἐπόπτης τε καὶ μυσταγωγός.

[216] Malherbe-Ferguson (1978) 154 n. 78.

[217] Cf. *Praem.* 2, where the Ten Commandments are said to be formed high above in the air and to have articulated speech.

18.b.   *Moses in the Darkness* (I.46-48, II.162-169)

This passage in which Gregory gives an exegesis of Moses' entrance into the darkness (Ex. 20:21) is generally claimed to be Philonic.[218] The examination of the Philonic background is organized as follows: first, Gregory's interpretation is set out; in the second section the focus of attention is Philo's exegesis of Ex. 20:21; the patristic exegetical tradition until Gregory is addressed in the third section, in which texts of Clement, Origen, and Gregory of Nazianzus are discussed.

18.b.1.   *Gregory on the Darkness*

Gregory interprets the darkness into which Moses enters and where God is (Ex. 20:21) as a symbol of God's invisibility and incomprehensibility.[219] In the *historia* he states that God is invisible and beyond human knowledge, remarking that everyone who intends to be together with God should go beyond all that is visible, lift up his mind to the invisible and incomprehensible, and believe that the divine is beyond human understanding (I.46). Next Gregory makes a distinction between God's existence, which is knowable, and his essence, which is unknown: one should believe in his existence, but not examine him with respect to his quality, quantity, origins or mode, because this is unreachable (I.47).[220] In the *theoria* the Cappadocian theologian expounds his view, writing that the mind leaves behind what is seen, not only what sense-perception comprehends, but also what the intellect thinks to see, and turns into the interior until it penetrates into the invisible and incomprehensible, and then it sees God. With a paradox Gregory states that the seeing of God consists in not-seeing, because the divine nature transcends all knowledge and is surrounded on all sides by incomprehensibility as by darkness. Therefore John, who penetrated the luminous darkness, says: 'No one has ever seen

---

[218]   Musurillo (1964) 86; Daniélou (1954a) 191 '... Grégoire dépende directement de lui (= Philo)'; (1968) 211 n. 3 'Grégoire s'inspire ici de Philon'; 212-213 n. 1; Malherbe-Ferguson (1978) 177 n. 192 'Gregory is inspired here by Philo.' See further Gobry (1991) 79-81, Runia (1993) 260-261, Meredith (1997) esp. 53.

[219]   Same interpretation of Ex. 20:21 in *Bas.* 129.5-9, *Cant.* 181.4-21, 322.11-323.9, *Inscr. Psal.* 44.18-19, *Thaum.* 10.10-14; see Daniélou (1953b) 1873-79, Andia (1996) 334-340, Meredith (1997) 52-53. For God's incomprehensibility in Gregory, see Daniélou (1954a) 190-199, Völker (1955) 36-38, Van Heck (1964) 103-110, Brightman (1973), Whittaker (1992), Dünzl (1993) 291-328, Carabine (1995) 236-258, Böhm (1996) 248-255. Cf. in Gregory *Beat.* 104.15-23, 140.15-141.1, *Cant.* 37.3, 86.13-14, 138.18-19, 357.4-6, *CE* 1.368-369, 2.91, 95, 138-140, 3.1.103-110, *Eccl.* 411-415, *Mort.* 45.12-15, *Prof.* 134.6-12, *Thaum.* 10.5-7. See Part II. II § 3.

[220]   Cf. II.110 the question about God's essence is beyond human understanding.

God.' (John 1:18), that is, knowledge of the divine essence is unreachable, not only for men, but for every rational nature (II.163). Gregory refers also to Ps. 17:12 'God made darkness his secret place' (II.164). The second commandment (Ex. 20:4) is explained within the same framework of God's unknowability. It forbids likening the divine to any of the things known by men, since every concept which comes from some comprehensible image by an approximate understanding and by guessing at the divine nature constitutes an idol of God and does not proclaim God himself (II.165, cf. I.47, II.234). The sound of the trumpet mentioned in Ex. 19:21 indicates the knowledge of God's power which comes from contemplation of the universe. The order of the marvels in heaven proclaims the wisdom manifest in the things that exist and declares the great glory of God in the visible things, according to the text 'The heavens declare the glory of God' (II.168-169; Ps. 18:2, cf. *CE* 2.219-225). God's activities in the world are indicative of his existence, but his essence is unattainable by the human mind (cf. II.110).[221]

18.b.2. *Philo's Interpretation of the Darkness*

Philo deals with God's incomprehensibility with a reference to Ex. 20:21 in two texts from the Allegorical Commentary, viz. *Post.* 14 and *Mut.* 7.[222] In *Post.* 12-20 he places the self-loving Cain, who left God's face (Gen. 4:16), opposite to the God-loving Moses, who issues the command 'to love God and to listen to and to cleave to him' (Deut. 30:20). Moses himself yearns so unceasingly to see God and to be seen by him that he implores him to make clearly known his own nature (Ex. 33:13), which is hard to guess. Although Moses knows that he longs for an object hard to catch and unattainable, he will struggle on for the attainment (13). He enters into the darkness where God is (Ex. 20:21), that is, into the impenetrable and unformed thoughts on the Existent, because the cause is neither in darkness nor in any place at all, but beyond place and time (14).[223] When the God-loving soul searches for the essence of the Existent, it makes a

---

[221] For this notion, cf. *Beat.* 140.13-141.27, *Cant.* 37.12-17, 89.16-18, 181.16-19, 334.15-336.1, *CE* 2.67, 71, 97-106, 3.5.59, 3.6.8, *Eccl.* 284.21-285.4, 415.17-29, *Eust.* 14.16-18, *Opif. hom.* 156B, *Ref. Eun.* 17. See Völker (1955) 175-179, Horn (1981) 969-971.

[222] For God's incomprehensibility in Philo, see Wolfson (1947) 2.94-164, Lilla (1982-87) 229-279, Montes-Peral (1987) 148-161, Carabine (1995) 191-222.

[223] *Post.* 14 ἤδη γοῦν καὶ εἰς τὸν γνόφον ὅπου ἦν ὁ θεὸς εἰσελεύσεται. τουτέστιν εἰς τὰς ἀδύτους καὶ ἀειδεῖς περὶ τοῦ ὄντος ἐννοίας. Colson translates as follows: '... that is into conceptions regarding the Existent Being that belong to the unapproachable region where there are no material forms' (PLCL 2.335). For God as αἴτιον, cf. *Opif.* 8, *Cher.* 87, *Post.* 38 etc.

search of that which is beyond form and beyond sight. From this quest a
very great good originates, namely the realization that God is invisible and
incomprehensible (15). By his request to God to manifest himself (Ex.
33:13) Moses shows very clearly that no created being is able to know God
in his essence (16). Even the mind falls short for comprehension of the
cause (19). It is said that God is nearby and far away: he is in contact with
the human kind by his creative and chastening powers,[224] but he has
driven the creatures far away from his essential nature so that man cannot
touch it with the pure and immaterial contact of understanding (20).

In *Mut.* 3-17 Philo comments on Gen. 17:1 'The Lord was seen by
Abraham.'[225] In his exegesis of the vision of the Lord, Philo explains that
this divine vision is not received by the eyes of the body, but by the eye of
the soul (3). The vision takes place without the sensible light, because what
is intelligible is only grasped by the intellect (6). One should not, however,
think that the Existent, which truly exists, is grasped by men. We have no
instrument by which we are able to perceive it, neither sense — for it is not
sensible —nor mind. Next, Philo brings in Moses as an example of one
who desires to see God. Moses, the seer and viewer of the unformed nature
— for Scripture records that he enters into the darkness (Ex. 20:21), that
is, the invisible and incorporeal essence — yearns to see the only good
clearly (7). Although Moses yearns to see God, he does not succeed.
Therefore he beseeches God: 'Manifest yourself to me, in order that I may
see you with knowledge.' (8; Ex. 33:13). God, however, answers: 'You will
see what is behind me, but you will not see my face.' (Ex. 33:13). This
means that all that is behind the Existent, both material and immaterial
things, are comprehensible, but God alone by his nature cannot be seen
(9).[226] And why should we wonder that the Existent is not comprehensible
by men, if even the mind in each of us is unknown to us? Who knows, Philo
asks rhetorically, the nature of the soul? (10). A consequence of the
assumption that the Existent is incomprehensible is that no proper name
can be assigned to it. To confirm this statement Philo refers to God's self-
revelation in Ex. 3:14 'I am he-who-is', that is 'my nature is to be, not to be
spoken.'[227](11). The existent is so unnameable that even his powers who
serve him do not tell us his proper name (14). So, the highest being is
ineffable, and if he is ineffable, he is also inconceivable and incomprehensible. Philo now returns to his starting-point: when it is written 'The

---

[224] For Philo's doctrine of the divine powers, see § 18.c.2.
[225] See Runia (1988a) 72-83, Williamson (1989) 85-102.
[226] Cf. *Post.* 169, *Fug.* 165.
[227] Cf. *Abr.* 50-51, *Mos.* 1.74-75, see § 6.a.2; see Runia (1995c) 207-216.

Lord was seen of Abraham', we should not think that the cause of all
appears. It is his royal power that appears, for 'Lord' is the title of God's
rule and kingship (15).

In the Allegorical Commentary Philo interprets the darkness as referring to God's incomprehensibility, but in *The Life of Moses* he offers a
different exegesis. Making a digression on Moses as leader of the Jewish
people, he refers to Ex. 20:21. Moses entered the unformed, unseen,
incorporeal and archetypal essence of existing things (*Mos.* 1.158). This
interpretation emphasizes the supra-natural status of Moses, who enters
into the noetic realm of the world of ideas. That Philo offers a less
theological exegesis in *Mos.* is due to the introductory character of the
treatise.[228]

18.b.3. *The Christian Tradition*

Philo's exegesis of the darkness as referring to God's incomprehensibility
is taken over by Clement of Alexandria, who refers to Ex. 20:21 in *Strom.*
2.6.1 and 5.78.3.[229] The context of the first text (*Strom.* 2.5.1-2.6.4) is
formed by a discourse on God's remoteness and the unknowability of his
nature. Herein Clement uses borrowings from Philo's *Post.* 5-18 and,
having cited Ex. 20:21, he gives the Philonic interpretation of the darkness
as the impenetrable and invisible thoughts on the Existent (cf. *Post.* 14).[230]
The other citation of the verse occurs at *Strom.* 5.78.3. Clement begins
section 78 with a quotation of Plato's statement in *Timaeus* 28C that 'it is a
hard task to find the maker and father of the universe, and having found
him, it is impossible to express him to all' (78.1).[231] For this reason Moses
forbids the people to ascend the mountain with him (78.2; Ex. 19:12).
That Moses enters into the darkness where God is indicates that God is
invisible and ineffable. The darkness, which is really the unbelief and
ignorance of the masses, blocks off the gleam of the truth, and therefore
their ascent of the mountain is forbidden. This last interpretation of the
darkness is not found in Philo,[232] but it is obvious that Clement explains
the darkness in the same way as Philo does, and the Philonic character of
his exegesis is reinforced by the fact that he quotes Philo *verbatim*.

---

[228]   See Part I. III.

[229]   See Gobry (1991) 81.

[230]   See the analysis by Van den Hoek (1988) 148-152; see also Mortley (1973) 61-67, and
Carabine (1995) 229-232.

[231]   For the role of this saying in the development of negative theology, see Nock (1962),
Runia (1986) 111-113.

[232]   Van den Hoek (1988) 175.

The next Christian author who comments on Ex. 20:21 is Origen. He does not comment on this verse in his *Homelies on Exodus*, but he does refer to it at other places.[233] At *Contra Celsum* 6.17 he explains Psalm 17:12 — 'God made darkness his secret place' — as denoting that thoughts on God are unclear and unknown. God hides himself as in darkness for those who cannot bear the splendours of knowledge of him, and are not able to see him. In order to make clear that knowledge of God has been rarely found in men it is written that Moses entered into the darkness where God was. And later on it is said: 'Moses alone will come near God, and the other people will not come near' (Ex. 24:2). Again the prophet shows that the depth of the doctrines of God is incomprehensible for those who do not have the spirit. Our saviour and Lord, the Word of God, shows the greatness of the knowledge of the Father. He is known worthily first by the Son alone, and second by those whose leading mind is illuminated by the Word and God himself. The Lord says: 'Nobody knows the Son, save the Father, and nobody knows the Father, save the Son and he to whom the Son wishes to reveal him' (Matt. 11:27, Luc. 10:22). By sharing in him who takes away from the Father what is called 'darkness', which 'He made his secret place' (Ps. 17:12), and 'the abyss', which is called his 'covering' (Ps. 103:6), and in this way unveiling the Father, everyone who is capable of knowing him knows the Father.

The notion of 'revealing' is also discussed in a fragment from a homily on Luke (*Luc. fr.* 162), where Origen argues that Christ reveals by removing the covering which lies on the heart and by taking away the darkness which God made his secret place (Ps. 17:12). So, one will be able, like Moses, to enter into the darkness, where God was (Ex. 20:21). Heretics view this verse as indicating that the Father of Jesus Christ was unknown to the old saints,[234] and hence it should be said to them that the words 'to whom the Son wishes to reveal' (Luc. 10:22, Mat. 11:27, cf. *CC* 6.17) refer not only to the future, but also to the past. The Father was known in the past as well.

In his discussion of the darkness mentioned in Joh. 1:5, Origen remarks that in Exodus darkness, obscurity, and tempest are said to be around God, and he cites Ps. 17:12. Next he connects the darkness with the knowledge of God, which is beyond the power of human nature (*Io. com.* 2.172). Origen's reference to Exodus in this text is rather vague.[235] All three terms

---

[233] See Meredith (1997) 49-52.
[234] That is, the Gnostics, cf. Irenaeus *Adv. Haer.* 1.19.1, 20.3.
[235] C. Blanc, the editor of the SC edition, refers to Ex. 19:9 (... ἐν στύλῳ νεφέλης), 19:16 (καὶ νεφέλη γνοφώδης) and 20:21.

— σκότος, γνόφος, θύελλα— occur in the description of the ninth plague (Ex. 10:22); σκότος and γνόφος are encountered in Ex. 14:20 with a reference to God. All three words are found in Deut. 4:11 in a description of legislation. It may, however, well be thought that Origen has primarily in mind Ex. 20:21[236] because in what follows he explains the darkness as the incomprehensibility of thoughts and knowledge of God for human beings. Using the word θύελλα, Origen is probably thinking of Ex. 19:16, where thunder and lightning are said to appear on the mountain.[237]

These texts show that in Origen's interpretation the darkness from Ex. 20:21 indicates that thoughts of God are hard to know. God is, however, not totally unknown because the Lord has made known his Father to men. The help of both God the Father and the Son is requisite for getting knowledge of God. Furthermore, the disposition of men matters; only with the right spirit is man able to know God. It is noticeable that Origen does not distinguish between God's existence and his essence, as Philo and Gregory of Nyssa do. The important notion in Origen that Christ, coming on earth, removes the darkness from God the Father is an aspect of the incarnation that seems to be absent in Gregory.

The notion of God's incomprehensibility and unknowability is also found in Gregory of Nazianzus, and forms a main theme in his 28th oration. It was written about 380, being earlier than the treatise on Moses' life by his namesake, and is entitled *On Theology*. In the beginning of this speech (2-3) the ascent of the mountain is explained as gaining knowledge of God. Nazianzen tells his own experience: he ascended the mountain and penetrated into the cloud, in which he was far away from matter and material things, and he turned to himself (3). A number of parallels with Gregory of Nyssa's *VM* are discernible here:[238] the ascent of the mountain in order to know God; the leaving behind of visible and material things as a requisite for the comprehension of God; the turning of the soul inwards. Both emphasize the necessary purification in body and soul in order to gain knowledge of God (*VM* II.154, *Or.* 28.1). Gregory of Nazianzus continues his speech with an anonymous reference to a theologian of the Greeks: it is hard to comprehend God, and impossible to express him.[239] In Nazianzen's view it is indeed impossible to express God, but it is

---

[236] In *Biblia Patristica* 3 no reference to this text is given for Ex. 20:21.
[237] The notion of God's incomprehensibility occurs also in *CC* 7.42, *Ps. fr.* PG 17.112C, *Princ.* 1.1.5. See Dillon (1988).
[238] The resemblance is noticed by Gallay (1978) 106-107 n. 2. Norris ((1991) 109) thinks that Gregory of Nyssa is indebted to Gregory of Nazianzus.
[239] Usually reference is made to Plato *Tim.* 28C (cf. Gallay (1978) 108 n. 1), but Pépin argues that Hermes Trismegistus is meant, to whose words there is more resemblance

more impossible to comprehend him. It is entirely impossible and impracticable to grasp such a great subject (4). In what follows he makes a distinction between God's existence, which man can infer from the visible things in the universe, and God's essence, which is impossible to grasp (5).[240] In chapter 7 he asks whether the divine is corporeal, and how it is infinite, limitless, formless, impalpable or invisible,[241] and his conclusion is that the divine is incorporeal (8-10). Men's corporeality is a hindrance to comprehension of the incorporeal God. The corporeal 'darkness' stands between men and God, as once the cloud stood between the Egyptians and the Hebrews (Ex. 14:19-20). Perhaps the same is meant by 'He made darkness his secret place' (Ps. 17:12), because the darkness indicates the thickness of the human body (12). Neither Nazianzen nor Basil interpret the darkness as the unknowability of God.

On the basis of this outline of the exegetical tradition the following concluding remarks can be made. Gregory's interpretation of the darkness as God's incomprehensibility is Philonic. Both Philo and Gregory interpret the darkness as God's incomprehensibility, calling God ἀκατάληπτος and ἀόρατος.[242] The Philonic interpretation does, however, recur in Clement, who quotes Philo's passages literally. Although Origen connects Ex. 20:21 with Ps. 17:12, as Gregory does, his exegesis differs from Gregory's.[243] He associates the darkness with the difficulty for human beings to know God, explaining that Christ has revealed God's darkness so that God could be known.[244] Even though the notion of God's incomprehensibility is important in Gregory of Nazianzus, he does not interpret the darkness as the unknowability of God's essence. Because the Philonic exegesis occurs also in Clement, Gregory's exegesis falls under category B2.

18.c. *The Tabernacle* (I.49-50, II.170-188)

After a description of the model of the tabernacle and its furnishings which Moses sees on Mount Sinai (I.49-50, II.170-173), Gregory offers a

---

(Pépin (1982), Hermes *ap.* Stobaeus 2.1.26 (Scott fr. 1)).

[240] Cf. 11 the divine is not comprehensible for the human intellect; 13 every rational creature longs for God, but it is impossible to comprehend him; 17 no one has found how God is in nature or essence.

[241] Cf. *Or.* 6.22 the Trinity is invisible, impalpable, incomprehensible.

[242] Philo *Post.* 15, 16, 169, *Mut.* 7, 10, 15; Gregory *VM* I.46, II.163, 167.

[243] Origen *CC* 6.17, *Luc. fr.* 162, *Io. com.* 2.172; Gregory *VM* II.164.

[244] Origen *Luc. fr.* 162.

Christological interpretation: the tabernacle is Christ, uncreated in pre-existence, but created in having received this material composition. Christ's coming on earth is thus the construction of the true tabernacle. In confirmation of this explanation Gregory refers to Joh. 1:14: 'The word was made flesh and dwelt among us.' (ἐσκήνωσε; σκηνή is the word used for the tabernacle, II.175).[245] The apostle Paul also brings Gregory to this exegesis, for the veil of the lower tabernacle is called the flesh of Christ (Hebr. 10:20), 'because, I think, it is composed of various colours, that is of the four elements.' Paul himself saw the tabernacle when he was in the impenetrable, supercelestial region (II.178; 2 Cor. 12:2-4).[246] The tabernacle, Gregory continues, is thus Christ, in whom all things are created, visible and invisible, whether thrones, authorities, principalities, dominions (Col. 1:16), or powers.[247] The furnishings of the tabernacle — the pillars (Ex. 26:15-25), the staves (Ex. 25:15), the rings (Ex. 25:12), the Cherubim who hide the ark with their wings (Ex. 25:18-20), and all the remaining things — are the superterrestrial powers, contemplated in the tabernacle, and which support the universe according to the divine will (II. 179). The Cherubim confirm this *theoria* on the tabernacle because, Gregory explains, we have learned that that is the name of those powers which are seen to stand near the divine nature and which were perceived by Isaiah and Ezekiel.[248] That the ark is covered by the wings of the Cherubim indicates the incomprehensibility of the contemplation of unutterable things (II.180). In what follows the Cappadocian exegete interprets the lower tabernacle as the Church (II.181-188).[249] Two issues from this exegesis can be associated with Philo, viz. the cosmological interpretation

---

[245] Same interpretation in *Cant.* 380.15-381.16, *Diem nat.* 236.6-12; in Basil *Ps. 45 hom.* 4.

[246] The Platonic word ὑπερουράνιος does not occur in 2 Cor. 12:2-4, where Paul mentions the third heaven, which, according to Gregory, is the intelligible creation (*Hex.* 81C, 121C), inhabited by the divine powers and angels (*Hex.* 81B, cf. *Inscr. psal.* 66.23-24, *Virg.* 255.6, *VM* II.180). In Gen. 1 these powers are referred to as the waters above the firmament, which is the border between the intelligible and sensible creation (cf. *Hex.* 89A), see Daniélou (1954a) 151-161.

[247] Cf. *Cant.* 182.4-10, 445.10-446.8; Daniélou (1954a) 162-172. Comparable interpretation in Gregory of Nazianzus (*Or.* 28.31), who remarks that Moses' tabernacle is a figure (cf. Hebr. 9:24) of the whole universe, that is, the construction of visible and invisible things. The holy denotes the intelligible and supercelestial nature (cf. Philo *Mos.* 2.28), inhabited by angels and archangels, thrones, dominions, principalities, authorities (Col. 1:16), lights, ascents, intellectual powers (Cf. *Or.* 38.9, Moreschini-Gally (1990) 122 n. 2). For Gregory of Nyssa's text of Col. 1:16, see Brooks (1991) 225-226.

[248] Isaiah mentions Seraphim, not Cherubim, but they are equated in the patristic tradition, cf. Clement *Strom.* 5.35.6. See also *CE* 1.306-313.

[249] Tabernacle as Church also in Origen *Ex. hom.* 9.3.

of the four colours as the four elements (18.c.1), and the explanation of the Cherubim as God's powers (18.c.2).[250]

18.c.1. *The Cosmological Interpretation of the Four Colours*

Philo, discussing Moses' priesthood in the second book of *The Life of Moses*, gives an extensive symbolic interpretation of the tabernacle in cosmo-logical terms (*Mos.* 2.77-108), in which he conceives of the four colours of the veil and of the other curtains (Ex. 26:1, 31, 36) as the four elements: linen indicates earth, purple water; blue is like air, which is naturally black, and scarlet is like fire since both are red. For it was necessary that the temple made with hands for the father and ruler of all was made with the same elements with which he made the universe (*Mos.* 2.88).[251] This cosmological interpretation of the four colours recurs in Josephus (*AJ* 3.183, *BJ* 5.212-213) and Clement of Alexandria (*Strom.* 5.32.3), the latter being clearly dependent on Philo.[252] Origen, too, interprets the veil of the interior tabernacle as the flesh of Christ on the authority of Paul (*Ex. hom.* 9.1) and also offers the exegesis of the four colours as the elements, referring to 'some before us' (*Ex. hom.* 13.3). Has Origen Philo in mind here? He does refer to Philo in anonymous terms at several places in his works,[253] but the reference is perhaps more inclusive, referring to Josephus and Clement as well.

It appears thus that the interpretation of the four colours as the elements, originally perhaps Jewish, is part of the Alexandrian tradition, since it is mentioned by Clement and Origen. Gregory derives it from the Alexandrians and places it in the service of his own exegesis of the tabernacle as Christ, being led by Paul's explanation of the veil as the flesh of Christ. Gregory's interpretation comes in category B2.

18.c.2. *The Cherubim as God's Powers*

Later on in the same section from *Mos.* Philo deals with the mercy seat and the Cherubim, which sit on it. Associating the word ἱλαστήριον (mercy seat) with mercy (ἵλεως) he explains the mercy seat as God's power of mercy (cf. *Fug.* 100).[254] The name of the Cherubim is rendered as

---

[250] Daniélou (1968) 232 n. 3, Musurillo (1964) 89, Malherbe-Ferguson (1978) 180 n. 227, 230.

[251] Cf. *Congr.* 117, *QE* 2.92.

[252] Van den Hoek (1988) 120-122.

[253] Runia (1993) 161-162.

[254] For God's power of mercy, cf. *Migr.* 124, *Fug.* 95, *Mut.* 129, *Somn.* 2.265, 292, *Mos.*

'recognition' and 'much knowledge'.[255] Next he points to an explanation of others who say that the Cherubim are symbols of the two hemispheres[256] but he himself favours another interpretation, in which they represent the two most august and highest powers of the Existent, the creative and the kingly. The Jewish exegete links these two powers with the two names of God employed in the LXX, namely God (θεός) and Lord (κύριος). The creative power is called God because through it the maker made the universe,[257] and the kingly is called Lord, by which he rules the creation (*Mos.* 2.96-100).[258] In a fragment from *De Deo*, preserved in an Armenian translation only, Philo combines the two Cherubim, explained as the two powers of God, with the Seraphim from Isaiah's vision, depicting them as bodyguards of God,[259] who is named He-who-is (§ 4-6).[260]

A discussion of the furnishings in the holy of holies is also given by Origen in *Rom. com.* 3.8 with reference to Rom. 3:25, where Christ is described as propitiation.[261] The mercy seat is the holy and pure soul of Jesus Christ, while the two Cherubim represent God's Word, that is his Son, and the Holy Spirit.[262] Origen gives the Philonic rendering of Cherubim as 'much science' (cf. *Num. hom.* 5.3, 10.3, *Cant. com.* 2.18.15),[263] and cites Hab. 3:2, which speaks of the two living creatures. The ark of the covenant, on which Jesus' soul sits, is the flesh of Christ, in which this holy soul lives. The celestial powers (*virtutes caelestes*) can also be viewed as God's ark of the covenant; they are capable of receiving God's Word and the Holy Spirit.[264] Origen interprets the Seraphim (Is. 6:2) in the same way as the Cherubim: they represent the Only Begotten Son of God and the

---

1.185, *Spec.* 1.229, 265, 294, 2.15.

[255] Cf. *QE* 2.62; see Grabbe (1988) 219, Strickert (1996).

[256] Cf. *Cher.* 25.

[257] Philo connects θεός with τίθημι, which he interprets as 'to create', cf. *Abr.* 122.

[258] For God's powers, cf. *Leg.* 1.96, 3.73, *Cher.* 27, *Sacr.* 59-60, *Deus* 77-81, *Plant.* 86, *Fug.* 100, *Mut.* 28-29, *Abr.* 119-146, *QG* 1.57, *QE* 2.62-67; see Wolfson (1947) 1.217-226, Pfeifer (1967) 53-57, Winston (1985) 19-21.

[259] For the powers as bodyguards, cf. *Sacr.* 59, *Deus* 109, *Abr.* 122, *Spec.* 1.47, *Legat.* 6, *QE* 2.67.

[260] See Siegert (1988) 26-27, 34-35, 71-79.

[261] Paul uses the word ἱλαστήριον, which denotes the mercy seat of the ark (Ex. 25:7).

[262] At *Num. hom.* 10.3 the mercy seat and the Cherubim symbolize knowledge of the Holy Trinity.

[263] Clement gives the Philonic translation as well (*Strom.* 5.35.6., cf. Van den Hoek (1988) 130, 132-133).

[264] The same exegesis is found in the Greek excerpts of *Rom. com.* 3.5-5.7 on the papyrus of Toura, where the ark of covenant is described in terms of powers. Hab. 3:2 is also cited, cf. Scherer (1957) 158.15-160.2

Holy Spirit (*Es. hom.* 1.3). He associates them with the two living creatures from Hab. 3:2 (*Princ.* 1.3.4, 4.3.14).[265]

When we compare Origen's interpretation with Gregory, it is obvious that Gregory's exegesis of the Cherubim as powers is not derived from Origen. His interpretation does have precedents in other Christian writers. Eusebius, for instance, sees in the Seraphim incorporeal and super-terrestrial powers, standing around God like bodyguards round the great king (*Es. com.* 1.41 (p. 38.10-15), *DE* 7.1.8-11, *Intro.* 1052D).[266] The same exegesis of the Seraphim occurs in the *Commentary on Isaiah* ascribed to Basil (428B-C), in which there is a reference to the interpretation of them as the two hemispheres, with which, as we have seen above, Philo is familiar. The exegesis of the Cherubim and Seraphim as God's super-terrestrial powers, being part of the Christian tradition, may have its origin in the Jewish interpretation of the Cherubim and Seraphim; Gregory's exegesis comes in category B2.

18.d. *The High-priestly Vestments* (I.51-55, II.189-201)

Having described and explained the tabernacle and its furnishings Gregory goes on to treat the high priest's vestments, which, in his view, is not a vestment perceptible by the senses but an ornament of the soul woven by virtuous pursuits (II.190). One point of his exegesis is of particular relevance to our subject. Gregory writes at § 191:

> The dye of the robe[267] is dark-blue. Some of those who before us have contemplated the passage say that the dye signifies the air. I, for my part, cannot accurately affirm whether such a colour as this has anything in common with the colour of the air. Nevertheless, I do not reject it. The perception does lead to the contemplation of virtue...(Translation Malherbe-Ferguson, slightly altered).[268]

---

[265] Cf. *Es. hom.* 1.2, 4.1. According to Daniélou Origen's source is a Jewish-Christian, who made use of Jewish speculations about the Seraphim, with which Philo was acquainted (Daniélou (1957) 28). The crying 'holy, holy, holy' of the Seraphim refers to the divine Trinity, cf. Gregory of Nyssa *CE* 1.310, Gregory of Nazianzus *Or.* 38.8. Irenaeus conceives of the Cherubim and Seraphim as the powers of God's word and wisdom (*Dem.* 10; see Rousseau (1995) 247-248).

[266] Same image in Philo *Sacr.* 59, *Deus* 109, *Abr.* 122, *Spec.* 1.47, *Legat.* 6, *QE* 2.67.

[267] Ex. 28:4, 31. See for the Hebrew word and diverse translations, Houtman (1986-96) 3.493-495.

[268] *VM* II. 191 ὑάκινθός ἐστιν ἡ τοῦ ποδήρους βαφή. φασὶ δὲ τινες τῶν πρὸ ἡμῶν τεθεωρηκότων τὸν λόγον τὸν ἀέρα σημαίνεσθαι τῇ βαφῇ. ἐγὼ δὲ εἰ μέν τι τὸ τοιοῦτον τοῦ χρώματος ἄνθος πρὸς τὸ ἀέριον χρῶμα συγγενῶς ἔχει, ἀκριβῶς οὐκ ἔχω διϊσχυρίζεσθαι. τὸν μέντοι λόγον οὐκ ἀποβάλλω. συντείνει γὰρ πρὸς τὴν κατ' ἀρετὴν θεωρίαν τὸ νόημα.

Next he explains the robe as the airy tunic purified of heavy and earthly parts, which is contrasted with the heavy and fleshy garment of life. Gregory writes that one should, through purity of life, make all the pursuits of life as thin as the thread of a spider's web. We should be near to what is ascending, light and airy so that we, having become light, shall be carried on high together with the Lord when we hear the last trumpet (1 Thess. 4:16-17). He who, according to the Psalmist, has melted away his soul like a spider's web (Ps. 38:12) has clothed himself with the airy tunic, which extends from the head to the feet because the Law does not want virtue to be cut short (II.191).[269] In what follows Gregory interprets the various parts of the vestment in the context of the virtuous life. The golden bells and the pomegranates (Ex. 28:34), for instance, represent the brilliance of good works, because there are two pursuits through which virtue is acquired, namely faith toward the divine and conscience toward life (II.192, cf. 1 Tim. 1:19). The various colours of the ephod (Ex. 28:7-8) symbolize many varied virtues (II.195-196).

In the passage cited above Gregory refers to some of his predecessors, using the plural form (τινες), which can also refer to a single person,[270] and the exegete to whom Gregory here refers is in all likelihood Philo, who interprets the priestly vestments in a cosmological way in *Mos.* 2.109-135.[271] He states that the whole vesture and its parts are a representation of the world and its particular parts (2.117). The tunic is totally dark-blue, an image of the air, for the air is naturally black and so to speak a robe, stretching down from the region below the moon to the ends of the earth, spreading out everywhere. And therefore the tunic spreads out from the breast to the feet round the whole body (2.118).[272] The flowers at the end of the robe are a symbol of the earth;[273] the pomegranates represent water, while the bells symbolize the harmonious alliance of earth and water (2.119). Finally, the ephod is a symbol of heaven (2.122).

As already noted above Gregory refers to Philo, about whose interpretation of the colour of the robe he expresses doubt without rejecting it totally. Taking over the connection between the dark-blue of the robe and

---

[269] For the airy tunic, cf. *An. et res.* 108A and *Melet.* 455.1-2.

[270] Runia (1993) 161 n. 23.

[271] Malherbe-Ferguson (1978) 183 n. 258, Runia (1993) 259-260.

[272] *Mos.* 2.118 οὗτος ὁ χιτὼν σύμπας ἐστὶν ὑακίνθινος, ἀέρος ἐκμαγεῖον· φύσει γὰρ ὁ ἀὴρ μέλας καὶ τρόπον τινὰ ποδήρης, ἄνωθεν ἀπὸ τῶν μετὰ σελήνην ἄχρι τῶν γῆς ταθεὶς περάτων, πάντη κεχυμένος· ὅθεν καὶ ὁ χιτὼν ἀπὸ στέρνων ἄχρι ποδῶν τὸ σῶμα κέχυται. Cf. 2.133, *Spec.* 1.85, 94, *QE* 2.117, 120.

[273] ἄνθινα (Ex. 28:34) is an addition in the LXX that does not occur in the Hebrew text, cf. Houtman (1996) 497.

the air, he uses it in the service of his own exegesis of the priestly garments in the context of the virtuous life: the blue points to the airy tunic made by the purity of the virtuous life. In doing so, Gregory uses the same procedure as in the interpretation of the colours of the tabernacle: he adapts an existing exegesis to his own aim.

A cosmological interpretation of the priestly vestment appears also in other Jewish and Christian authors but their interpretations differ from Philo in details. In the Wisdom of Solomon the robe represents the whole universe (Sap. 18:24). Josephus interprets the blue of the priest's tunic as the arch of heaven; the pomegranates represent lightning, and the sound of the bells indicates thunder. The priest's upper garment is a symbol of the nature of the universe, made of four elements (*AJ* 3.184). Clement of Alexandria sees in the robe a symbol of the world of senses (*Strom.* 5.37.1).[274] In Origen's exegesis the diverse colours of the tabernacle and of the priest's vestments indicate various virtues with which the Church should be decorated. Linen represents virginity; scarlet the glory of confession; purple the splendour of charity; dark-blue the hope of the kingdom of heaven (*Ex. hom.* 9.3). Discussing the priestly vestments in *Ex. hom.* 9.4, Origen explains that the robe extending to the feet indicates that one should be vested with chastity.[275] In none of these interpretations does Philo's exegesis of the blue robe as the air occur, which strengthens the conclusion that Gregory in the passage at hand refers specifically to Philo (category B3).

19. *The Golden Calf and the Killing by the Levites* (I.56-60, II.202-218)

The next episode treated by Gregory is the story of the golden calf made by the Israelites during Moses' stay on Sinai, where he receives the tables of stone that contain the law. After his return to the apostate people, Moses breaks the tables; then he destroys the calf, pulverizes it, and having mixed it with water he gives it the Israelites to drink (II.202; Ex. 32:19-20). Gregory, remarking that these events also happen today, explains that the error of idolatry disappears, being swallowed by pious mouths (II.203).[276] Next Moses arms the Levites against the idolaters, and orders them to kill

---

[274] See Van den Hoek (1988) 134-137.

[275] Irenaeus sees in the priest's garment reaching to the feet a reference to Christ, who is clothed with a garment down to the feet (Apoc. 1:13; *Adv. Haer.* 4.20.11).

[276] In II.316 Gregory interprets the destruction of the calf as the destroying of the power of avarice.

brother, friend, and neighbour (Ex. 32:27).[277] The Cappadocian exegete conceives of this killing by the Levites as the purification of evil habits by death; brother, friend, and neighbour are the innermost thoughts whose life causes death, and whose death causes life (II.208).

Gregory comments also on the earrings from which the calf was made: Moses had given the Israelites an ornament for the ear, which is the Law, but Aaron destroyed it by disobedience and made an idol out of it (II.212).[278] Being led by Paul who calls the tables 'hearts' (2 Cor. 3:3), Gregory sees in the tables a symbol of human nature, which was unbroken and immortal at the beginning. The tables, however, have been broken but the true lawgiver, having become the stonecutter of his own flesh, restores the broken table of human nature to its original status (II.215-217).[279]

Regarding the interpretation of the killing by the Levites, Daniélou notices that Philo offers the same exegesis in *Ebr.* 67-71,[280] where he explains the story allegorically. The Levites are an example of those who are disobedient to their mother, which stands for custom, but obedient to their father, which means right reason. They do not murder human beings but cut away from their own minds all that is near and dear to the flesh. The 'brother' is not a man but brother of the soul, that is the body. The 'neighbour' represents the troop and company of the senses, which try to overwhelm the soul so that it will not lift up its head heavenwards. The 'nearest' is the uttered word, which implants false opinions for the destruction of truth.[281]

A closer examination of Philo's passage shows that Daniélou is not entirely correct in his reference to Philo because the Jewish exegete does not interpret brother, friend, and neighbour as the innermost thoughts, as Gregory does. Philo gives each of the three persons a separate meaning and applies to them a triad, which he uses elsewhere in his treatises as well.

---

[277] Gregory uses ἀδελφός, φίλος, and πλησίος in stead of ἀδελφός, πλησίος, and ἔγγιστα from Ex. 32:27.

[278] Simonetti (1984) 319 remarks that Philo interprets the earrings in a negative way at *Post.* 166.

[279] For Gregory's thought on the original nature of man, see § 6.b.

[280] Daniélou (1968) 249 n. 1; see also Musurillo (1964) 105, Malherbe-Ferguson (1978) 183 n. 279, Simonetti (1984) 319.

[281] Same interpretation in *Fug.* 90-92. In *Migr.* 1-2 Philo mentions the same triad of body, senses, and uttered word as symbolic interpretation of land, kinsfolk, and father's house from Gen. 12:1 (cf. *Her.* 69). In *Mos.* 2.161-173 he narrates the story of the golden calf and the action of the Levites, omitting Aaron's leading role in making the idol. In *Post.* 159 he interprets the burning of the calf as the burning up of the bodily pleasures by the lover of virtue. Simonetti (1984) 318 notes that this interpretation is in harmony with the discourse Gregory develops in *VM.* Clement of Alexandria, Origen, Basil, and Gregory of Nazianzus do not interpret the story allegorically.

Both exegetes do give an allegorical interpretation of the killing by the
Levites but the differences are too great to settle Gregory's dependence on
Philo.

19.a. *Moses sees God* (II.219-255)

The passage from Exodus 33 which records that Moses asks God to manifest himself (Ex. 33:12-32) is of capital interest for Gregory's mysticism,
and by explaining this passage he elaborates the central theme of the
treatise: the desire of the soul for God is unending. It is striking that
Gregory does not retell the passage in the *historia*, perhaps because of the
absence of a literal meaning (cf. II.122). The scriptural account relates that
in answer to Moses' question God says that Moses cannot see his face
because man cannot see God's face and live (Ex. 33:20). God goes on to
say that there is a place with a rock, and, when Moses is in the hole of the
rock, God will cover him with his hand until God passes. Next God will
take away his hand, and Moses will see God's back but his face will not be
seen (II.220; Ex. 33:21-23).

Gregory argues that this passage cannot be interpreted in a literal sense,
because speaking about God's back implies that he is corporeal and
corruptible; and this is out of the question, for God is incorporeal and
incorruptible (II.222). Hence, the passage should be contemplated in its
spiritual sense. It signifies the ascent of the soul that is released from its
earthly attachment to the nature of the Good (II.224).[282] During this
ascent the soul becomes higher than itself, 'stretching itself to things that
lie before it' (II.225; Phil. 3:13).[283] Moses is an example of the ascending
soul. He never stops in his ascent but always finds a step higher than the
one he had attained (II.227). In § 228-230 Gregory summarizes the steps in
Moses' life from his childhood until he beseeches God to appear to him
(Ex. 33:20). The Cappadocian father compares Moses' longing to the
desire of a soul that loves the beautiful and longs to be filled with the
stamp of the archetype (II.231), requesting to enjoy the beauty not in
mirrors or reflections, but face to face (II.232).[284]

---

[282] Same exegesis in *Cant.* 355.16-356.16.

[283] Malherbe-Ferguson (1978) 186 n. 321 refers to Philo *QE* 2.51 'For the beginning and
end of happiness is to be able to see God. But this cannot be happen to him who has not
made his soul . . a sanctuary and altogether a shrine of God.' This reference seems to be
unconvincing, because Philo's main point differs from Gregory's interpretation.

[284] *VM* II.232 αἴτησις τὸ μὴ διὰ κατόπτρων τινῶν καὶ ἐμφάσεων, ἀλλὰ κατὰ πρόσωπον....
Winston (1994) 110 remarks that Philo, describing Moses' desire to see God, uses the
same image of a mirror in *Leg.* 3.101: μηδὲ κατοπτρισαίμην ἐν ἄλλῳ τινὶ τὴν σὴν ἰδέαν ....

Gregory continues by saying that the passage teaches us that the divine is infinite and enclosed by no boundary.[285] Gregory's argumentation can be summarized as follows:

1. What has a limit ends somewhere, and is surrounded by something that is different in nature.
2. What surrounds is much larger than what is surrounded.
   Gregory illustrates this by some examples: fish are surrounded by water, and birds by air; the water is the limit for that which swims, and the air for that which flies.
3. The divine nature is beautiful/good, and what is outside the beautiful/good is evil in nature.

On the basis of these assumptions Gregory makes a *reductio ad absurdum* in order to prove God's infinity: if the beautiful/good (i.e. God) has a limit, it must be surrounded by something different in nature (i.e. evil), and is ruled by it. This is absurd. Therefore, Gregory concludes that no comprehension of the infinite nature can be thought (II.236-238).[286] Because God is without any limit, the ascent of the soul is also without end (II.239). The soul's desire is for God, but this desire is never fulfilled. Moses is an example of the soul who longs for God.

Next Gregory goes on to explain the place, the rock and its hole, God's hand, and his passage. The mention of the place points to the limitless and infinite. The place of God is so great that one who is running in it is never able to stop his course (II.242). Gregory states paradoxically that the running is also called standing still because God says 'I shall station you on the rock' (Ex. 33:21). This means that the firmer one remains in the Good the more one progresses in the course of virtue. He who is uncertain in his conception about reality and does not stay in the Good firmly will not ascend the height of virtue (II.243). The rock is explained as Christ (1 Cor. 10:4), who is absolute virtue, and the more steadfast one stays on the rock the faster one completes the course (II.244).[287] The hole in the rock is the heavenly house, which is laid up for those who have dissolved their earthly

---

Cf. 1 Cor 13:12 βλέπομεν γὰρ ἄρτι δι᾽ ἐσόπτρου ἐν αἰνίγματι, τότε δὲ πρόσωπον πρὸς πρόσωπον. The connection of 1 Cor. 13:12 with Ex. 33:20 occurs also in Clement *Strom.* 5.7.5-7.

[285] See Schoedel (1979) 83-84, Sweeney (1992) 499-501, Böhm (1996) 137-149.

[286] For God's infinity, see Mühlenberg (1966) 89-145, Ullmann (1987), Böhm (1996) 107-211. Cf. in Gregory *Abl.* 52.16-22, *Cant.* 157.14-158.12, 246.8, 247.18, 337.2, 387.3, *CE* 1.167-171, 1.236-237, 1.362-3, 1.367, 1.669, 2.67, 2.125, 2.528, 3.1.103-104, 3.1.110, 3.3.46, 3.5.54-55, 3.6.3. *Deit. Euag.* 339.12, *Eccl.* 411.9, *Infan.* 85.19.

[287] Gregory refers to Ps. 39:3 ('He brought me out of the miry clay, and set my feet on the rock'), cf. *Cant.* 331.15-16. Origen also combines Ex. 33:21 with Ps. 39:3 (*Ier. hom.* 16.2).

tabernacle and finished their course (II.245-246; 2 Tim. 4:7).[288] God's hand, which covers Moses, points to God's creative power of the existent things, the Only Begotten God (II.249). Finally, Gregory interprets the seeing of God's back as the following of God, referring to the prescript from Deut. 13:5 to go behind the Lord God.[289] David was also obedient to this command because he says 'My soul clings to your back part' (II.250; Ps. 62:9).[290] In this context the Cappadocian theologian appeals also to sayings of Jesus like 'Come, follow me' (II.251; Luc. 18:22).

The biblical account in Ex. 33 is discussed by Philo in *Spec.* 1.32-50. Philo begins with the statement that the father and ruler of all is hard to fathom and hard to comprehend (cf. Plato *Tim.* 28C)[291]. Nevertheless, the quest for God should not be abandoned. In the search for God Philo distinguishes two main questions: whether the divine exists, and what it is in its essence. The first question can be solved easily, but the second is difficult and perhaps impossible. Both questions should be examined (32). We can gain knowledge of God's existence on the basis of the creation, in the same way as we can gain knowledge of the sculptor on the basis of the sculpture (33-35).[292] God's essence is difficult to catch and to grasp, but the search for it should be undertaken. For nothing is better than the search for the true God, even if the discovery of him is beyond human capacity (36). We do not have a clear vision of God as he really is, but we should not relinquish the quest, because the search even without finding God is valuable in itself (40).[293] Philo illustrates the search for God with the story in Ex. 33, where Moses asks God to manifest himself (41; Ex. 33:13). In Philo's exegesis God answers: 'I praise your desire, but the request cannot fitly be granted to any that are brought into creation. I freely bestow what is in

---

[288] Irenaeus explains that Ex. 33:20-23 signifies two things: that man cannot see God, and that through God's wisdom man will see him in the last times on the height of the rock, that is in his coming as a man (*Adv. Haer.* 4.20.9). Origen, referring to Paul, also interprets the rock as Christ. The hole in the rock is he who reveals God to men, and makes him known to them. God's back parts are the things that come to pass in the last times (*Cant. Com.* 4.2.12, cf. *Ex. hom.* 12.3, *Ier. hom.* 16.2, *Ps. 36 hom.* 4.1). Commenting on Ex. 33:20, Basil writes that it is impossible for men to be capable of the sight of the glorious appearance because of the weakness of the flesh (*Ps. 33 hom.* 11).

[289] The notion of following God is Pythagorean (Iamblichus *De vita Pythagorica* 86) and occurs also in Philo (*Abr.* 60, 204, *Spec.* 4.187, *Praem.* 98), who combines it with Deut. 13:5 as well (*Migr.* 131, 146). Cf. Clement *Strom.* 2.70.1, Marcus Aurelius 3.16, 7.31, 12.31.

[290] Origen, too, combines this verse from Ps. 62 with the seeing of God's back part (*Ps. fr.* PG 12.1489B).

[291] See Runia (1986) 111-113.

[292] The cosmological argument for God's existence also in *Leg.* 3.97-99, *Spec.* 3.187-189, *Praem.* 41-42.

[293] Cf. *Leg.* 3.47, *Post.* 21

accordance with the recipient; for not all that I can give with ease is within man's power to take, and therefore to him that is worthy of my grace I extend all the boons which he is capable of receiving. But the apprehension of me is something more than human nature, yea even the whole heaven and universe will be able to contain.' (43-44; tr. Colson). Thereupon Moses asks God to see his glory, explaining God's glory as God's powers (45; Ex. 33: 18). God replies that his powers are incomprehensible in their essence, but they do present an impression of their activities. They supply quality and shape to things that are without quality and shape (47). God urges Moses not to hope to apprehend him or his powers in their essence (49). Philo ends his exegesis of Ex. 33 by remarking that Moses, having heard God's answer, did not stop his longing for God, but kept the desire for the invisible aflame (50).[294]

In other passages Philo offers an interpretation of Ex. 33:23 'You will see my back part, but you will not see my face.' This verse denotes that it is possible for human beings to know what follows God and is behind him, but God's essence is incomprehensible. God's powers, who follow him, make known his existence, but not his essence. One who wishes to see God's essence will be blinded before he can see (*Fug.* 165, cf. *Post.* 169, *Mut.* 9).[295]

When we compare Philo's exegesis of Ex. 33 with Gregory's interpretation we can see that both interpret Moses' longing for God as the unending quest of the soul for God. In II.239 Gregory urges that one should always rekindle the desire to see God. This can be regarded as an echo of Philo's remark that Moses keeps the desire to see God aflame (*Spec.* 1.50). An important difference is that Gregory bases the unending ascent of the soul on God's infinity, for which he gives an elaborated argumentation. Further, Ex. 33:23 is interpreted differently: Philo explains this verse as indicating the incomprehensibility of God's essence, whereas Gregory interprets the seeing of God's back as the following of God. Furthermore, the Cappadocian exegete offers a detailed interpretation of the rock, the hole, God's hand and passage largely within the Christian tradition (e.g. the rock as Christ), referring to New Testament texts. The framework of Gregory's exegesis of Ex. 33 is largely Philonic, but the details of the exegesis differ. His exegesis comes in category B3.

---

[294] Cf. *Fug.* 161-162, where Moses' quest for God is called an endless labour.
[295] Gregory of Nazianzus offers an interpretation of this verse along Philo's line of thought (*Or.* 28.3).

20. *Moses envied* (I.61-62, II.256-263)

The following event, which concerns Miriam's and Aaron's envy of Moses (Num. 12), is not interpreted in allegorical terms by Gregory. He tells us that Moses, fortified with the shield of virtue, is not wounded by the darts of envy because he is following God (II.261-263).[296] Philo, briefly referring to this story in *Leg.* 3.103, allegorizes Miriam as sense-perception and Aaron as speech. That Gregory does not take over this Philonic interpretation is in line with the observation made earlier that in the discussion of the meeting between Moses and Aaron Gregory does not give Philo's interpretation of Aaron as speech and Moses as thought (II.43-47).[297] The Jewish author does not narrate the episode about Miriam's and Aaron's envy in *Mos.*

21. *The Quails* (I.63-64, II.264)

Gregory continues by retelling the story about the quails, which are sent by God in response to the Israelite complaints (Num. 11:31-35). In his account in the *historia* some cases of Philonic phraseology are encountered. The expression 'excess of the pleasures of the stomach' may be a reminiscence of similar words in *Leg.* 2.76 and 77, where Philo offers an exegesis of the serpents from Num. 21, which is partly followed by Gregory in II.276.[298]

Leg. 2.76 περὶ τῶν γαστρὸς ἡδονῶν[299] *VM* I.63
2.77 ἀμετρία τῶν ἡδονῶν ἡ τῶν κατὰ γαστέρα ἡδονῶν ἀμετρία

A second Philonic topic is the remark that the quails fly close to the ground, which is found in Philo *Mos.* 1.209.

Mos. 1.209 *VM* I.63
ὀρτυγομητρῶν νέφος συνεχὲς ἐκ θαλάτ- ὀρνέων τὶ πλῆθος, πρόσγειον ποιουμένων
της ἐπιφερόμενον ἅπαν τὸ στρατόπεδον τὴν πτῆσιν, ἐφιεὶς τῷ στρατοπέδῳ
ἐπεσκίαζε τὰς πτήσεις προσγειοτάτας αἰφνηδὸν καὶ κατ' ἀγέλας ἐφίπτασθαι,
ποιουμένων εἰς τὸ εὔθηρον. ἐφ' ὧν ἡ εὐκολία τῆς ἄγρας εἰς κόρον
τὴν τῶν κρεῶν ἐπιθυμίαν προήγαγεν.

---

[296] For the digression on envy in II.256-258, cf. Gregory of Nazianzus *Or.* 36.4-5. For a survey of the patristic exegesis of this passage, see Dorival (1994) 299-300.
[297] See § 7.
[298] See § 24.
[299] For the phrase ἡδοναὶ γαστρός, cf. *Ios.* 61, *Mos.* 2.23, *Spec.* 2.163, 3.43.

Although this notion may have a textual trigger in Num. 11:31 ('about two cubits from the earth'), it is striking that both authors use the same words to express it, and, in all likelihood, Gregory derives the phrase from Philo (with a slight alteration in number).[300] Furthermore, both Philo and Gregory remark that the quails can be captured easily because they fly close to the earth. Neither Gregory nor Philo interpret the story of the quails in allegorical terms; Gregory passing over the episode in virtual silence in the *theoria*.[301]

22. *The Spies* (I.65, II.265-268)

The next episode depicts the exploration of the promised land by spies, who return with a bunch of grapes; some of them report positively, others negatively (Num. 13:25-33). In Gregory's allegorical exegesis the spies who bring positive messages are the reasonings born of faith, which confirm hope for the good things laid down; by contrast, those who reject better hopes are the reasonings of the adversary (II.266). The bunch of grapes, hanging on the wood (Num. 13:23), points to the bunch suspended from the wood in the last days, whose blood becomes a saving drink for those who believe (II.268).[302]

Influence from Philo is not traceable in Gregory's treatment of the story. Philo brings up the story briefly in *Somn.* 2.170-171, referring to Num. 13:18-21. The desert, being free from passions and wrongdoing, is a symbol of philosophy. Right reason is placed on the mountain in order to explore the land of virtue, whether it is well fitted for increasing lessons and for forming stems of doctrines, or for the opposite. The cities of the land are actions, while the bunch of grapes (Num. 13:24) is a symbol of joy, cut off from the whole trunk of wisdom (*Somn.* 2.170-171).[303]

---

[300] The expression is not found in the description of the event in Josephus (*AJ* 3.299), Eusebius (*Ps. com.* 920D-921A), Gregory of Nazianzus (*Or.* 4.19), or Basil (*Enar. es.* 157A, *Ieiun.* 180B). Origen does not deal with the story from Num. in *Num. hom.*

[301] The order in which Gregory narrates the several events from Numbers differs from the biblical order, see Dorival (1994) 23. It is remarkable that a sentence in I.64 has an exact parallel in the Catenae on Ps. 77 ascribed to Origen (PG 17.140A); this fragment is not authentic (see CPG no 1426.II; Mühlenberg (1978) 3.25; Devreesse (1970) 6). It concerns the sentence ὧν τὸ ὑπόδειγμα αὐτοῖς τε ἐκείνοις καὶ τοῖς πρὸς ἐκείνους ὁρῶσιν ἱκανὸν πρὸς σωφροσύνην ἐγένετο, after the description of the punishment of the Israelites for their craving for meat (Num. 11:33).

[302] Cf. *Cant.* 98.14-99.1. Interpretation of the bunch of grapes, based on John. 15:1, as referring to the passion of Christ in Clement *Paed.* 2.19.3.

[303] In *Mut.* 224 the bunch of grapes is a specimen and part of the whole virtue. Philo recounts the story of the spies of the promised land in *Mos.* 2.210-236.

23. *Water from the Rock* (I.66, II.269-270)

In Num. 20:2-13 the marvel of the water springing from the rock when Moses strikes it with his staff is told for the second time.[304] In Gregory's narrative at I.66 we find a phrase that also occurs in Philo's description of the marvel, namely the words ἀκρότομος πέτρα (flinty rock).[305] This phrase is not found in the scriptural account in Numbers or Exodus, but it does occur in Deut. 8:15 and Ps. 113:8, where reference is made to the marvel.[306] Because Gregory shows familiarity with Philo's writings, it is possible that his use of this phrase is caused by his reading of the Jewish exegete,[307] but it would be going too far to label this expression as Philonic since Gregory may well be inspired by Deut. 8:15 or Ps. 113. Gregory explains that the story, spiritually perceived, indicates the mystery of repentance. It is possible for those who have turned to the Egyptian pleasures to repent and thus find the rock, which gives water again (II.269-270). Gregory's interpretation of the story of the rock in terms of the mystery of repentance seems to be original.[308]

24. *The Brazen Serpent* (I.67-68, II.271-277)

When the Israelite people long for the Egyptian pleasures, serpents, which inject deadly poison into those they bite, appear. Interpreting this incident, Gregory explains that the unruly desire (ἡ ἐπιθυμία τῶν ἀτόπων)[309] brings forth serpents (II.272), interpreting them as beastly desires (II.276).[310] The brazen serpent made by Moses at God's order is an antidote for the poison. Gregory explains the brazen serpent as a symbol of the mystery of the cross, appealing to John 3:14 'as Moses lifted up the

---

[304]   The story is also told in Ex. 17:1-7, treated by Gregory in I.35, II.135-136 (see § 15). The remark of Daniélou (1968) 291 n.1 that Gregory does not speak about the first episode in which the rock appears seems to be incorrect.

[305]   *VM* I.66 πάλιν αὐτοῖς θαυματοποιῆσαι τὴν ἀκρότομον ἐκείνην πέτραν εἰς ὑδάτων φύσιν μεταβαλόντα.
Mos. 1.210 Μωυσῆς ... θεοφορηθεὶς τὴν ἀκρότομον πέτραν παίει. Cf. *Leg.* 2.86 (discussion of Deut. 8:15-16), *Somn.* 2.222 (citation Deut. 8:15), and *Decal.* 16.

[306]   Kreitzer (1993) discusses this phrase in connection with Paul's christological interpretation of the rock in 1 Cor. 10:4.

[307]   Basil and Gregory of Nazianzus do not use the phrase in their narratives of the event. It does occur in Clement *Paed.* 2.19.1.

[308]   Daniélou (1968) 291 n. 3.

[309]   For this expression, cf. *Or. dom.* 34.2.

[310]   *VM.* II.276 Θηρία δὲ λέγω τὰς ἐπιθυμίας... ἡ δὲ ἐγκειμένη τῇ σαρκὶ κατὰ τοῦ πνεύματος ἐπιθυμία εἰς τὸ παντελὲς οὐκ ἀπόλωλε. II.277 . . τῆς ἐπιτυμίας τὰ δήγματα. .

serpent in the wilderness, even so must the Son of man be lifted up.' (II.277; Num 21:4-9, cf. *Cant.* 8.3-6).[311]

Daniélou and the other commentators on Gregory remark that the interpretation of the serpents as desires comes from Philo, who gives an interpretation of the story in *Leg* 2.76-81.[312] The point of departure in this passage is the serpent from Gen. 3:1, which is likened to pleasure, because the movement of pleasure is variable as that of the serpent (2.71).[313] Philo discusses the story from Numbers as an example of the pleasure of eating and drinking. When the mob-like part of us desires the dwellings in Egypt, it encounters pleasures which bring death, not the death that separates soul from body, but the death that destroys the soul by vice (2.77). Healing of the passion is brought about by the serpent made by Moses, that is, the principle of self-control (σωφροσύνη) because self-control is opposite to pleasure (2.79).[314] After explaining why the serpent should be made of brass Philo ends with a summarizing sentence: 'When the mind, bitten by pleasure, i.e. the serpent of Eve, is strong enough to see in his soul the beauty of self-control, i.e. the serpent of Moses, and through this God himself, he will live' (2.81).

In all probability Gregory is inspired by Philo's exegesis of the serpents because other Church fathers (Clement, Origen, Basil, and Gregory of Nazianzus) do not offer an allegorical exegesis of the serpents that bite the people. Further, there are more reminiscences of Philo's passage in Gregory's writings: (a) the expression 'excess of the pleasures of the stomach' (I.63),[315] and (b) the notion of ποικίλη ἡδονή compared to a serpent (*Or. dom.* 53.21-25).[316] Influence from Philo's *Leg.* is also discernible in other passages from *VM*,[317] and in the introduction we saw that

---

[311] Christological interpretation of the brazen serpent is very common among the Church fathers, cf. Justin *Dial.* 91, 94, 112, 131, Iraeneus *Adv. Haer.* 4.2.7, 4.24.1, Origen *Pasc.* 14, 15, Basil *Spir. sanct* 14.31, *Ep.* 260, see the overview in Dorival (1994) 398-399.

[312] Daniélou (1968) 295 n.1, Malherbe-Ferguson (1978) 191 n. 390, Simonetti (1984) 332.

[313] Serpent as pleasure in Philo also in *Opif.* 157, *Leg.* 3.68, *Agr.* 97.

[314] Cf. 2.86, 93, 99, *Agr.* 97-98. σωφροσύνη is also important for Gregory, cf. *VM.* I.64. In II.279 he refers to a σωφρονέστερος βίος as a remedy for the passion of desire.

[315] See § 21.

[316] Gregory *Or. dom.* 53.22-23 αἱ δὲ ποικίλαι καὶ πολύτροποι τῶν ἡδονῶν ἰδέαι, Philo *Leg.* 2.74 πολύπλοκος γὰρ καὶ ποικίλη ὥσπερ τοῦ ὄφεως ἡ κίνησις, οὕτως καὶ ἡδονῆς (cf. 2.76). Cf. Basil *Ps. 28 hom.* 7 (301A) αἱ ὑλώδεις ψυχαί, ἐν αἷς, ὥσπερ τινὰ θηρία, τὰ ποικίλα πάθη τῶν ἁμαρτιῶν ἐμφωλεύει,... (Gregory uses ἐμφωλεύω in *Or. dom.* 53.18, Philo in *Agr.* 97, where he interprets the serpent as pleasure). Same interpretation of the serpent as pleasure in Gregory *Eccl.* 348.15. In *VM* II.282 Gregory refers to the serpents as ἡδοναί.

[317] See § 3.2, 3.3, 21.

Gregory, referring to Philo in *CE* 3.7.8-9, has probably a passage from the same work in mind.[318] The Cappadocian exegete does not take over Philo's interpretation of the serpents entirely. He speaks about ἐπιθυμία, whereas Philo speaks about ἡδονή, but both desire and pleasure are passions. Gregory does not follow Philo in the interpretation of the brazen serpent as the principle of self-control, giving preference to the common Patristic tradition. We can conclude that Gregory's exegesis falls under the category 'Philonic exegesis altered' (B3).

25. *Rebellion against Moses* (I.69, II.278-283)

After the passion of desire is healed, Gregory continues, another passion arises, namely arrogance. Some people make themselves priests, thrusting out those who had received this ministry from God. The biblical story shows that they are swallowed up by the yawning chasm in the earth and destroyed. All of those left on the earth are burned to ashes by lightning. Therefore, arrogance is not unreasonably defined as a downward ascent (II.280; Num. 16:31-35, Lev. 10:1-2).

With regard to the description of the punishment, Musurillo refers to Philo *Mos.* 2.280-285.[319] There is indeed a similarity between Philo and Gregory, namely the mention of the lightning, while the scriptural account only speaks about a light from the Lord.[320]

Mos. 2.283	*VM* II.280
μικρὸν δ᾽ ὕστερον τοὺς τῆς στάσεως ἡγεμόνας πεντήκοντα πρὸς τοῖς διακοσίοις ἄνδρας κεραυνοὶ κατασκήψαντες αἰφνίδιον ἀθρόους ἐξανάλωσαν. 287 τὸ δὲ τέλος καὶ τοῖς καταποθεῖσι καὶ τοῖς ὑπὸ τῶν κεραυνῶν διεφθαρμένοις ταὐτὸν ἀπέβαινεν. ... οἱ δ᾽ ὅλοι δι᾽ ὅλων ἀναλωθέντες ὑπὸ τοῦ κεραυνίου πυρός.[321]	τὸ δὲ ὅσον ὑπὲρ γῆς ἦν τοῦ τοιούτου συντάγματος, κεραυνοῖς κατεπρήσθη, διδάσκοντος, οἶμαι, τοῦ λόγου διὰ τῆς ἱστορίας ὅτι πέρας ἐστὶ τῆς καθ᾽ ὑπερηφανίαν ἐπάρσεως ἡ εἰς τὸ ὑπόγειον κάθοδος.[322]

---

[318] See Part II. I § 1.
[319] Musurillo (1964) 129, see also Daniélou (1967a) 344.
[320] Gregory does this in *Inscr. Psal.* 44.25.
[321] *Mos.* 2.283 'And, shortly after, thunderbolts fell suddenly on the two hundred and fifty men who had led the sedition and destroyed them in a mass. [287] Whether they were swallowed up or destroyed by the thunderbolts, the result was the same...consumed absolutely and entirely by the flame of the thunderbolt.' (translation Colson).
[322] *VM* 280 'All of those left on the earth were burned to ashes by lightning. The Scripture teaches in the history, I think, that when one arrogantly exalts himself he ends by falling even below the earth.' (translation Melherbe-Ferguson).

Both Philo and Gregory see lightning in the light from the Lord ,[323] and it would seem that Gregory's reference to lightning here can be labelled as Philonic phraseology.

26. The Miracle of Aaron's Staff (I.70-71, II.284-286)

Next Gregory narrates God's confirmation of the appointment of Aaron as priest. Of the twelve staffs — one for each tribe — placed in the tabernacle by God's order, only Aaron's staff blooms and brings forth fruit. This fruit is a nut (I.70; Num. 17:16-26). In Gregory's interpretation the nut indicates 'the kind of life that must characterize the priesthood — namely, a life self-controlled, tough and dried in appearance, but containing on the inside (hidden and invisible) what can be eaten' (II. 285; tr. Malherbe-Ferguson).[324]

Daniélou remarks that Gregory's exegesis of the nut is derived from Philo's *Mos.* 2.183-184,[325] where the Jewish exegete explains that, in a nut, seed and edible part are identical and this signifies perfect virtue. 'For, just as in a nut, beginning and end are identical, beginning represented by seed and end by fruit, so it is with the virtues. There, too, it is the case that each is both a beginning and an end; a beginning in that it springs from no other power but itself, an end in that it is the aspiration of the life which follows nature.' (2.181; tr. Colson). Next Philo remarks that the fruit of the nut, enclosed by a bitter shell and an inner layer, is not easy to get at (2.182). This is a symbol of the practising soul because a soul, striving for virtue, first encounters toil, and toil is bitter, stiff and hard but the good springs from it (2.183).[326] So, he who flees from toil flees also from the good. Virtue does not live in souls of those who live voluptuously (2.184).[327]

---

[323] The lightning is not found in the descriptions of the event by Josephus (*AJ* 4.55), Origen (*Num. hom.* 9.1), Eusebius (*Ps. com.* 1316B), or Basil (*Auctor* 340A).

[324] Gregory gives the same interpretation of the pomegranates from the high priest's vestment in II.193: the philosophical life is outwardly unpleasant but full of good hopes (cf. *Cant.* 230.13-17, 282.12-283.7)

[325] Daniélou (1968) 300 n. 1; see also Malherbe-Ferguson (1978) 191 n. 397, Simonetti (1984) 333.

[326] The notion of toil in the virtuous life is also present at *Post* 156, where Philo discusses the bitter water in Marah; see § 13.

[327] In Origen's interpretation the bitter outer part of the nut is the literal interpretation of the law (*Num. hom.* 9.7). He explains Aaron's staff as Christ (*Num. hom.* 9.9, cf. Justin *Dial.* 86). An exegesis of the nut growing from Aaron's staff does not occur in Clement of Alexandria, Eusebius, Gregory of Nazianzus or Basil.

To some extent Gregory's symbolic interpretation of the nut fits in with
the second exegesis found in Philo: for both authors the hardness of the
nut refers to the hardness of the virtuous life but they elaborate this
reference in a different way. Philo conceives of the hardness of the nut as
being the toil that a virtuous soul has to encounter, and this toil should be
seen as something good. In Gregory's interpretation the hardness of the
shell of the nut indicates the outward austerity of the life of the priests. A
difference is also discernible in the context: Philo speaks in general terms
about the soul that strives for virtue, whereas Gregory specifically mentions
the priest's life. The similarities are sufficient, however, to justify placing
Gregory's exegesis in category B3, 'a Philonic exegesis which has been
altered'.

27.　*The Royal Way* (I.72, II.287-290)

When, Gregory continues, the people are purified of the passion of
arrogance, they cross through the foreign life under the leadership of the
law. It leads them along the royal highway, from which they do not deviate
to right or left (Num. 20:17, 21:22). The law requires that he who follows it
does not leave this road, which is, as the Lord says, narrow and hard
(II.287; Mat.7:14).[328] Gregory links the royal way from Numbers with the
Aristotelian definition that virtue is found in the middle, illustrating this
with the example of courage, which lies in between cowardice and rashness
(II.288).[329] In the same way wisdom is in the middle between shrewdness
and simplicity, while self-control is situated between licentiousness and the
extremity of one who even regards marriage as adultery (II.289). He who
lives in this world, which lies in wickedness (1 John 5:19), makes the
journey of virtue safely if he keeps to the highway and does not turn aside
to any byways (II.290).[330]

The connection between the royal way and Aristotelian ethics is also
found in Philo.[331] The Jewish exegete deals with it in *Deus* 140-181,[332]

---

[328]　Connection between the royal way and Mat. 7:14 occurs also in Clement *Strom.* 4.5.3.

[329]　The definition of virtue is found in *Ethica Nicomachea* II.6. Aristotle also gives the
examples of courage and self-control (II.7.1107b1-7). Gregory refers to this theory in
Cant. 284.5-8, *Eccl.* 375.4-12, *Inscr. Psal.* 103.17-104.4, *Virg.* 282.24-284.3. Basil speaks about
the mean of virtue in *Ps. 7 hom.* 7.

[330]　Cf. *Cant.* 453.3 ἡ τραχεῖα τῆς ἀρετῆς ὁδός.

[331]　Daniélou (1968) 303 n. 2, Musurillo (1964) 132, Malherbe-Ferguson (1978) 192 n.
401, 402, 403, 408.

[332]　The passage is commented on by Winston-Dillon (1983) 341-358.

where his starting point is Gen. 6:12b: '. . all flesh destroyed his way upon the earth.'[333] In Philo's interpretation 'his' refers to God, and the verse means that men destroyed the perfect way of the eternal and indestructible, the way that leads to God. This way is wisdom, which is a straight highway, having as goal knowledge of God (143). Philo interprets Edom, through whose land the royal way runs, as the earthly one, who does not permit Israel to journey along the royal way (144).[334] He who despises the earthly things and external goods of Edom travels by the royal way without turning to the right or to the left, but keeping the middle path because deviations — whether of excess or of deficiency — are blameworthy (162). Next Philo links the royal way with the doctrine of virtue as in the middle, explaining that courage is the middle between rashness and cowardice, self-control between extravagance and parsimony; prudence lies in between slyness and folly; and piety between superstition and impiety (164).[335]

It is, indeed, highly probable that in his interpretation of the royal way Gregory is indebted to Philo because, to the best of my knowledge, no other Church father (Clement, Origen, Eusebius, Gregory of Nazianzus, or Basil) connects the biblical royal way with Aristotelian ethics.[336] The two authors partly share two of the examples of individual virtues, namely courage and self-control (though these examples occur in Aristotle as well). Furthermore, it is likely that the metaphorical use of λεώφορος contrasted with ἀνοδία with regard to the practice of virtue is borrowed from Philo, of whom the use of the word ἀνοδία — literally meaning 'a road that is no road' — seems typical. At *Det.* 18 he explains that toil by itself is not good, but needs to be combined with skill. Just as one should not practice music unmusically or grammar ungrammatically, so one

---

[333] This is a fine example of verbal association in Philo, see Runia (1984) 244.
[334] Cf. *Post.* 101-102, where the royal way leading to God is said to be philosophy. In the law this way is called the utterance and the word of God, for it is written 'You should not deviate from the word I command you this day to the right hand nor to the left hand' (Deut. 28:14). Philo refers also to the royal way in *Gig.* 64, *Spec.* 4.168, and *QE* 2.26.
[335] Same definition of ἀνδρεία in *Spec.* 4.146; see Billings (1919) 77-78 with references to Plato and Chrysippus. Same definition of εὐσέβεια in *Spec.* 4.147, in Gregory *Virg.* 283.7. In *Migr.* 146-147 Philo connects the royal way with the Aristotelian definition of virtue as well.
[336] Origen deals with the royal way in *Num. hom.* 12.4, discussing Num. 21:21-23. He interprets Sihon, the king of the Amorites, as the devil, the prince of this world (John 14:30). The Israelites promise not to turn into his fields or his vineyards, that is they will travel through this world without making use of the works of the devil. The royal way is he who has said: 'I am the way, the truth, and the life' (John 14:6). Gregory makes the connection between the royal way and John 14:6 in *Cant.* 330.14-331.3.

should not exercise prudence in a bad way, or self-control thriftily, or courage with rashness, or piety in a superstitious way, or any other knowledge according to virtue in an ignorant way: these are all no-ways (ἀνοδίαι). The contrast between λεώφορος and ἀνοδία recurs in *Agr.* 101, where Philo expounds the expression 'on the road' from Gen. 49:17, which runs: 'Let Dan be a serpent on the road.' Having explained that the serpent is here a symbol of self-control,[337] he writes that lack of endurance and all other things that are conceived and brought forth by immoderate pleasures[338] do not allow the soul to go by the straight highway. But endurance, self-control and other virtues secure a safe journey for the soul. Therefore, it is written that self-control keeps to the right road because lack of endurance makes use of a road that is no road. Finally, in *Mos.* 2.138 Philo speaks about the blameless life, which does not travel on the rough road — or more properly said the no-way — of vice, but on the highway of virtue.[339] It can be concluded that Gregory's interpretation of the royal way as referring to the definition of virtue as the middle between two extremities, combined with the metaphorical usage of the expressions highway and no-way, is derived from the writings of Philo (category A + B3).

28. *Balaam* (I.73-74, II.291-296)

Gregory continues the story by recounting that Balak, king of the Midian-ites, launches an attack against the Israelites with the help of sorcery, calling in Balaam, a soothsayer (μαντίς) and augur (οἰωνιστίς), who is assisted by demons (I.73, II.292). This seer is called in to curse the king's enemies but he learns that his sorcery is too weak to harm those who have God as their ally. When he is inspired by divine inspiration,[340] his utter-ances become a prophecy of better things that are to occur later on (I.74; Num. 22-24). Spiritually conceived this history teaches that sorcery is ineffective against those who live in virtue (II.292). The story of Balaam's speaking ass shows that those who have been overtaken by demonic deceit accept teaching from irrational animals instead of using their reason (II.293; Num. 22:22-35). The history of Balaam teaches that he who wishes

---

[337] Cf. *Leg.* 2.79, see § 24.

[338] Note the metaphorical use of conceiving and giving birth, see § 1.1 and § 3.3.

[339] Cf. *Spec.* 1.215, 3.29, *Praem.* 117, 167, *QE* 2.13, 2.26.

[340] *VM* I.74 . . ἔνθους γενόμενος. Philo also uses the word ἔνθους in the context of Balaam's speaking (*Mos.* 1.277, 288). The word has a Platonic background (cf. e.g. *Ion* 533E, see Billings (1919) 66-68, Wolfson (1947) 2. 22-54, Levison (1995a)).

to curse those who live in virtue is not able to produce any harmful sound, but his curse is turned into a blessing (II.295).[341]

Daniélou remarks that Gregory's portrait of Balaam as an augur has been drawn from Philo.[342] Indeed, Philo pictures Balaam as an augur (*Mos.* 1.264, 282, 287), a soothsayer (1.264, 276, 277, 282, 285), and a magician (1.276). When Balaam utters his prophetic words, he is divinely inspired, acting as an interpreter of the words of another (1.277, 283, 288). Philo interprets the figure of Balaam in allegorical terms as well, e.g. in *Cher.* 32-36. Balaam, whose name is translated as 'vain people' (cf. *Conf.* 65, 159, *Migr.* 113), is an example of one who thinks that it is the pursuits of life which bring good or ill, and not the divine Logos, the helmsman of all. He rides an ass, that is the unreasoning rule of life; the angel, who stands in his way, is God's Logos (cf. *Deus* 182), the source through which both good and ill come to fulfilment.[343]

The portrait of Balaam as soothsayer and augur has scriptural precedents (Num. 22:7, 24:1, Jos. 13:22) and is also found in other Church fathers, for instance in Origen. He depicts Balaam as famous in the magical art, and as a soothsayer, who stays in contact with demons (*Num. hom.* 13.4, 14.3). He also gives the Philonic rendering of the name (*Num. hom.* 14.4).[344] It can be concluded that Gregory's picture of Balaam as augur is in agreement with the LXX and the patristic tradition without any special influence of Philo.

29. *The Action of Phinehas* (I.75, II.297-304)

In the last episode from Moses' life Gregory deals with the story of the daughters of Moab, with whom the Israelites fornicate. In reaction to the fornication Phinehas throws a spear through a Midianitish woman and an Israelite man (Num. 25:1-8). In his interpretation of the story Gregory states that the inventor of evil entices nature to evil through pleasure, which is like a bait to evil; when it is thrown out lightly, it draws gluttonous souls to the fish-hook of destruction (II.297). Those who had prevailed

---

[341] In *VM* II.316 the magical art of Balaam is interpreted as the deceit of life, by which human beings are transformed to irrational forms of animals (cf. for the notion of man becoming beast II.70), see § 10.

[342] Daniélou (1967a) 344.

[343] For Philo's treatment of Balaam, see Levison (1995b) 190-195 and Remus (1996).

[344] Cf. Basil *Ep.* 210, *Enar. es.* 125A, 629C, 653C. For the figure of Balaam in Philo, Josephus, the rabbis, and the Church fathers, see Karpp (1954), Baskin (1983) 93-113, Dorival (1996) 414-419.

over the enemy's army are now themselves wounded by feminine darts of pleasure (II.298). Phinehas purges the sin with blood, not with the blood of a guiltless animal which has no part in the stain of licentiousness, but with the blood of the wrongdoers (II.300). The lesson from this story, Gregory teaches, is that no passion is so strong as the disease of pleasure (II.301). Therefore, we should conduct our lives as far removed from it as possible (II.303).[345]

In Gregory's treatment there are some reminiscences of Philo's recount in *Mos.* 1.294-299, namely the notion of pleasure as a bait to evil, combined with the image of hooking, and both authors consider the adultery of the Israelites a stain which should be purged. The comparable texts are the following:

Mos. 1.295

πρὸς μεῖζον κακόν, ἀσέβειαν, ἄγειν αὐτοὺς ἐσπούδασεν ἡδονὴν δέλεαρ προθείς.
296 ἀγκιστρεύσονται τὴν νεότητα τῶν ἀντιπάλων.[346]
303 τὸ μὲν μίασμα τοῦ ἔθνους ἐκκαθαίρουσι

VM II.297

πάλιν δι' ἡδονῆς πρὸς τὸ κακὸν δελεάζων τὴν φύσιν. ὄντως γὰρ πάσης κακίας οἷόν τι δέλεαρ ἡ ἡδονὴ προβληθεῖσα, εὐκόλως τὰς λιχνοτέρας ψυχὰς ἐπὶ τὸ ἄγκιστρον τῆς ἀπωλείας ἐφέλκεται.
300 καθαρίσας τὴν ἁμαρτίαν, αἵματι . .
οὐκ . . . τοῦ μηδὲν μετεσχηκότος τοῦ τῆς ἀκολασίας μιάσματος,

Even though the notion of pleasure as bait to evil can be regarded as a *topos*,[347] Gregory's phrases do appear to recall Philo's text. The mention of hooking and the purification of the stain are also elements common in both authors. So, we have here the final example of Philonic phraseology in Gregory 's *VM*.[348]

---

[345] In *Diem lum.* 240.4-6 Gregory tells that sin is pierced by the javelin of baptism, like the prostitute by the zealous Phinehas.

[346] For the expression δέλεαρ ἡδονῆς, cf. *Post.* 72, *Deus* 168, *Agr.* 103, *Migr.* 29, for the image of hooking *Deus* 115, *Mut.* 172, *Spec.* 4.67.

[347] Cf. Plato *Tim.* 69D (ἡδονήν, μέγιστον κακοῦ δέλεαρ, see Billings (1919) 69 n. 4, Runia (1986) 260). Malherbe-Ferguson (1978) 192 n. 415 refer to Lucian *Apologia* 9 (...ὑπ' ἄλλης τινὸς ἐλπίδος τοιαύτης δελεασθείς...) and Julian *Oratio* 6.185a (ὑπὸ . . τῶν Λωτοφάγων ἡδονῆς . . . δελεασθέντες...). See also Josephus *C. Ap.* 2.284 τῆς ἡδονῆς . .δελέατος.

[348] Philo describes Phinehas' action in *Mos.* 1.301-304. Allegorical interpretation in *Leg.* 3.242, *Post.* 182-183, *Ebr.* 73, *Mut.* 108; see Dorival (1994) 461-462 and Seland (1995) 132-136.

30. *Epilogue* (I.75-77, II.305-321)

In the epilogue Gregory repeats his definition of the perfect life given in the introduction: the way of perfection for the soul consists in a continuous progress to what is better (II.305-306). After having stressed the notion of progress by giving a summary of the events in Moses' life (II.308-313), Gregory tells us that Moses ascends the top of the mountain and crowns his work, like a good sculptor who has made well the whole statue of his own life (II.313).[349] In the scriptural verses describing Moses' end he is called 'servant of the Lord' (Deut. 34:5), and Gregory explains that this is the end or goal of the virtuous life: to be called servants of God by virtue of the lives we live (II.314-315). Characteristic of the service to God is that neither the eye is dimmed, nor the face is corrupted (Deut. 34:7). That Moses attained perfection is also testified by the divine voice which says: 'I have known you more than all others' (Ex. 3:12, 17). Furthermore, he is called 'friend of God' (Ex. 33:11) by God himself. All these things demonstrate that Moses has ascended the highest mountain of perfection.[350] True perfection is to become God's friend, which is the only thing worthy of honour and desire (II.319-320).

Philo, too, deals with Moses' death. At the end of *Mos.* he recounts the death of the Jewish leader in the context of Moses' prophecies because Moses prophesies his own death (*Mos.* 2.288-291). Philo describes it as a migration from earth to heaven. Moses leaves his mortal life for immortality. At that moment God resolves Moses' duality of soul and body into a unity, transforming his whole being into mind, pure as the sunlight (2.288).

When we compare Gregory and Philo, we see that they present Moses' death from a different point of view. Gregory presents Moses' death as a culminating point after a continuous process of many ascents. This agrees with Gregory's view of the virtuous life as a continuous ascending process, in which perfection is never reached. The death of Moses is a climax in this ascent: at that moment Moses becomes perfect and for this reason he is called 'friend of God'. Philo's view is different: during his lifetime Moses is already perfect and Philo calls Moses the most perfect of men (*Mos.* 1.1, cf.

---

[349] For the image of the sculpturing of one's own life, see Plotinus *Enn.* 1.6.9.

[350] Malherbe-Ferguson refer to Philo *QE* 2.40 (interpretation of Ex. 24:12a), where Philo remarks that a holy soul is divinized by ascending to a region above the heavens. Marcus (PLCL suppl. 2.82 n. n) remarks that the Greek translation of the Armenian word for 'divinize', θεοῦσθαι, seems not to occur elsewhere in Philo. Philo's remark differs from Gregory, who presents Moses' life as a continuous growth and ascent.

Leg. 2.91, 3.100, *Mut.* 128). The idea of a ascending line in Moses' life is absent in Philo's description of Moses' death. At that moment Moses begins an ascent from earth to heaven.

CHAPTER THREE

SURVEY OF RESULTS AND CONCLUSIONS

Now that we have completed our analysis of the Philonic background of Gregory's *VM*, it is the aim of this chapter to give a survey of the results and to draw conclusions. The distinction used in the analysis between phraseology (A) and exegesis (B) has proved useful, and will be maintained in this chapter. We begin, therefore, with an overview of Philonic phrases and expressions in *VM*. Then, Gregory's use of Philo's exegesis is treated on the basis of four exegetical themes. Next, the relationship of *VM* with Philo's *Mos.* and other treatises is discussed. Finally, we try to answer the questions why and how Gregory makes use of Philo, in other words what is his goal in using Philo and what is his working method.

1. *Philonic Phraseology*

From the analysis it appears that in a very great number of cases Gregory uses the same or nearly the same phrases as Philo in the same context, and these phrases are neither found in the scriptural narrative, nor in passages in Christian writers dealing with the same topic. For this reason these expressions can rightly be labelled as Philonic. Gregory uses expressions derived from Philo's *Mos.* in the following cases (cases with a asterisk are disputable, see the analysis):

	Gregory	Philo's *Mos.*
Moses' royal education	I.18	1.8, 20, 25
description of Jethro	I.19	1.59
burning bush	I.20	1.65
the Egyptian sorcerers	I.24, 26, II.63,64	1.92, 94
co-operation of the 4 elements in the plagues	I.25	1.96
Moses' cry	I.29	1.173
crossing the Red Sea *	I.31	1.177, 253
bloodless victory of the Israelites	I.32	1.180
power of the wood at Marah *	I.33	1.185
Moses as mystagogue *	I.42	2.71
the quails	I.63	1.209
the flinty rock *	I.66	1.210

the Egyptian army	II.122	1.168
the death of the rebellious	II.280	2.283, 287
pleasure as bait	II.297, 300	1.295, 296, 303

Some expressions are borrowed from other works of Philo, namely the following:

the sea of life *	I.11	*Spec.* 1.224
the harbour of virtue	I.13	*Sacr.* 90
articulated voice of the trumpet	I.44	*Decal.* 33
excess of the pleasures of the stomach	I.63	*Leg.* 2.76, 77
the swell of life	II.8	*Sacr.* 13
woman in labour pains	II.11	*Leg.* 1.75-76
the killing of the Egyptian man	II.14	*Leg.* 3.37-38
shepherding of the movements of the soul	II.18	*Sacr.* 45
Moses as athlete *	II.36	*Leg.* 3.12-14
definition of clay *	II.59	*Conf.* 89
high way of virtue contrasted with no-way	II.290	*Det.*18, *Agr.*101

The total number of (possible) borrowings from Philo is about twenty-five. Because there is a cumulative element in the matter — the more expressions that seem to be Philonic the more it is likely that Gregory derives them from Philo — the dubious cases may also be plausibly attributed to Philo's influence. On the basis of the occurrence of so many Philonic expressions in Gregory, the conclusion can safely be drawn that he was acquainted with the Philonic corpus, or at least with some of its writings. This conclusion is thus fully in agreement with the determination of Philo's influence in other writings of Gregory.[1] The great number of citations from *Mos.* shows that Gregory has studied this work; furthermore, at one place (II.191) he probably gives an, albeit anonymous, reference to Philo's *Mos.*[2] The overview given above indicates quite clearly that the greater part of the expressions from *Mos.* occurs in the *historia.* This result is not unexpected, for Gregory's *historia* fits in well with the literal exposition of Moses' life in Philo's *Mos.* Besides the quotations from Philo's treatise on Moses' life, Gregory takes over expressions from other works, especially from *Leg.* and *Sacr.* A few phrases come in the category of metaphorical language, for instance the harbour of virtue, the sea of life, or the highway of virtue. A comparison of the original expressions in Philo with Gregory's 'citations' shows his method of quoting: it is characteristic

---

[1] See Part II. I.
[2] See II § 18.d.

of him that he does not take over expressions from Philo *verbatim*, but makes slight alterations. He uses synonyms: δι' ἑνὸς ἔργου in Philo (*Mos.* 1.59) becomes διὰ μιᾶς πράξεως in Gregory (*VM* I.19).[3] He can also alter the word order (ὕδατος καὶ γῆς (*Conf.* 89) becomes γῆς ἤ ὕδατος (*VM* II.59)),[4] or change the number (τὰς πτήσεις προσγειοτάτας ποιουμένων (*Mos.* 1.209) becomes πρόσγειον ποιουμένων τὴν πτῆσιν (*VM* I.63)).[5] J. Whittaker has shown that the making of such alterations in quotations and borrowings was common practice in Antiquity, as he can show on the basis of Alcinous' *Didaskalikos*.[6] Such alterations were made to emphasize independence. Gregory is clearly an exponent of this manner of appropriating earlier texts.

2. *Exegetical Themes*

In addition to Philonic phraseology, Gregory makes use of Philonic exegesis. In the working method we have presented three categories of Philonic influence on Gregory.[7]

B 1: Gregory offers exactly the same exegesis as Philo does;

B 2: the Philonic exegesis occurs also in other Christian exegetes and belongs to the patristic tradition;

B 3: Gregory offers a Philonic interpretation that is not found in the Christian tradition before him, but he alters the Philonic exegesis in some way.

From the analysis it emerges that category B1 does not occur in Gregory's *VM*. Category B2 is represented by a large number of cases. Gregory's interpretation of male and female as virtue and vice, for instance, occurs in Origen.[8] The exegesis of the darkness in Ex. 20:21 as indicating God's incomprehensibility is also found in Clement.[9] The last category (B3) is the most interesting: Gregory takes over a Philonic interpretation but makes alterations. We discuss this category on the basis of four themes, namely the exegesis of Egypt and of Pharaoh, the notion of pagan education, the interpretation of the serpent, and finally the exegesis of the royal way.

---

[3] See II § 5.1.
[4] See II § 8.
[5] See II § 21.
[6] Whittaker (1989).
[7] See I.
[8] See II § 1.2.
[9] See II § 18.b.

The most important and the most elaborate theme that Gregory derives from Philo is the interpretation of Egypt and related persons and events, such as Pharaoh and the exodus from Egypt. The Cappadocian exegete conceives of Egypt as the land of passions, and its king, Pharaoh, stands for the lover of passions, who only values material and fleshly things (II.35). He takes enjoyment in the Israelites' labour, which consists in making bricks out of clay. The brick-making is a symbol of being involved in a life according to pleasure (II.59-60).[10] Gregory denotes the pursuit of a material life with the verb αἰγυπτίζειν (II.66, 69, 83) and sees in the whole Egyptian person every form of evil (II.127). It is Moses' task to struggle against Pharaoh like an athlete, to destroy his tyranny, and to free the people from the slave labour he imposes (II.26-27).[11] In his fight against Pharaoh he performs a miracle with his staff, which, when cast on the ground, becomes a serpent. The Egyptian magicians do the same but their serpents are eaten up by Moses' one. Gregory explains the Egyptian serpents as the sophistical tricks of deceit made by the adversary against the divine law (II.63-64).[12] The deliverance of the Israelites from Egypt is a symbol of the liberation of the soul from the tyranny of the passions (II.26), and the downfall of the Egyptian army symbolizes the destruction of the passions (II.122-125).[13] The bitter water at Marah, where the Israelites arrive after the crossing of the Red Sea, indicates that a life without pleasures is at first difficult for one who has left behind the pleasures of Egypt, but later on the virtuous life becomes more pleasant and sweeter (II.132).[14]

In general terms this entire complex of allegory connected with Egypt is taken over from Philo by Gregory. In exploiting this allegory, he also employs Philonic imagery: the soul has to fight as an athlete (II.36) against the tyranny of the passions (II.26-27), which are cruel despots (II.128), trying to overwhelm the soul so that it may sink in the sea of life (I.11).[15] Verbal agreements, already mentioned above, suggest that Gregory's employment is based on a direct reading of Philo. A vital consideration here is that other Church fathers, notably Origen, do not offer an allegorical exegesis of this theme as Philo and Gregory do.

Although the general framework of Gregory's interpretation of Egypt can be regarded as Philonic, there are, of course, modifications and

---

[10] See II § 7.1.
[11] See II § 6.c.
[12] See II § 9.
[13] See II § 12.4.
[14] See II § 13.
[15] See II § 6.c, 7.2, 12.4.

deviations. It goes without saying that the Christian symbolism used by Gregory is absent in Philo. The Cappadocian theologian interprets, for instance, the stretching out of Moses' arms as pointing to the arms of Christ on the cross (II.78). Other examples are the lamb as a prefiguration of Christ (II.95),[16] and the crossing of the Red Sea as a symbol of the sacrament of baptism (II.125).

Further, there are a number of points in Philo's exegesis that are not taken over by Gregory. It seems, for instance, that he avoids interpretations in terms of the body. Though he follows the Jewish exegete in the interpretation of Pharaoh as a lover of material life, he does not take over Philo's designation of the king as a lover of the body. Likewise, he neither interprets the Egyptian river, nor Egypt itself, nor Moses' basket as the body, as Philo does (*Somn.* 2.109, *Det.* 38, 170).[17] This alteration is mostly likely due to the influence of Gregory's Christian faith, with its more positive attitude to the body and its belief in the bodily resurrection. We note too that, like Philo, Gregory allegorizes the Egyptian army as the passions but he does not connect the horsemen, the so-called *tristiai* (Ex. 14:7), with the six movements of the body, as Philo does (*Ebr.* 111, *Leg.* 2.99-102).

Some further differences may be noted. Philo gives an extensive allegorical exegesis of the seven daughters of Jethro in *Mut.* 110-120. They represent the seven powers of the irrational soul, namely the five senses, the reproductive power, and speech. The daughters keep the sheep of their father, that is they bring external objects to the mind, their father. When they draw water for the sheep they are attacked by friends of envy and malice, who wish to entice the mind. This interpretation does not recur in Gregory.

At a few places Philo allegorically interprets the meeting between Moses and Aaron, making use of the Stoic distinction between λόγος προφορικός (uttered speech) and λόγος ἐνδιάθετος (inward speech, mind; SVF 2.135). Aaron as Moses' brother and his spokesman represents speech, while Moses is a symbol of mind or intellect, for speech is the brother of mind, and intellect is the fountain of speech. Moses needs speech in order to fight against Pharaoh and the Egyptian sorcerers (*Det.* 38-40, *Migr.* 77-85, 169, *Mut.* 208). The encounter between the two brothers is interpreted in a different way by Gregory, for whom Aaron is the angel who brings help in the struggle against the Egyptians (II.45-47). Gregory does take over

---

16 See II § 10.
17 See II § 2.2, 7.1.

Philo's designation of the activities of the Egyptian sorcerers as sophistical tricks.

A conspicuous deviation from Philo is that Gregory never translates and interprets biblical names, as Philo does in his allegorical writings. The Jewish exegete renders, for instance, Pharaoh as 'scatterer' (*Leg.* 3.236, 243),[18] Zipporah, Moses' wife, as 'bird' (*Cher.* 41), Jethro as 'superfluous' (*Mut.* 103), and Amalek as 'a people licking out' (*Leg.* 3.186).[19] These renderings form a basis for the allegorical interpretation of the person in question. Philo does not, however, give such translations in *Mos*, which is due to the introductory character of the treatise.[20] They are also mentioned in Origen's writings,[21] but in Gregory's *VM* they are totally absent.

It will be valuable to compare Gregory's interpretation of Egypt with Origen's exegesis in his *Homilies on Exodus*. Basing himself on New Testament texts, Origen regards the leader of Egypt as the devil, the prince of this world, and the ruler of darkness. Egypt represents this world, the present age, the dark works of this age, or the darkness of ignorance (*Hom. Ex.* 1.5, 2.1, 3.3, 5.5, 7.3, 8.1).[22] Along the same lines he sees in the Egyptian river the billows of this age (2.3). The departure from Egypt is thus the abandoning of this world in order to serve God (3.3); it is leaving the image of the earthly man and receiving the image of the heavenly man, laying aside the whole old man with his deeds and putting on the new, who has been created in accordance with God (1.5; 1 Cor. 15:49, Eph. 4:22-24). The Alexandrian theologian often connects Egypt with the notion of 'flesh': it is a symbol of our flesh (1.5); Pharaoh lets the girls live, that is, he wishes to augment what belongs to flesh and bodily matter (2.3). Being a slave to luxury of flesh is called an Egyptian disease (7.2). The sons of Israel, symbol of the rational sense or the virtues of the soul, are forced to do the works of the flesh by the devil's order (1.5). Further, Origen conceives of the Egyptian firstborn as representing the first movements of the soul made according to the flesh, which should be destroyed (4.8). The horses from the Egyptian army are all those who are born in the flesh, while the horsemen are the devil and his angels (6.2). Some interpretations of Origen concern the exegesis of Scripture: the bitterness of the water at Marah, for instance, is the literal interpretation of the law (7.1). At

---

[18] See II § 7.1.
[19] See II § 17.
[20] See Part I. III.
[21] Origen translates, for instance, Amelek as 'people licking out' (*Num. hom.* 19.1), Zipporah, although with regard to the midwife Zipporah, as 'bird' (*Ex. hom.* 2.1), and Pharaoh as 'scatterer' (*Pasc.* 49).
[22] See II § 7.1.

several places in the homilies Moses himself is regarded as the law (2.4, 3.2 etc.).

When we compare this overview of Origen's exegesis of the Egypt theme with Gregory's interpretation, they appear to differ strikingly. Origen's interpretation has hardly left any traces in Gregory, apart from the fact — but this goes without saying — that both share Christian symbolism. A few Philonic interpretations are, however, found in both Origen and Gregory, for instance the explanation of the male as virtue and the female as passions (*Leg.* 3.3, 243, Origen *Ex. hom.* 2.1, 2.3, Gregory *VM* II.2). The point of the Cappadocian father in his exegesis of the theme of Egypt is the struggle of the soul against passions and vices, and this has determined his exegetical focus. We shall see that this notion is also central in two other exegetical themes, namely education and the interpretation of the serpent.

The theme of education also shows Philo's influence. It is brought up at several places by Gregory, appearing for the first time in the exegesis of Moses' basket. Its interpretation as education, which consists of several disciplines, the so-called ἐγκύκλιος παιδεία, can be regarded as a transposition of Philo's exegesis of the work of Bezaleel, which also consists of various disciplines (*Somn.* 1.205).[23] Next Gregory sees in Pharaoh's daughter a symbol of pagan education and philosophy. It seems that he transposes Philo's interpretation of Hagar as school education to Pharaoh's daughter, and Moses' natural mother occupies Sarah's place (*Leg.* 3.244-245). That Gregory uses the same word for Moses' return to his mother as Philo does for Abraham's return to Sarah corroborates the suggestion that Gregory is here indebted to Philo.[24] Furthermore, Gregory transposes Philo's image of a woman who is in the pangs of labour but never gives birth to Pharaoh's daughter.[25] Later on, Moses' wife, originating from an alien people, symbolizes pagan education and philosophy. Gregory, interpreting the circumcision of Moses' son, emphasizes that alien elements in pagan philosophy should be removed (II.37-38). We can here assume the same Philonic background as in the interpretation of Pharaoh's daughter, but we have to take into account that Origen has a comparable interpretation in *Gen. hom.* 11.2, where he interprets a marriage with a woman from a foreign people as the use of pagan disciplines such as literature, grammar,

---

[23] See II § 2.2.
[24] See II § 3.2.
[25] See II § 3.3.

geometry, arithmetic, and dialectic.[26] The idea of the use of pagan education is also brought up in the explanation of the deprivation of the Egyptians. Just as the Jews took away the wealth of the Egyptians in order to build the tabernacle, so one who leads a virtuous life should take the richness of pagan education in order to beautify the divine sanctuary of mystery (II.115). This interpretation is derived from Origen's *Epistula ad Gregorium Thaumaturgum* 1-2 (88B-89B).[27]

The fact that the notion of education appears at several places in *VM* indicates that for Gregory the use of (pagan) education and philosophy is important in the virtuous life. He explains that education, symbolized by Moses' basket, protects against the passions of life (II.7-8). In his interpretation of Moses' wife he remarks that pagan philosophy can be useful for giving birth to virtue, but it has to be purified of wrong ideas. It teaches, for instance, that God exists but also that he is material; this last notion should be rejected as an impure element, just as Moses' wife circumcises her son (II.40).

The third theme in which Philo's influence can be seen is the interpretation of the serpent, which Philo identifies as a symbol of pleasure, for instance in his interpretation of the story with the serpent which appears in paradise and deceives Eve (*Leg.* 2.73). Likewise, in the explanation of the transformation of Moses' staff into a serpent he identifies the beast with passion and pleasure, from which Moses, the lover of virtue, flees (*Leg.* 2.88-93). Gregory does not make use of this exegesis of Philo but conceives of the change as the incarnation of Christ (II.31-34). In a third biblical narrative in which serpents play a role Gregory does partly follow Philo. It concerns the serpents sent by God against the Israelites as a punishment for their complaints (Num. 21:4-9).[28] They are interpreted by Philo as pleasures bringing death, which are overcome by the principle of self-control, symbolized by the serpent made by Moses (*Leg.* 2.76-79). This interpretation does not occur in other Church fathers. Gregory's interpretation, in which the serpents represent desires, proceeds along the same lines, but, according to the Christian tradition based on John 3:14, he sees in the serpent made by Moses a reference to Christ (II.276). As in the other themes, the central idea is the struggle against the passions.

---

[26] See II § 7.3.
[27] See II § 11.
[28] See II § 24.

The fourth theme in which Gregory is indebted to Philo is the interpretation of the royal way (Num. 20:17, 21:22).[29] Gregory connects the
biblical royal way with the Aristotelian definition of virtue as the middle
between two extremes (II.287-290), and it seems that Philo is the only
interpreter before Gregory who also makes this connection. Philo's
metaphorical use of the highway of virtue contrasted with the road-that-is-
no-road is also taken over by Gregory. The interpretation of the Jewish
exegete, in which the notion of virtue is dominant, fits in very well with the
general theme of Gregory's treatise.

3. *Gregory and Philo's* De Vita Moysis

So far we have observed a number of exegetical themes in which Gregory
draws partly on the allegorical writings of his Jewish predecessor. But what
is the relationship with Philo's treatise on Moses' life? Although Gregory's
treatise bears partly the same title, there are significant differences
between the two works. Whereas Philo gives a thematic account of Moses'
life, dealing with him as a philosopher-king in book one, and discussing his
offices of lawgiver, high priest, and prophet in book two, Gregory gives a
literal sketch of Moses' life in book one (*historia*), and allegorizes Moses'
life as the spiritual ascent of the soul in book two (*theoria*). Regarding the
interpretation of Moses' life, it is noticeable that Philo hardly employs
allegorical exegesis, whereas book two of Gregory consists entirely in
allegorical exegesis. This difference in the approach to Moses' life accords
with the difference in goal and aim. It is Philo's aim to make known the
life of the Jewish legislator to people who are ignorant of him (*Mos.* 1.1),
and the treatise seems to be aimed at a broad audience, including non-
Jews. It has an introductory function and should be read before studying
Philo's other writings.[30] The theme of Gregory's treatise, perhaps
addressed to a monk, is the perfection of the virtuous life. It shows how
Moses' life is a model for a life according to virtue that is to be imitated. It
seems to be written for Christian readers. Because of the virtual absence of
allegory in Philo's *Mos.* influence of this work in Gregory is mostly
restricted to phraseology, as we have seen above. The few cases in which
Philo offers a symbolic interpretation, mostly with reference to the Jewish
nation, are explained by Gregory in a different way. Philo interprets, for
instance, the twelve springs and the seventy trees at Elim as the tribes and

---

[29] See II § 27.
[30] See Part I. III.

the elders of the nation (1.189), whereas Gregory sees in them the apostles (II.134).[31] The interpretation of the raising of Moses' hands at the victory over Amalek also relates to the Jewish people: just as in the universe heaven rules over earth, so this nation will be victorious over their adversaries (1.217). In Gregory's interpretation the raising and going down of Moses' hands refer to the spiritual and literal meaning of the law (II.149).[32]

In the framework of the treatment of Moses as high priest, Philo offers an extensive explanation of the tabernacle and its furnishings in cosmological terms (2.77-108). Gregory, though basically not interested in the cosmological exegesis, does invoke it at one point, namely the interpretation of the four colours of the veil as the four elements, combining it with the explication of the veil as the flesh of Christ (Hebr. 10:20) in order to confirm his exegesis of the tabernacle as Christ (II.178).[33] Because Clement of Alexandria and Origen — the latter also refers to the apostle's interpretation of the veil as the flesh of Christ — give the same explanation of the four colours of the veil, it remains unclear whether Gregory depends on Philo directly.

After the interpretation of the tabernacle Philo goes on to explain the vestment of the high priest in a cosmological way as well. The dark blue of the robe refers to the air; the ephod is a symbol of heaven (2.122), and the twelve stones on the high priest's breast represent the twelve signs of the zodiac (2.124). In his treatment of the priest's garments, Gregory, in all likelihood, refers to Philo's interpretation, where he writes that some before him say that the dark-blue of the robe signifies the air. Because this interpretation does not occur in other discussions on the same subject, for instance in those of Josephus and Origen, it is highly probable that Gregory is referring to Philo here. Gregory doubts whether this interpretation is correct, although he does not reject it totally, because it can contribute to the virtuous life. He explains the blue of the robe as referring to the light and airy tunic in which man is clothed when he hears the last trumpet and, having become light, goes on high through the air together with the Lord (1 Thes. 4:16-17). The airy tunic extends from the head to the foot because the law does not wish virtue to be cut short.[34]

The notion of virtue appears also in the final symbolic interpretation from Philo's *Mos.* that has left traces in Gregory, namely the interpretation

---

[31] See II § 14.
[32] See II § 17.
[33] See II § 18.c.1.
[34] See II § 18.d.

of the nut of Aaron's staff. Philo explains that the nut, enclosed by a bitter shell, is not easy to get at (2.182). This is a symbol of the soul striving for virtue which encounters bitter toil; the good, however, springs from toil (2.183). Like Philo, Gregory sees the hardness of the outer part of the nut as referring to the hardness of the virtuous life (II.185).[35] In the same way the bitter water at Marah symbolizes the bitter toil of the beginnings of the virtuous life (*Post.* 154-156), and this interpretation is also taken over by Gregory (II.132).[36]

To sum up, on the exegetical level only two indubitable examples of influence from Philo's *Mos.* on Gregory's *VM* can be found: 1. the dark-blue of the high priest's robe as referring to the air; 2. the hardness of the nut of Aaron's staff as a symbol of the austerity of the virtuous life. Further, the idea of Moses as the example for the virtuous life is also encountered in *Mos.* 1.158-159.[37] Obviously Gregory is not interested in Philo's symbolic interpretation concerning the Jewish people. Likewise the cosmological explanation of the tabernacle, its furnishings, and the priest's vestments has little appeal. He takes over from Philo's explanation in *Mos.* what is useful for his own purpose and adapts his predecessor's interpretation accordingly.

4. *Gregory and Philo's Allegorical Commentary*

In the foregoing we have seen that Philo's *Mos.* is not very influential in Gregory's exegesis, in which Gregory makes more use of other Philonic treatises. In order to answer the question which writings of Philo Gregory specifically uses in his allegorical interpretation the borrowings are listed:

Moses' basket	II.7	*Somn.* 1.205
Pharaoh's daughter	II.11	*Leg.* 3.244-45
Exodus of Egypt	II.26-27	*Her.* 268-272
Pharaoh as lover of passions	II.35	*Leg.* 3.13 etc.
The Israelites' labour	II.60	*Conf.* 83-100
The Egyptian sorcerers	II.63-64	*Det.* 38, *Migr.* 82-85
Marah	II.132	*Post.* 154-157
Serpents as pleasures	II.276	*Leg.* 2.76-81
The royal way	II.287-290	*Deus* 140-181

---

[35] See II § 26.
[36] See II § 13.2.
[37] See Part II. III § 3.

We can extend this list a little by giving the Philonic interpretations that occur also in other Christian writers:

Male and female	II.2	*Leg.* 3.3, 243 etc.
Moses' wife as education	II.38	*Leg.* 3.244-45, *Congr.* 15-18
Doorposts as tripartition of the soul	II.96	*QE* 1.12
Girdle round the loins	II.108	*Leg.* 3.154, *QE* 1.19
Egyptian army	II.122	*Leg.* 2.99-102, *Ebr.* 111
Darkness as God's invisibility	II.163	*Post.* 14, *Mut.* 7

We see that nearly all of these writings belong to the Allegorical Commentary, with the exception of *QE*, which belongs to the Questions and Answers. Treatises that belong to the Exposition of the Law are totally absent. That Gregory mostly makes use of the Allegorical Commentary is not unexpected, for in this series of writings Philo offers the most extensive allegorical interpretations. The same exclusive use of the Allegorical Commentary can be seen in the writings of Origen: Runia lists about twelve places at which Origen refers — although in anonymous terms — to Philonic interpretations from the Allegorical Commentary.[38] For Origen Philo is first and foremost an exegete of Scripture, and our research shows that this is also the case for Gregory. The popularity of the Allegorical Commentary among the Christians appears also from the fact that three papyri found in Egypt and possessed, in all likelihood, by Christians contain treatises of the Allegorical Commentary.[39]

The only work belonging to the Exposition of the Law which Gregory appears to use on a regular basis is the *De opificio mundi*, which he uses in those of his writings that are concerned with the creation account.[40] This work is much more philosophical than the others in the same series. In our context it is noteworthy that Gregory does not make use of the two biographies in the Exposition, of Abraham and Joseph (the other two are lost).

The treatise that occurs more than once in the list of borrowings is *Leg.*, and, as we already have seen, it is this work that also dominates in the Philonic phrases that are not derived from *Mos.* We have to admit, however, that the prominent place of this treatise can be qualified, because some interpretations from *Leg.* occur also in other treatises,[41] and some

---

[38] Runia (1993) 161-163; Van den Hoek (2000).
[39] See Runia (forthcoming), Van Haelst (1976) no 695-696. No 696 (= P.Oxy. 9.1173) contains also *Merced.* (= *Spec.* 1.280-4).
[40] See Part II. I § 2.
[41] For instance, the interpretation of Pharaoh as a lover of the body, see II § 7.1.

belong to the patristic tradition.[42] In spite of this fact it seems that Gregory is mostly indebted to Philo's *Leg.* because, perhaps, this work deals with themes that are attractive for Gregory, for instance the interpretation of the serpent as pleasure (*Leg.* 2.74) and the horses as passions (*Leg.* 2.99). These interpretations fit in very well with the theme of the struggle of the soul against the passions in Gregory's *VM.*

5. *Gregory's Goal in using Philo*

The answer to the question why Gregory feels the need to make such an extensive use of Philo in his interpretation of Moses' life may be found in the scope and aim of his treatise. It is Gregory's goal to show how Moses' life can function as a model for a virtuous life. A life according to virtue consists in the struggle against the passions and the attempt to attain *apatheia* (freedom from passions), which was part of man's original nature created after the image of God.[43] For this reason his exegesis of Moses' life is centred on the theme of fighting against passions. We can call this interpretation ethical: how should one conduct a virtuous life. Parts of the interpretation of Moses' life as given by Philo suit Gregory's theme very well, e.g. the interpretations of Egypt as land of the passions, and of serpents in terms of desire. Because Philo's allegory is more in keeping with his own theme, Gregory stays closer to Philo's line of thought than to Origen's interpretation, though he does make a number of omissions and adaptations. He omits parts of Philo's allegory that do not suit his aim, like the allegorization of Jethro's daughters as the senses, Moses and Aaron as thought and speech, the cosmological interpretation of the tabernacle, and the interpretation of the promised country. Gregory centres on the ethical interpretations of Philo, whereas Philo himself has a broader approach, offering also physical and cosmological explanations.

Even though for both Philo and Gregory Moses is the example of the perfect man, who reaches *apatheia*, and who is honoured with the title 'friend of God' (Ex. 33:11, *Mos* 1.156, *VM* II.319), there are noticeable differences in their views on Moses. For Philo, Moses is the philosopher *par excellence*, the writer of the Torah, leader of the Jewish people in the exodus from Egypt. His special status is described in a digression on his leadership in *Mos.* (1.148-162). Philo presents him as a king and super-sage.[44] Gregory

---

[42] For instance, the interpretation of male and female as virtue and passions, see II § 1.2.
[43] See II § 6.c.
[44] See Part I Introduction.

sees in Moses an example of a virtuous life, presenting him as continuously growing in virtue: Moses ascends higher and higher, which culminates first in his ascent of Mount Sinai and later in his death at the mountain (cf. for instance, II.152, 167, 228, 307). This ascending line in Moses' life is absent in Philo's portrait. This difference can be well seen in the descriptions of Moses' death. In the epilogue Gregory gives a summary of the ascents in Moses' life, writing that he who lifted up his own life through such ascents never failed to become even higher than he was previously (II.307). Moses' death is another ascent. By contrast, Philo does not see Moses' death as a culminating point after many earlier ascents. He tells that at the moment of his death Moses rises up to heaven (*Mos.* 2.291).[45]

6. *Gregory's Working Method*

After the question why Gregory makes use of Philo we have to ask *how* he makes use of Philo; in other words, what is the working method which Gregory employs in his use of Philo. Keywords are *selection, adaptation, transposition,* and *Christianization.* First of all, it is clear that he makes a *selection* from Philo's interpretations: having his own aim in mind, Gregory takes over those aspects from the exegesis of Philo that suit his theme, namely the virtuous life. This theme emerges in a various number of the Philonic texts that Gregory uses. For instance, in *Leg.* 3.3, where the saving of the male children by the midwives is interpreted as building up the affairs of virtue; later on in the same treatise in a passage about Abraham's intercourse with Hagar, Abraham is presented as striving for virtue. In *Post.* 154-157 the bitterness of Marah represents the bitter toil of the virtuous life,[46] and the bitter shell of the nut growing from Aaron's staff is explained in the same way (*Mos.* 2.183).[47] For Gregory the virtuous life consists in the struggle against passions, and other Philonic texts which are used by him are related to this theme. Here we can also refer to two passages from *Leg.*: in 2.77 the serpents from Num. 21 are interpreted as the passions of pleasure,[48] and in *Leg.* 2.99-102 the horses of Pharaoh's army represent the passions (cf. *Ebr.* 111).[49] Further, Philo explains the girdle round the middle as an instrument to restrain the passions (*QE*

---

[45] See II § 30.
[46] See II § 13.
[47] See II § 26.
[48] See II § 24.
[49] See II § 12.4.

1.19).[50] The notion of liberation from the tyranny of the passions is dominant in Philo's exegesis of the brick-making in Egypt (*Conf.* 83-100, cf. *Her.* 268-272).[51] When we see this overview of Philonic texts, it appears that the theme of the virtuous life, which is formed by the fight against passions, is the common denominator.

Gregory, however, does not take over Philo's interpretations wholesale, but, even though he maintains Philo's line of thought in most cases, he makes various *alterations* and *adaptations*. A slight alteration that is characteristic of Gregory's working method can be observed in the exegesis of the serpents from Num. 21: in Philo they represent ἡδονή, whereas Gregory interprets them as ἐπιθυμία. But both pleasure and desire are passions, so Gregory clearly maintains Philo's line of exegesis. At the same time this Philonic interpretation is Christianized: the remedy for the passions is the coming of Christ.[52] An adaptation to Gregory's own aim is discernible in his use of Philo's interpretation of the colour of the high priest's robe. Gregory, taking over Philo's connection of the colour with the air, explains the blue as referring to the airy tunic made by the purity of the virtuous life. In this way he makes an element from Philo's cosmological exegesis serviceable to his own aim and purpose. As in other interpretations, he refers to a relevant passage from the New Testament: man is clothed in the airy tunic when he is carried on high together with the Lord and hears the last trumpet (1 Thess. 4:16-17).[53]

Another procedure that Gregory uses is *transposition*, in which he transposes Philo's interpretation of a biblical object or figure to another object or figure. Following this procedure, he transfers Philo's exegesis of the ark made by Bezaleel to Moses' basket,[54] and Philo's interpretation of Hagar and Sarah to Pharaoh's daughter and Moses' mother.[55] This procedure also occurs in Gregory's use of Philonic imagery: the image of the woman who is in labour, but never gives birth is transposed to Pharaoh's barren daughter.[56]

Finally, as we announced above, Gregory imports *Christian* themes into the Philonic material that he appropriates. A great number of Gregory's Christian interpretations belong to typology: the wood in Marah points to the wood of Christ's cross (II.132), the brazen serpent is a symbol of Christ

---

[50] See II § 10.a.
[51] See II § 8.
[52] See II § 24.
[53] See II. § 18.d.
[54] See II § 2.2.
[55] See II § 3.2.
[56] See II § 3.3.

(II.277), and the bunch of grapes refers to Christ's passion (II.268). All these explanations are part of the wider Christian tradition. But more narrowly characteristic of Gregory's *VM* is the emphasis on Christ's incarnation as bringing about the destruction of the tyranny of the passions and the liberation of the soul (II.27). Gregory interprets the transformation of Moses' staff into a serpent and the change in the colour of his hand (Ex. 4: 1-7) as referring to the coming of Christ (II.28-34). This interpretation seems to be original. Mary's virginity is also underlined: that the bush is not burned denotes that the virginity of Mary is not affected by giving birth (II.21). The same mystery is also indicated by the marvel that the manna is found on the earth, while the earth remains unchanged (II.139).

Setting out our method of research, we mentioned the problem of the so-called 'Gedanke-Zitat'; i.e. Gregory takes over an idea from a predecessor, but he rewords and elaborates it differently so that verbal similarities disappear. In *VM* a number of such 'thought-citations' are discernible. Gregory explains, for instance, the exodus from Egypt as the liberation of the soul from the tyranny of the passions, and the Israelites' labour in Egypt as being involved in the passionate life. We have found that a comparable exegesis occurs in Philo's *Her.* 268-272, where Philo, commenting on God's saying in Gen. 15:13, also interprets the exodus as deliverance from the passions. Although no verbal parallels between the two texts occur, Philo's thought recurs plainly in Gregory's passage, and we can rightly name it a 'thought-citation'. Gregory's interpretation of Pharaoh as a lover of passions and the material life can be regarded as a 'thought-citation' as well. It should be noted, however, that Gregory does quote expressions of Philo, as appears from the overview of Philonic phraseology. In the Philonic exegesis of the Israelite labour, for instance, he gives a definition of clay which is also formulated by Philo in the same context (II. 59; Philo *Conf.* 89).

We have already observed that Gregory mainly makes use of Philo as an exegete of Scripture. Philo allegorically interprets the Pentateuch with the help of contemporary philosophy, mainly Platonism and Stoicism. Gregory, also employing the method of allegorical exegesis, speaks nearly the same philosophical language and for that reason he is able to make use of Philo's exegesis after nearly four centuries. As we have amply seen, however, he is not a slavish and uncritical imitator but makes Philo's exegesis serviceable to his own purpose: to present the virtuous life of a Christian.

ABBREVIATIONS

1. *Philo's Writings*

Abr.	*De Abrahamo*
Aet.	*De aeternitate mundi*
Agr.	*De agricultura*
Anim.	*De animalibus*
Cher.	*De Cherubim*
Cir.	*De circumcisione* (= *Spec.* 1.1-12)
Concup.	*Non concupisces* (= *Spec.* 4.79-135)
Conf.	*De confusione linguarum*
Congr.	*De congressu eruditionis gratia*
Consti.	*De constitutione principum* (= *De justitia* 2 = *Spec.* 4.151-237)
Contempl.	*De vita contemplativa*
Coph.	*De cophini festo* (= *Spec.* 2.215-223)
Decal.	*De Decalogo*
Det.	*Quod deterius potiori insidiari soleat*
Deus	*Quod Deus sit immutabilis*
Ebr.	*De ebrietate*
Exsec.	*De exsecrationibus* (= *Praem.* 127-172)
Flacc.	*In Flaccum*
Fort.	*De fortitudine* (= *Virt.* 1-50)
Fug.	*De fuga et inventione*
Furt.	*De furto* (= *Spec.* 4.1-40)
Gig.	*De gigantibus*
Her.	*Quis rerum divinarum heres sit*
Hom.	*De homicidas* (= *Spec.* 3.83-119)
Hum.	*De humanitate* (= *Virt.* 51-174)
Hypoth.	*Hypothetica*
Ios.	*De Iosepho*
Jud.	*De judice* (= *Spec.* 4.55-78)
Jus. 1	*De justitia* 1 (= *Spec.* 4.136-150)
Jus. 2	*De justitia* 2 (= *Consti.*)
Leg. 1-3	*Legum allegoriae* 1, 2, 3
Legat.	*Legatio ad Gaium*
Merced.	*De mercede meretricis non accipienda in sacrarium* (= *Spec.* 1.280-4)

Migr.	*De migratione Abrahami*
Mon. 1	*De monarchia* 1 (= *Spec.* 1.13-65)
Mon. 2	*De monarchia* 2 (= *Spec.* 1.66-78)
Mos. 1-2	*De vita Moysis* 1, 2
Mut.	*De mutatione nominum*
Nob.	*De nobilitate* (= *Virt.* 187-227)
Opif.	*De opificio mundi*
Paen.	*De paenitentia* (= *Virt.* 175-186)
Par. col.	*De parentibus colendis* (= *Spec.* 2.224-262)
Perh.	*Non perhibetis falsum testimonium* (= *Spec.* 4.41-54)
Piet.	*De pietate*
Plant.	*De plantatione*
Post.	*De posteritate Caini*
Praem.	*De praemiis et poenis*
Prob.	*Quod omnis probus liber sit*
Prov. 1-2	*De Providentia* 1, 2
QE 1-2	*Quaestiones et solutiones in Exodum* 1, 2
QG 1-4	*Quaestiones et solutiones in Genesim* 1, 2, 3, 4
Sac. hon.	*De sacerdotum honoribus* (= *Spec.* 1.131-161)
Sacerd.	*De sacerdotibus* (= *Spec.* 1.79-130)
Sacr.	*De sacrificiis Abelis et Caini*
Sacrif.	*De sacrificantibus* (= *Spec.* 1.257-345)
Sep. 1-2	*De septenario* 1, 2 (= *Spec.* 2.39-40, 41-223)
Sobr.	*De sobrietate*
Somn. 1-2	*De somniis* 1, 2
Spec. 1-4	*De specialibus legibus* 1, 2, 3, 4,
Stup.	*De stupro* (= *Spec.* 3.65-71
Vic.	*De victimis* (= *Spec.* 1.162-256)
Virt.	*De virtutibus*

2. Gregory's Writings

Abl.	*Ad Ablabium quod non sint tres dei*, in: GNO 3.1. 37-57
An. et Res.	*De anima et resurrectione*, in: PG 46.12-160
Bas.	*In Basilium fratrem*, in: GNO 10.1.109-134
Beat.	*De beatitudinibus*, in: GNO 7.2.75-170
Cant.	*In Canticum canticorum*, in: GNO 6
CE	*Contra Eunomium libri I - III*, in: GNO 1, 2.3-311
Deit. Euag.	*De deitate adversus Euagrium*, in: GNO 9.331-341
Deit. fil.	*De deitate filii et spiritus sancti*, in: GNO 10.2.115-144

Diem lum.	*In diem luminum,* in: GNO 9.221-242
Diem nat.	*In diem natalem,* in: GNO 10.2.233-269
Eccl.	*In Ecclesiasten homiliae,* in: GNO 5.277-422
Ep.	*Epistulae,* in: GNO 8.2
Eust.	*Ad Eustathium, De sancta trinitate,* in: GNO 3.1.3-16
Hex.	*Apologia in Hexaemeron,* in: PG 44.61-124
Infant.	*De infantibus praemature abreptis,* in: GNO 3.2.67-97
Inscr. Psal.	*In inscriptiones Psalmorum,* in: GNO 5.24-175
Maced.	*Adversus Macedonianos, De spiritu sancto,* in: GNO 3.1.89-115
Marc.	*Vita s. Macrinae,* in: GNO 8.1.370-414
Mart. Ia, Ib, II	*In XL Martyres* Ia, Ib, II, in: GNO 10.1.135-169
Melet.	*Oratio funebris in Meletium episcopum,* in: GNO 9.441-457
Mort.	*De mortuis oratio,* in: GNO 9.28-68
Opif. hom.	*De hominis opificio,* in: PG 44.125-256
Or. cat.	*Oratio catechetica,* in: GNO 3.4
Or. dom.	*De oratione dominica,* in: GNO 7.2.1-74
Perf.	*De perfectione,* in: GNO 8.1.173-214
Prof.	*De professione Christiana,* in: GNO 8.1.129-142
Ref. Eun.	*Refutatio confessionis Eunomii,* in: GNO 2.312-410
Simpl.	*Ad Simplicium, De fide,* in: GNO 3.1.61-67
Thaum.	*De vita Gregorii Thaumaturgi,* in: GNO 10.1.3-57
Theoph.	*Ad Theophilum, Adversus Apolinaristas,* in: GNO 3.1.119-128
Trid. spat.	*De tridui inter mortem et resurrectionem domini nostri Iesu Christi,* in: GNO 9.273-306
Virg.	*De virginitate,* in: GNO 8.1.247-343, Aubineau (1966)
VM	*De vita Moysis,* in: GNO 7.1, Daniélou (1968), Simonetti (1984)

3. *Other Writings*

Basilius Caesariensis

Auctor	*Quod Deus non est auctor*
Eun.	*Contra Eunomium*
Enar. Es.	*Enarratio in prophetam Esaiam*
Ep.	*Epistula*
Hex. Hom.	*Homiliae in Hexaemeron*
Ieiun.	*De Ieiunio*
Libris	*De legendis gentilium libris*
Ps. hom.	*Homiliae in Psalmos*
Spir. sanc.	*De Spiritu sancto*

Clemens Alexandrinus
Paed.	*Paedagogos*
Prot.	*Protrepticus*
Strom.	*Stromateis*

Eusebius Caesariensis
DE	*Demonstratio evangelica*
Eccl. th.	*De ecclesiastica theologia*
Es. com.	*Commentarii in Esaiam*
HE	*Historia Eccelsiastica*
Intro.	*Generalis elementaria introductio*
Pas.	*De solemnitate Paschali*
PE	*Preparatio evangelica*
Ps. com.	*Commentarii in Psalmos*

Gregorius Nazianzenus
Or.	*Oratio*
Poem. mor.	*Poemata moralia* (= *Poemata theologica* II)

Iosephus
AJ	*Antiquitates Judaicae*
BJ	*Bellum Judaicum*
C. Ap.	*Contra Apionem*

Irenaeus
Adv. Haer.	*Adversus Haereses*
Dem.	*Demonstratio*

Iustinus Martyr
Apo.	*Apologia*
Dial.	*Dialogus cum Tryphone*

Methodius Olympius
Res.	*De resurrectione*
Symp.	*Symposium*

Origenes
Cant. com.	*Commentarii in Canticum canticorum*
CC	*Contra Celsum*
Ep. ad Greg.	*Epistula ad Gregorium Thaumaturgum*
Es. hom.	*Homiliae in Esaiam*
Ex. fr.	*Fragmenta in Exodum*
Ex. hom	*Homiliae in Exodum*
Gen. hom.	*Homiliae in Genesim*
Ier. hom.	*Homiliae in Ieremiam*
Io. com.	*Commentarii in Ioannem*
Ios. hom.	*Homiliae in Iosue*
Lev. hom.	*Homiliae in Leviticum*

Luc. fr.	*Fragmenta in Lucam*
Mat. com.	*Commentarii in Matthaeum*
Num. hom.	*Homiliae in Numeros*
Pasc.	*De Pascha*
Princ.	*De principiis*
Ps. hom.	*Homiliae in Psalmos*
Ps. fr.	*Fragmenta in Psalmos*
Reg. hom.	*Homiliae in primum Regnorum librum*
Rom. com.	*Commentarii in Romanos*

Plato

Phdr.	*Phaedrus*
Rep.	*Respublica*
Symp.	*Symposium*
Theat.	*Theatetus*
Tim.	*Timaeus*

Plotinus

Enn.	*Enneades*

Porphyrius Tyrius

Vita Plot.	*Vita Plotini*

Xenophon

Mem.	*Memorabilia*

4. *Bibliographical Abbreviations*

ALGHJ	Arbeiten zur Literatur und Geschichte des hellenistischen Judentums
ANRW	*Aufstieg und Niedergang der römischen Welt*
BJS	Brown Judaic Studies
CPG	*Clavis Patrum Graecorum*
FC	Fontes Christiani
FHG	Fragmenta Historicorum Graecorum, ed. C. Müllerus
GCS	Die Griechischen Christlichen Schriftsteller der ersten drei Jahrhunderte
GG	Goodhart, H.L. - Goodenough, E.R., 'A general bibliography of Philo Judaeus'
GNO	Gregorii Nysseni Opera
GOThR	*Greek Orthodox Theological Review*
HThR	*Harvard Theological Review*
JSNT.S	Journal for the Study of the New Testament Supplement Series

JThS	*Journal of Theological Studies*
LCL	Loeb Classical Library
LG	*Lexicon Gregorianum*
NTSup	Novum Testamentum Supplements
OCT	Oxford Classical Texts
OPA	Les œuvres de Philon d'Alexandrie
PCH	Philo von Alexandrien: die Werke in deutscher Übersetzung
PG	Patrologia Graeca, ed. J.P. Migne
PLCL	Philo in ten volumes (and two supplementary volumes), LCL
PCW	Philonis Alexandrini opera quae supersunt, ed. L.Cohn-P.Wendland
RAC	*Reallexikon für Antike und Christentum*
RAM	*Revue d'Ascétique et de Mystique*
RE	*Real-Encyclopaedie der classischen Altertumswissenschaft*
RecSR	*Recherches de Science Religieuse*
RevSR	*Revue des Sciences Religieuses*
SBLSPS	*Society of Biblical Literature. Seminar Papers Series*
SC	Sources Chrétiennes
SP	*Studia Patristica*
SPh	*Studia Philonica*
SPhA	*The Studia Philonica Annual*
SVF	Stoicorum Veterum Fragmenta, ed. I. von Arnim
TWNT	*Theologisches Wörterbuch zum Neuen Testament*
VC	*Vigiliae Christianae*
VCSup	Supplements to Vigiliae Christianae

BIBLIOGRAPHY

1. Bibliographies, Indices, Lexica

LEISEGANG, J. *Indices ad Philonis Alexandrini opera.* PCW vol. 7 (Berlin 1926-30).

GOODHART, H.L., and E.R. GOODENOUGH. 'A General Bibliography of Philo Judaeus'. In: E.R. GOODENOUGH. *The Politics of Philo Judaeus: Practice and Theory* (New Haven 1938) 125-321.

EARP, J.W. *Philo Indices to Volumes I-X.* In: PLCL 10.189-520 (Cambridge MA-London 1962).

MAYER, G. *Index Philoneus* (Berlin 1974).

Biblia Patristica. Index des citations et allusions bibliques dans la littérature patristique, 5 vols. and suppl. (Paris 1986-1991).

RADICE, R., and D.T. RUNIA. *Philo of Alexandria: an Annotated Bibliography 1937-1986.* VCSup 8 (Leiden 1988).

ALTENBURGER, M., and F. MANN. *Bibliographie zu Gregor von Nyssa: Editionen – Übersetzungen – Literatur* (Leiden 1988).

BORGEN, P., K. FUGLSETH, K., and R. SKARSTEN. *The Philo Index.* A Complete Greek Word Index to the Writings of Philo of Alexandria Lemmatised & Computer-generated (Michigan-Leiden 2000).

MANN, F., (ed.). *Lexicon Gregorianum.* Wörterbuch zu den Schriften Gregors von Nyssa. Band I – III (Leiden 1999-2001).

RUNIA, D.T. *Philo of Alexandria: an Annotated Bibliography 1987-1996.* VCSup 57 (Leiden 2000).

2. Editions of Philo

Philonis Iudaei in libros Mosis, de mundi opificio, historicos, de legibus; eiusdem libri singulares. Ed. A. TURNEBUS (Paris 1552).

Philonis Iudaei opera quae reperiri potuerunt omnia. Ed. T. MANGEY. 2 vols. (London 1742).

Fragments of Philo Judaeus. Ed. J.R. HARRIS (Cambridge 1886).

Philonis Alexandrini opera quae supersunt. Ed. L. COHN, P. WENDLAND, and S. REITER. 6 vols. (Berlin 1896-1915).

Philo von Alexandrien: die Werke in deutscher Übersetzung. Ed. L. COHN, I. HEINEMANN *et al.* 7 vols. (Breslau/Berlin 1909-64).

Philo in Ten Volumes (and two supplementary volumes). English translation by
F.H. COLSON, G.H. WHITAKER (and R. MARCUS). 12 vols. (London
1929-62).

Les œuvres de Philon d'Alexandrie. Ed. R. ARNALDEZ, J. POUILLOUX, and C.
MONDÉSERT (Paris 1961-92).

3. *Editions of Gregory*

Gregorii Nysseni opera auxilio aliorum virorum doctorum edenda curavit W.
JEAGER (Leiden 1952-).
1. *Contra Eunomium libri*. Ed. W. JEAGER. Pars prior: Libri I et II
   (1960).
2. *Contra Eunomium libri*. Ed. W. JEAGER. Pars altera: Liber III;
   Refutatio confessionis Eunomii (1960).
3.1. Opera dogmatica minora. Pars 1. Ed. FR. MUELLER (1958).
3.2. Opera dogmatica minora. Pars 2. Ed. J.K. DOWNING, J.A.
   MCDONOUGH, and H. HÖRNER (1987).
3.4. Opera dogmatica minora. Pars 4. *Oratio catechetica*. Ed. E. MÜHLEN-
   BERG (1996).
5. *In Inscriptiones Psalmorum; In Sextum Psalmum*. Ed. J. MCDONOUGH.
   In Ecclesiasten Homiliae. Ed. P. ALEXANDER (1986).
6. *In Canticum canticorum*. Ed. H. LANGERBECK (1986).
7.2. *De oratione dominica; De beatitudinibus*. Ed. J.F. CALLAHAN (1992).
8.1. Opera ascetica, Ed. W. JAEGER, J.P. CAVARNOS, and V.W. CALLA-
   HAN (1986).
8.2. *Epistulae*. Ed. G. PASQUALI (1959).
9. Sermones. Pars 1. Ed. G. HEIL, A. VAN HECK, E. GEBHARDT, and A.
   SPIRA (1967, 1992).
10.1. Sermones. Pars 2. Ed. G. HEIL, J.P. CAVARNOS, and O. LENDLE
   (1989).
10.2. Sermones. Pars 3. Ed. E. RHEIN, F. MANN, D. TESKE, and H.
   POLACK (1996).

3.1 *Gregory's De Vita Moysis*

Grégoire de Nysse La vie de Moïse ou Traité de la perfection en matière de vertu,
introduction, texte critique et traduction de J. DANIÉLOU, SC 1 (Paris
1942, 1955², 1968³).

Gregor von Nyssa Der Aufstieg des Moses. Übersetzt und eingeleitet von M.
BLUM (Freiburg i. Br. 1963).

Gregorii Nysseni De vita Moysis. Ed. H. MUSURILLO. GNO 7.1 (Leiden 1964, 1991).

Gregory of Nyssa The Life of Moses, translation, introduction and notes by A. J. MALHERBE, and E. FERGUSON. The Classics of Western Spirituality (New York 1978).

Gregorio di Nissa Le vita di Mosè. A cura di M. SIMONETTI (Milano 1984).

Gregorio de Nisa, Sobre la vida de Moisés. Introducción, traducción y notas de LUCAS F. MATEO-SECO (Madrid 1993).

4. *Other Authors*

ARISTOTELES
Ethica Nicomachea. Ed. I. BYWATER. OCT (Oxford 1894, repr. 1970).

BASILIUS CAESARENSIS
PG 29-32 (Paris 1886, 1888, 1885, 1886).

Homélies sur l'hexaéméron. Ed. S. GIET. SC 26 (Paris).

Contre Eunome, suivi de Eunome, Apologie. Ed. B. SESBOÜÉ, G.-M. DE DURAND, and L. DOUTRELEAU. 2 vols. SC 299, 305 (Paris 1982-83).

De spiritu sancto. Über den heiligen Geist. Ed. H.J. SIEBEN. FC 12 (Freiburg i. Br. 1993).

The Letters, with an English translation by R. J. DEFERRARI. 4 vols. LCL (Cambridge MA-London 1926-34).

CLEMENS ALEXANDRINUS
Stromata 1-6. Ed. O. STÄHLIN, and L. FRÜCHTEL. GCS 52 (Berlin 1960).

Stromata 7-8. Ed. O. STÄHLIN, L. FRÜCHTEL, and U. TREU. GCS 17 (Berlin 1970).

Les Stromates. Stromate V. 2 vols. Ed. A. LE BOULLUEC, and P. VOULET. SC 278, 279 (Paris 1981).

Les Stromates VII, ed. A. LE BOULLUEC. SC 428 (Paris 1997).

Le Pédagogue. Livre I. Ed. H.I. MARROU, and M. HARL. SC 70 (Paris 1960).

Le Pédagogue. Livre II. Ed. C. MONDÉSERT, and H.I. MARROU. SC 108 (Paris 1965).

Le Pédagogue. Livre III. Ed. C. MONDÉSERT, C. MATRAY, and H.I. MARROU. SC 158 (Paris 1970).

Le Protreptique. Ed. C. MONDÉSERT. SC 2 (Paris 1976).

DIOGENES LAERTIUS
Lives of Eminent Philosophers. With an English translation by R.D. HICKS. 2 vols., LCL (Cambridge MA-London 1925).

EUNOMIUS
The Extant Works. Ed. R.P. VAGGIONE. Oxford Early Christian Texts (Oxford 1987).
EUSEBIUS CAESARENSIS
PG 23, 24 (Paris 1857).
Werke, IV, Gegen Marcell; Über die Kirchliche Theologie; Die Fragmente Marcells. Ed. E. KLOSTERMANN. Zweite Auflage G.C. HANSEN. GCS (Berlin 1972).
Werke, VIII, Die Praeparatio evangelica. 2 vols. Ed. K. MRAS. GCS (Berlin 1954, 1956).
Werke, IX, Der Jesajakommentar. Ed. J. ZIEGLER. GCS (Berlin 1975).
The Ecclesiastical History with an English translation by K. LAKE. Vol. 1. LCL (Cambridge MA-London 1926).
EZEKIEL TRAGICUS
The Exagoge of Ezekiel, by H. JACOBSON (Cambridge 1983).
GREGORIUS NAZIANZENUS
PG 35-38 (Paris 1857, 1858, 1860, 1862).
Discours 1 – 3. Ed. J. BERNARDI. SC 247 (Paris 1978).
Discours 6-12. Ed. M.-A. CALVET-SEBASTI. SC 405 (Paris 1995).
Discours 20-23. Ed. J. MOSSAY. SC 270 (Paris 1980).
Discours 24-26. Ed. J. MOSSAY. SC 284 (Paris 1981).
Discours 27-31. Ed. P. GALLAY. SC 250 (Paris 1978).
Discours 32-37. Ed. C. MORESCHINI, and P. GALAY. SC 318 (Paris 1985).
Discours 38-41. Ed. C. MORESCHINI, and P. GALLY. SC 358 (Paris 1990).
Discours 42-43. Ed. J. BERNARDI. SC 384 (Paris 1992).
Lettres. Ed. P. GALLAY. 2 vols. (Paris 1967).
GREGORIUS THAUMATURGUS
Remerciement à Origène. Lettre d'Origène à Grégoire. Ed. H. CROUZEL, SC 148 (Paris 1969).
HERACLITUS
Die Fragmente der Vorsokratiker. Ed. H. DIELS, and W. KRANZ. Vol. 1 (Dublin-Zürich 1966[12]).
HERMETICA
Hermetica. Ed. with English translation and notes by W. SCOTT. (Oxford 1924-1936 repr. Boston 1993).
HOMERUS
Ilias. Ed. D.B. MONRO, and W. ALLEN. OCT, 2 vols. (Oxford 1920[3]).
IAMBLICHUS
De vita Pythagorica. Ed. L. DEUBNER (Leipzig 1937).
IOANNES CHRYSOSTOMUS
Sur l'incompréhensibilité de Dieu. Ed. J. DANIÉLOU, A.M. MALINGREY, and R. FLACELIÈRE. SC 28bis (Paris 1970).

IOSEPHUS
Josephus, with an English translation by H. St. J. THACKERAY, and R. MARCUS. 9 vols., LCL (Cambridge MA-London 1926-65).

IRENAEUS
Epideixis/Adversus Haereses. Ed. N. BROX. FC 8, 4 vols. (Freiburg i. Br. 1993-97).

IULIANUS IMPERATOR
Oevres Complètes II.I: discours de Julien Empereur. Ed. G. ROCHEFORT (Paris 1963).

IUSTINUS MARTYR
Opera. Ed. J.C.T. OTTO. 2 vols. (Jena 1842-43).

LUCIANUS
Opera, vol. 1,. Ed. C. JACOBITZ (Leipzig 1921).

MARCUS AURELIUS
The Communings with himself of Marcus Aurelius Antoninus together with his Speeches and Sayings. Ed. C.R. HAINES. LCL (Cambridge MA-London 1930).

METHODIUS
Methodius. Ed. G. N. BONWETSCH. GCS (Leipzig 1917).

ORIGENES
PG 12, 17 (Paris 1857).

Contre Celse. Ed. M. BORRET. 5 vols., SC 132, 136, 147, 150, 227 (Paris 1967-76).

Vier Bücher von den Prinzipien. Ed. H. GÖRGEMANS, and H. KARPP. Texte zur Forschung 24 (Darmstadt 1992).

Sur la Pâque. Traité inédit publié d'après un papyrus de Toura par O. GUÉRAUD, and P. NAUTIN (Paris 1979).

Homelien zum Hexateuch in Rufins Übersetzung. Ed. W.A. BAEHRENS. 2 vols., GCS 29, 30 (Berlin 1920-21).

Homélies sur la Genèse. Ed. L. DOUTRELEAU. SC 7 bis (Paris 1996).

Homélies sur l'Exode. Ed. M. BORRET. SC 321 (Paris 1985).

Homélies sur le Lévitique. Ed. M. BORRET. 2 vols., SC 286, 287 (Paris 1981).

Homélies sur les Nombres. Ed. L. DOUTRELEAU. 3 vols. SC 415, 442, 461 (Paris 1996–2001).

Homélies sur Josué. Ed. A. JAUBERT. SC 71 (Paris 1960).

Homélies sur Jérémie. Ed. P. HUSSON, and P. NAUTIN. 2 vols. SC 232, 238 (Paris 1976-77).

Homélies sur les Psaumes 36 à 38. Ed. E. PRINZIVALLI, H. CROUZEL, and L. BRÉSARD. SC 411 (Paris 1995).

Commentaire sur le Cantique des Cantiques. Ed. L. BRÉSARD, and H. CROUZEL. 2 vols. SC 375, 376 (Paris 1991-92).

Commentaire sur St. Jean. Tome I (Livres i-v). Ed. C. BLANC. SC 120bis (Paris 1996).

Commentaire sur St. Jean. Tome II (Livres vi et x). Ed. C. BLANC. SC 157 (Paris 1970).

Commentaire sur St. Jean. Tome V (Livres xxviii et xxxii). Ed. C. BLANC. SC 385 (Paris 1992).

Commentarii in Epistulam ad Romanos, Römerbriefkommentar. Ed. T. HEITHER. 5 vols. FC 2 (Freiburg i. Br. 1990-96).

PLATO

Platonis Opera. Ed. J. BURNET 5 vols. OCT (Oxford 1900-07).

PLOTINUS

Plotini Opera. Ed. P. HENRY, and H.-R. SCHWYZER. 3 vols. OCT (Oxford 1964-82).

Plotinus, with an English translation by A.H. ARMSTRONG. 7 vols. LCL (Cambridge MA-London 1966-88).

PROCOPIUS GAZAEUS

PG 87 (Paris 1860).

PSEUDO-CLEMENTINA

Die Pseudoklementinen II, *Rekognitionen* in Rufins Übersetzung.. Ed. B. REHM, and G. STRECKER. GCS (Berlin 1994).

RABBINICA

Midrash Rabbah Exodus. Translated by S.M. LEHRMAN. (London-Bourne-mouth 1951).

STOBAEUS, JOANNIS

Anthologium. Ed. C. WACHSMUTH, and O. HENSE. 5 vols. (Berlin 1884-1912).

STOICI

Stoicorum Veterum Fragmenta. Ed. I. VON ARNIM. 4 vols. (Stuttgart 1903-24, repr. 1978-1979).

XENOPHON

Opera omnia, vol. 2. Ed. E.C. MARCHANT. OCT (Cambridge 1921, repr. 1983).

Scripta minora. With an English translation by E.C. MARCHANT. LCL (Cambridge MA-London 1925).

5. General Bibliography

ABRAMOWSKI, L. Art. 'Eunomios'. In: *RAC* 6 (Stuttgart 1966) 936-947.

ALEXANDRE, M. *Philon d'Alexandrie De congressu eruditionis gratia.* OPA 16 (Paris 1967).

——. 'La théorie de l'exégèse dans le *De Hominis opificio* et l' *In Hexaemeron*'. In: HARL (1971) 87-110.

——. 'De grec au latin: Les titres des œuvres de Philo d'Alexandrie'. In: J.-C. FREDOUILLE *et al. Titres et articulations de texte dans les œuvres antiques.* Actes du Colloque International de Chantilly, 13-15 décembre 1994 (Paris 1997) 255-285.

AMIR, Y. *Die hellenistische Gestalt des Judentums bei Philon von Alexandrien* (Neukirchen 1983).

ANDIA, Y. DE. *Henosis. L'union à Dieu chez Denys l'Aréopagite.* Philosophia Antiqua 71 (Leiden 1996).

ARNALDEZ, R., C. MONDÉSERT, J. POUILLOUX, AND P. SAVINEL. *Philon d'Alexandrie De vita Moysis* I-II. OPA 22 (Paris 1967).

AUBINEAU, M. 'Le thème du bourbier dans la littérature grecque profane et chrétienne'. *RecSR* 47 (1959) 185-215.

——. *Grégoire de Nysse Traité de la virginité.* SC 119 (Paris 1966).

BAER, R.A. *Philo's Use of the Categories Male and Female.* ALGHJ 3 (Leiden 1970).

BALÁS, D.L. Μετουσία Θεοῦ. *Man's Participation in God's Perfections according to Saint Gregory of Nyssa.* Studia Anselmiana 55 (Rome 1966).

——. 'Eternity and Time in Gregory of Nyssa's *Contra Eunomium*'. In: DÖRRIE, ALTENBURGER and SCHRAMM (1976) 128-155.

BALTHASAR, H. VON. *Présence et pensée. Essai sur la philosophie religieuse de Grégoire de Nysse* (Paris 1942).

BARCLAY, J.M.G. 'Manipulating Moses: Exodus 2:10-15 in Egyptian Judaism and the New Testament'. In: R. CARROLL (ed.). *Text as Pretext: Essays in Honour of Robert Davidson.* Journal for the Study of the Old Testament Supplement Series 138 (Sheffield 1992) 28-46.

BARDENHEWER, O. *Geschichte der altkirchlichen Literatur.* 5 vols. (Freiburg i. Br. 1913-32).

BARNES, M.R. 'Eunomius of Cyzicus and Gregory of Nyssa: Two Traditions of Transcendent Causality'. *VC* 52 (1998) 59-87.

BASKIN, J.R. 'Origen on Balaam: the Dilemma of the Unworthy Prophet'. *VC* 37 (1983) 22-35.

BEAUCHAMP, P. 'La cosmologie religieuse de Philon et la lecture de l'Exode par le Livre de la Sagesse: le thème de la manne'. In: *Philon d'Alexandrie* (1967) 207-218.

BIENERT, W. A. *'Allegoria' und 'Anagoge' bei Didymos dem Blinden von Alexandria.* Patristische Texte und Studien 13 (Berlin 1972).

BILLINGS, T.H. *The Platonism of Philo Judaeus* (diss. Chicago 1919).

BIRNBAUM, E. 'What does Philo mean by "Seeing God"? Some Methodological Considerations'. *SBLSPS* 34 (1995) 535-552.

——. *The Place of Judaism in Philo's Thought. Israel, Jews, and Proselytes.* BJS 290 (Atlanta 1996).

BITTER, R.A. 'De androgynie van de mens bij Philo van Alexandrië, Clemens van Alexandrië, Origenes en de Russische Orthodoxie'. In: G. QUISPEL (ed.). *De Hermetische Gnosis in de loop der eeuwen* (Baarn 1992) 53-95.

BLANC, C. *Origène Commentaire sur St. Jean. Tome I (Livres i-v).* SC 120bis (Paris 1996).

BÖHM, T. 'Die Wahrheitskonzeption in der Schrift *De vita Moysis* von Gregor von Nyssa'. *SP* 27 (1993) 9-13.

——. *Theoria Unendlichkeit Aufstieg. Philosophische Implikationen zu* De vita Moysis *von Gregor von Nyssa.* VCSup 35 (Leiden 1996).

BORGEN, P. *Bread from Heaven. An Exegetical Study of the Concept of Manna in the Gospel of John and the Writings of Philo.* NTSup 10 (Leiden 1965).

——. 'Philo of Alexandria: a Critical and Synthetical Survey of Research since World War II'. *ANRW* II 21.1 (Berlin-New York 1984a) 98-154.

——. 'Philo of Alexandria'. In: M.E. STONE (ed.). *Jewish Writings of the Second Temple Period: Apocrypha, Pseudepigrapha, Qumran Sectarian Writings, Philo, Josephus* (Assen 1984b) 233-282.

——. *Philo of Alexandria. An Exegete for his Time.* NTSup 86 (Leiden 1997).

BORRET, M. *Origène Homélies sur l'Exode.* SC 321 (Paris 1985).

BORNKAMM. Art. 'μυστήριον'. In: *TWNT* 4 (Stuttgart 1942).

BOTTE, B. 'La vie de Moïse par Philon'. *Cahiers Sioniens* 8 (1954) 173-180.

BRÉHIER, É. *Les idées philosophiques et religieuses de Philon d'Alexandrie* (Paris 1908).

BRIGHTMAN, R.S. 'Apophatic Theology and Divine Infinity in St. Gregory of Nyssa'. *GOThR* 18 (1973) 97-114.

BROEK, R. VAN DEN, T. BAARDA, and J. MANSFELD. *Knowledge of God in the Graeco-roman World.* Études préliminaires aux religions orientales dans l'Empire romain 112 (Leiden 1988).

BROOKS, J.A. *The New Testament Text of Gregory of Nyssa* (Atlanta 1991).

BROTTIER, L. 'L' épisode des fléaux d' Egypte (Ex. 7-11) lu par Philon d'Alexandrie et les Pères Grecs'. *Recherches Augustiniennes* 24 (1989) 39-64.

BURDACH, K. 'Faust und Moses', *Sitzungsberichte der preußischen Akademie der Wissenschaften, Philosophisch-historische Klasse* 23, 35, 36 (1912) 358-403, 627-659, 736-89.

BURRIDGE, R. A. *What are the Gospels? A Comparison with Graeco-Roman Biography* (Cambridge 1992).

CANÉVET, M. *Grégoire de Nysse et l'herméneutique biblique* (Paris 1983).

CARABINE, D. *The Unknown God. Negative Theology in the Platonic Tradition: Plato to Eriugena.* Louvain Theological and Pastoral Monographs 19 (Leuven-Grand Rapids 1995).

CHESNUT, G.F. 'The Ruler and the Logos in Neopythagorean, Middle Platonic and Late Stoic Political Philosophy'. *ANRW* II.16.2 (Berlin-New York 1978) 1310-1332.

——. *The First Christian Histories: Eusebius, Socrates, Sozomen, Theodoret, and Evagrius* (Macon 1986²).

COHEN, J. *The Origins and Evolution of the Moses Nativity Story.* Numen Book Series 58 (Leiden 1993).

COHN, L. *Einteilung und Chronologie der Schriften Philos* (Leipzig 1899).

COHN, L., P. WENDLAND, and S. REITER. *Philonis Alexandrini opera quae supersunt.* 6 vols. (Berlin 1896-1915).

CROUZEL, H. 'Grégoire de Nysse est-il le fondateur de la théologie mystique? Une controverse récente'. *RAM* 33 (1957) 189-202.

——. 'Le thème du mariage mystique chez Origène et ses sources'. *Studia Missionalia* 26 (1977) 37-57.

DÄHNE, A.F. 'Einige Bemerkungen über die Schriften des Juden Philo'. *Theologische Studien und Kritieken* 6 (1833) 984-1040.

DALEY, B.E. '"Bright Darkness" and Christian Transformation: Gregory of Nyssa on the Dynamics of Mystical Union'. *SPhA* 8 (1996) 83-98.

D'ANGELO, M.R. *Moses in the Letter to the Hebrews.* Society of Biblical Literature. Dissertation Series 42 (Missoula 1979).

DANIÉLOU, J. *Sacramentum futuri. Études sur les origines de la typologie biblique* (Paris 1950).

——. 'Ἀκολουθία chez Grégoire de Nysse'. *RevSR* 27 (1953a) 219-249, cf. (1970) 19-49.

——. 'Mystique de la ténèbre chez Grégoire de Nysse'. In: *Dictionnaire de spiritualité* 2 (Paris 1953b) 1872-1885.

——. *Platonisme et théologie mystique. Doctrine spirituelle de saint Grégoire de Nysse* (Paris 1944, 1954²a).

——. 'Moïse. Exemple et figure chez Grégoire de Nysse'. *Cahiers Sioniens* 8 (1954b) 385-400.

——. 'La colombe et la ténèbre dans la mystique byzantine ancienne'. *Eranos Jahrbuch* 23 (1954c) 389-418.

——. 'La chronologie des sermons de Saint Grégoire de Nysse'. *RevSR* 29 (1955) 346-372.

——. 'Le mariage de Grégoire de Nysse et la chronologie de sa vie'. *Revue des Études Augustiniennes* 3 (1956) 71-78.

——. 'Trinité et angélologie dans la théologie Judéo-Chrétienne'. *RecSR* 45 (1957) 5-41.

——. 'La notion de confins (*methorios*) chez Grégoire de Nysse'. *RecSR* 49 (1961) 161-187.

——. 'Grégoire de Nysse à travers les lettres de Saint Basile et de Saint Grégoire de Nazianze'. *VC* 19 (1965a) 31-41.

——. 'Bulletin d'histoire des origines Chrétiennes'. *RecSR* 53 (1965b) 296-298.

——. 'La chronologie des œuvres de Grégoire de Nysse'. *SP* 7 (1966) 159-69.

——. 'Philon et Grégoire de Nysse'. In: *Philon d'Alexandrie* (1967a) 333-345.

——. 'Les tuniques de peau chez Grégoire de Nysse'. In: G. MÜLLER, and W. ZELLER (eds.). *Glaube, Geist, Geschichte. Festschrift für Ernst Benz zum 60. Geburtstage am 17. November 1967* (Leiden 1967b) 355-367.

——. *Grégoire de Nysse La vie de Moïse*. SC 1 (Paris 1942, 1955², 1968³).

——. Art. 'Exodus'. In: *RAC* 7 (Stuttgart 1969) 22-44.

——. *L'être et le temps chez Grégoire de Nysse* (Leiden 1970).

——. 'Orientations actuelles de la recherche sur Grégoire de Nysse', In: HARL (1971) 3-17.

——. 'La θεωρία chez Grégoire de Nysse'. *SP* 11 (1972) 130-145; repr. in (1970) 1-17.

DANIÉLOU, J., A.-M. MALINGREY, and R. FLACELIÈRE. *Jean Chrysostome Sur l'incompréhensibilité de Dieu*. SC 28bis (Paris 1970).

DEVREESSE, R. *Les anciens commentateurs grecs des Psaumes*. Studi e Testi 264 (Città del Vaticano 1970).

DIEKAMP, F. *Die Gotteslehre des heiligen Gregor von Nyssa. Theil I* (Münster 1896).

——. 'Literaturgeschichtliches zur Eunomianischen Kontroverse'. *Byzantinische Zeitschrift* 18 (1909) 1-13, 190-194.

DILLON, J.M. 'The Knowledge of God in Origen'. In: VAN DEN BROEK, BAARDA and MANSFELD (1988) 219-228.

——. *The Middle Platonists. 80 B.C. to A.D. 220*. Revised edition with a new afterword (London 1996).

DÖRRIE, H. Art. 'Gregor von Nyssa'. in: *RAC* 12 (Stuttgart 1983) 863-895.

DÖRRIE, H., M. ALTENBURGER, and U. SCHRAMM. *Gregor von Nyssa und die Philosophie. Zweites Internationales Kolloquium über Gregor von Nyssa* (Leiden 1976).

DORIVAL, G. *Les Nombres. Traduction du texte grec de la Septante, Introduction et Notes. La bible d'Alexandrie* 4 (Paris 1994).

DOWNING, F.G. 'Ontological Asymmetry in Philo and Christological Realism in Paul, Hebrews and John'. *Journal of Theological Studies* 41 (1990) 423-440.

DROBNER, H. 'Die Deutung des alttestamentlichen Pascha (Ex. 12) bei Gregor von Nyssa im Lichte der Auslegungstradition der griechischen Kirche'. In: H.R. DROBNER, and CHR. KLOCK (eds.). *Studien zu Gregor von Nyssa und der christlichen Spätantike*. VCSup 12 (Leiden 1990).

DÜRING, I. *Aristotle in the Ancient Biographical Tradition* (Göteborg 1957).

DÜNZL, F. 'Gregor von Nyssa's Homilien zum Canticum auf dem Hintergrund seiner Vita Moysis'. *VC* 44 (1990) 371-381.

——. *Braut und Bräutigam. Die Auslegung des Canticum durch Gregor von Nyssa* (Tübingen 1993).

ELERT, W. *Der Ausgang der altkirchlichen Christologie*. Eine Untersuchung über Theodor von Pharan und seine Zeit als Einführung in die alte Dogmengeschichte (Berlin 1957).

ELLIS, E.E. 'Χριστός in 1 Corinthians 10.4-9'. In: M.C. DE BOER (ed.). *From Jesus to John; Essays on Jesus and New Testament Christology in Honour of Marinus de Jonge*. JSNT.S 84 (Sheffield 1993) 168-173.

FABRICIUS, J.A. *Bibliotheca Graeca* (Hamburg 1705-28, 1795⁴).

FERGUSON, E. 'God's Infinity and Man's Mutability: Perpetual Progress according to Gregory of Nyssa'. *GOThR* 18 (1973) 59-78.

FESTUGIÈRE, A.J. *La révélation d'Hermes Trismégiste, 4 Le Dieu inconnu et la gnose* (Paris 1954).

FONTAINE, J., and C. KANNENGIESSER, (eds.). *Epektasis. Mélanges patristiques offerts au Cardinal J. Daniélou* (Paris 1972).

FRASER, P.M. *Ptolemaic Alexandria*. 3 vols. (Oxford 1972).

GAÏTH, J. *La conception de la liberté chez Grégoire de Nysse* (Paris 1953).

GALLAY, P. *Grégoire de Nazianze Discours 27-31*. SC 250 (Paris 1978).

GAMBLE, H. Y. *Books and Readers in the Early Church: a History of Early Christian Texts* (New Haven 1995).

GARRISON, R. *The Graeco-Roman Context of Early Christian Literature*. JSNT.S 137 (Sheffield 1997).

GFRÖRER, A.F. *Philo und die jüdisch-alexandrinische Theosofie*. 2 vols. (Stuttgart 1835²).

GINZBERG, L. *The Legends of the Jews*. 7 vols. (Philadelphia 1909-38).

GOBRY, I. 'La ténèbre (γνόφος): l'héritage alexandrin de Saint Grégoire de Nysse'. *Diotima: Revue de recherche philosophique* 19 (1991) 79-82.

GOODENOUGH, E.R. 'The Political Philosophy of Hellenistic Kingship'. *Yale Classical Studies* 1 (1928) 55-102.

——. 'Philo's Exposition of the Law and his *De vita Moysis*'. *HThR* 27 (1933) 109-125.

——. *An Introduction to Philo Judaeus* (Oxford 1962).

GRABBE, L. *Etymology in Early Jewish Interpretation: the Hebrew Names in Philo*. BJS 115 (Atlanta 1988).

GRANT, R.M. 'Theological Education at Alexandria', in: B.A. PEARSON, and J.E. GOEHRING (eds.). *The Roots of Egyptian Christianity* (Philadelphia 1986) 178-198.

GUYOT, H. *L'infinité divine depuis Philon le Juif jusque'à Plotin*. Thèse (Paris 1906).

HAELST, J. VAN *Catalogue des papyrus littéraires juifs et chrétiens* (Paris 1976).

HÄGG, T. *The Novel in Antiquity* (Oxford 1983).

HARL, M. Review of GNO 7.1. De Vita Moysis. Ed. Musurillo. *Gnomon* 38 (1966).

——. 'Les trois quarantaines de la vie de Moïse, schéma idéal de la vie du moine-évêque chez les Pères Cappadociens'. *Revue des Études Grecques* 80 (1967) 407-412.

——. (ed), *Écriture et culture philosophique chez Grégoire de Nysse. Actes du colloque de Chevetogne (22 – 26 Septembre 1969).* (Leiden 1971).

——. 'Citations et commentaires d'Exode 3, 14 chez les Pères Grecs des quatre premiers siècles'. In: VIGNAU (1978) 87-108.

——. 'Le nom de l' arce de Noé dans la Septante'. In: *AΛEXANΔPINA: hellénisme, judaïsme et christianisme à Alexandrie; mélanges offerts à Claude Mondésert* (Paris 1987) 15-43.

HECK, A. VAN. *Gregorii Nysseni De pauperibus amandis, orationes duo* (Leiden 1964).

HEIBGES. Art. 'Hermippos, der Kallimacher'. In: *RE* 8.844-854 (Stuttgart 1913).

HEINE, R.E. *Perfection in the Virtuous Life. A Study of the Relationship between Edification and Polemical Theology in Gregory of Nyssa's De Vita Moysis* (Cambridge MA 1975).

——. *Origen Homilies on Genesis and Exodus.* The Fathers of the Church 71 (Washington 1982).

HEINEMANN, I. 'Die Lehre vom ungeschriebenen Gesetz im Jüdischen Schrifttum'. *Hebrew Union College Annual* 4 (1927) 149-171.

HENRICHS, A. 'Philosophy, the Handmaiden of Theology'. *Greek, Roman, and Byzantine Studies* 9 (1968) 437-450.

HILGERT, E. 'The Quaestiones: Texts and Translations'. In: D.M. HAY (ed.). *Both Literal and Allegorical: Studies in Philo of Alexandria's Questions and Answers on Genesis and Exodus.* BJS 232 (Atlanta 1991) 1-15.

HILHORST, A. 'Was Philo Read by Pagans? The Statement on Heliodorus in Socrates *Hist. Eccl.* 5.22'. *SPhA* 4 (1992) 75-77.

HOEK, A. VAN DEN. *Clement of Alexandria and his Use of Philo in the Stromateis: an Early Christian Reshaping of a Jewish Model.* VCSup 3 (Leiden 1988).

——. 'How Alexandrian was Clement of Alexandria? Reflections on Clement and his Alexandrian Background'. *Heythrop Journal* 31 (1990) 179-194.

——. 'Techniques of Quotation in Clement of Alexandria. A View of Ancient Literary Working Methods'. *VC* 50 (1996) 223-243.

——. 'The "Catechetical" School of Early Christian Alexandria and its Philonic Heritage'. *HThR* 90 (1997) 59-87.

——. 'Philo and Origen: a Descriptive Catalogue of their Relationship'. *SPhA* 12 (2000) 44-121.

HÖRNER, H. 'Über genese und derzeitigen Stand der großen Edition,der Werke Gregors von Nyssa'. In: HARL (1971) 18-50.

HORN, G. 'Le 'miroir', la 'nuée': deux manières de voir Dieu après Grégoire de Nysse'. *RAM* 8 (1927) 113-131.

HORN, H.J. Art. 'Gottesbeweis'. In: *RAC* 11 (Stuttgart 1981) 951-977.

HOUTMAN, C. 'Exodus 4:24-26 and its Interpretation'. *Journal of Northwest Semitic Languages* 11 (1983) 81-105.

——. *Exodus. Vertaald en verklaard.* Commentaar op het Oude Testament, 3 vols. (Kampen 1986-96).

HUNT, A.S. (ed.). *The Oxyrhynchus Papyri* IX (London 1912).

JACOBSON, H. *The Exagoge of Ezekiel* (Cambridge 1983).

KAMESAR, A. 'San Basilio, Filone, e la tradizione ebraica'. *Henoch* 17 (1995) 129-139.

KARPP, H. Art. 'Bileam'. In: *RAC* 2 (Stuttgart 1954) 362-373.

KEES, R.J. *Die Lehre von der Oikonomia Gottes in der* Oratio catechetica *Gregors von Nyssa.* VCSup 30 (Leiden 1995).

KEIZER, H.M. *Life Time Entirety. A Study of* αἰών *in Greek Literature and Philosophy, the Septuagint and Philo* (diss. Amsterdam 1999).

KRAPPE, A.H. 'Tiberius and Thrasyllus'. *American Journal of Philology* 48 (1927) 359-366.

KREITZER, L. '1 Corinthians 10:4 and Philo's Flinty Rock'. *Communio Viatorum* 35 (1993) 109-126.

KUGEL, J.L. *The Bible as it was* (Cambridge MA-London 1997).

LE BOULLUEC, A. *Clément d'Alexandrie Les Stromates V.* 2 vols. SC 278, 279 (Paris 1981).

——. 'Moïse menacé de mort. L'énigme d'Exode 4, 24-26 d'après la Septante et selon les Pères'. *Cahiers de la Biblia Patristica* 1 (Strasbourg 1987) 75-104.

LE BOULLUEC, A., and P. SANDEVOIR. *L'Exode. Traduction du texte grec de la Septante, Introduction et Notes.* La bible d'Alexandrie 2 (Paris 1989).

LEVISON, J.R. 'Inspiration and the Divine Spirit in the Writings of Philo Judaeus'. *Journal for the Study of Judaism* 26 (1995a) 271-323.

——. 'The Prophetic Spirit as an Angel according to Philo'. *HThR* 88 (1995b) 189-207.

LILLA, S. 'La theologia negativa dal pensiero classico a quello patristico bizantino'. *Helicon* 22-27 (1982-87) 211-279.

LIPATOV, N.A. 'The Problem of the Authorship of the Commentary on the Prophet Isaiah attributed to St. Basil the Great'. *SP* 27 (1993) 42-48.

LORENZ, A. *Arius Judaizans?* Untersuchungen zur dogmengeschichtlichen Einordnung des Arius (Göttingen 1979).

LOUTH, A. *The Origins of the Christian Mystical Tradition. From Plato to Denys* (Oxford 1981).

LUNDBERG, P. *La typologie baptismale dans l'ancienne église* (Leipzig-Uppsala 1942).

MACK, B.L. 'Imitatio Mosis. Patterns of Cosmology and Soteriology in the Hellenistic Synagogue'. *SPh* 1 (1972) 27-55.

MACLEOD, C.W. 'The Preface to Gregory of Nyssa's *Life of Moses*'. *JThS* 33 (1982) 183-191.

MALHERBE, A.J., and E. FERGUSON. *Gregory of Nyssa The Life of Moses.* The Classics of Western Spirituality (New York 1978).

MANSFELD, J. *Prolegomena. Questions to be Settled before the Study of an Author, or a Text* (Leiden 1994).

MARTENS, J. '*Nomos empsychos* in Philo and Clement of Alexandria'. in: W.E. HELLEMAN (ed.). *Hellenization Revisited. Shaping a Christian Response within the Greco-Roman World* (Lanham 1994) 323-338.

MASSEBIEAU, L. 'Le classement des œuvres de Philon'. *Bibliothèque de l'École des Hautes Études, Sciences Religieuses* I (1889) 1-91.

MATILLA, S.L. 'Wisdom, Sense Perception, Nature and Philo's Gender Gradient'. *HThR* 89 (1996) 103-129.

MAY, G. 'Die Chronologie des Lebens und der Werke des Gregor von Nyssa'. In: HARL (1971) 51-66.

MÉASSON, A. *Du chair ailé de Zeus à l'Arche d'Alliance: images et mythes platoniciens chez Philon d'Alexandrie.* Études Augustiniennes (Paris 1986).

MEREDITH, A. *The Cappadocians* (Crestwood 1995).

——. 'Licht und Finsternis bei Origenes und Gregor von Nyssa'. In: T. KOBUSCH, and B. MOJSISCH (eds.). *Platon in der abendländischen Geistesgeschichte* (Darmstadt 1997) 48-59.

——. *Gregory of Nyssa.* The Early Church Fathers (London 1999).

MERKI, H. ' Ὁμοίωσις θεῷ. *Von der platonischen Angleichung an Gott zur Gottähnlichkeit bei Gregor von Nyssa* (Freiburg 1952).

MIRRI, P., 'La vita di Mosè di Filone Alessandrino e di Gregorio Nissene: note sull' uso dell' allegoria'. *Annali della Facoltà di Lettere e Filosofia della Università di Perugia* 20 (1982) 31-53.

MOMIGLIANO A. *The Development of Greek Biography.* Expanded edition (Cambridge MA 1993).

MONTES-PERAL, L.A. *Akataleptos theos: der unfassbare Gott.* ALGHJ 16 (Leiden 1987).

MOORE, W., and H.A. WILSON. *Select Writings and Letters of Gregory, Bishop of Nyssa.* The Nicene and Post-Nicene Fathers II.5 (1892, repr. 1988).

MORRIS, J. 'Philo the Jewish Philosopher'. In: E. SCHÜRER, and G.VERMES *et al. The History of the Jewish People in the Sge of Jesus Christ (175 B.C. – A.D. 135)* vol 3, part 2 (Edinburgh 1987) 809-889.

MORTLEY, R. *Connaissance religieuse et herméneutique chez Clément d'Alexandrie* (Leiden 1973).

MORESCHINI, C., and P. GALLAY. *Grégoire de Nazianze Discours 38-41.* SC 358 (Paris 1990).

MOSÈS, A. *Philon d'Alexandrie De gigantibus – Quod Deus sit immutabilis.* OPA 7-8 (Paris 1963).

MOSSAY, J. *Grégoire de Nazanze Discours 20-23.* SC 270 (Paris 1980).

MUCKLE, J.T. 'The Doctrine of St. Gregory of Nyssa on Man as the Image of God'. *Mediaeval Studies* 7 (1945) 55-84.

MÜHLENBERG, E. *Die Unendlichkeit Gottes bei Gregor von Nyssa. Gregors Kritik am Gottesbegriff der klassischen Metaphysik* (Göttingen 1966).

——. *Psalmenkommentare aus der Katenenüberlieferung, Band III: Untersuchungen zu den Psalmenkatenen.* Patristische Texte und Studien 19 (Berlin 1978).

MUSURILLO, H. *Gregorii Nysseni De vita Moysis.* GNO 7.1 (Leiden 1964).

NAUTIN, P. *Homélies pascales II.* SC 36 (Paris 1953).

——. *Origène Homélies sur Jérémie.* 2 vols. SC 232, 238 (Paris 1976-77).

——. *Origène. Sa vie et son œuvre* (Paris 1977).

——. 'Je suis celui qui est (Exode 3,14) dans le théologie d'Origène'. In: VIGNAU (1978) 109-119.

NEMESHEGYI, P. *La paternité de Dieu chez Origène* (Tournai 1960).

NESTLE, D. Art. 'Freiheit'. In: *RAC* 8 (Stuttgart 1972) 269-306.

NIKIPROWETZKY, V. *Le commentaire de l'Écriture chez Philon d'Alexandrie: son caractère et sa portée; observations philologiques.* ALGHJ 11 (Leiden 1977).

NOCK, A.D. 'The Exegesis of *Timaeus* 28C'. *VC* 16 (1962) 79-86.

NORRIS, F.W. *Faith gives Fullness to Reasoning. The Five Theological Orations of Gregory Nazianzen.* VCSup 13 (Leiden 1991).

OMONT, H. *Catalogues des manuscripts grecs de Fontainebleau sous François I et Henri II* (Paris 1889).

OTIS, B. 'Gregory of Nyssa and the Cappadocian Conception of Time'. *SP* 14 (1976) 327-357.

PEARCE, S. 'Belonging and not Belonging: Local Perspectives in Philo of Alexandria'. In S. JONES, and S. PEARCE, (edd.). *Jewish Local Patriotism and Self-identification in the Graeco-Roman Period.* Journal for the Study of the Pseudepigrapha. Supplement Series 31 (Sheffield 1998) 79–105.

PÉPIN, J. 'Grégoire de Nazianze, lecteur de la littérature hermétique'. *VC* 36 (1982) 251-260.

PERI, C. 'La vita di Mosè di Gregorio di Nissa: un vaggio verso l'areté cristiana'. *Vetera Christianorum* 11 (1974) 313-332.

PETIT, F. review of Daniélou *Grégoire de Nysse La vie de Moïse*, (Paris) 1955², *Recherches de Théologie ancienne et médiévale* 25 (1958) 366-369.

PFEIFER, G. *Ursprung und Wesen der Hypostasenvorstellungen im Judentum.* Arbeiten zur Theologie I.31 (Stuttgart 1967).

PFEIFFER, R. *History of Classical Scholarship.* Vol. 1 (Oxford 1968).

Philon d'Alexandrie. Lyon 11-15 septembre 1966. Colloques nationaux de centre national de la recherche scientifique (Paris 1967).

PUECH, H.CH. 'La ténèbre mystique chez le Ps.-Denys et dans la tradition patristique'. *Études carmélitaines* 23 (1938) 33-53. Repr. in: *En quête de la Gnose* (Paris 1978) I. 119-141.

QUASTEN, J. *Patrology.* 4 vols. (Utrecht-Antwerpen 1950-86).

RAHNER, H. *Symbole der Kirche. Die Ekklesiologie der Väter* (Salzburg 1964).

REGENBOGEN, O. Art. 'Πίναξ, 3) Literarisch'. In: *RE* 20 (Stuttgart 1950) 1409-82.

REMUS, H. 'Moses and the thaumaturges: Philo's *De vita Moysis* as a rescue operation'. *Laval théologique et philosophique* 52 (1996) 665-680.

RICHARDSON, W. 'The Philonic Patriarchs as Nomos Empsychos'. *SP* 1 (1957) 515-25.

RIEDWEG, C. *Mysterienterminologie bei Platon, Philon und Klemens von Alexandrien.* Untersuchungen zur antiken Literatur und Geschichte 26 (Berlin-New York 1987).

RIST, J.M. *The Road to Reality* (Cambridge 1967, repr. 1980).

ROBINSON, B.P. 'Symbolism in Exod. 15:22-27 (Marah and Elim)'. *Revue biblique* 94 (1987) 376-388.

RÖDER, J-A. *Gregor von Nyssa Contra Eunomium I 1-146*, eingel., übers. und komment. Patrologia 2 (Frankfurt/Main 1993).

ROUSSEAU, A. *Irénée de Lyon Demonstration de la prédiction apostolique.* SC 406 (Paris 1995).

ROYSE, J.R. 'The Original Structure of Philo's *Quaestiones*'. *SPh* 4 (1976-77) 41-78.

RUNIA, D.T. 'The Structure of Philo's Allegorical Treatises: a Review of two Recent Studies and Some Additional Comments'. *VC* 38 (1984) 209-256.

——. *Philo of Alexandria and the* Timaeus *of Plato*. Philosophia Antiqua 44 (Leiden 1986).

——. 'Naming and Knowing: Themes in Philonic Theology with Special Reference to the *De mutatione nominum*'. In: VAN DEN BROEK, BAARDA and MANSFELD (1988a) 66-91.

——. 'God and Man in Philo of Alexandria'. *JThS* 39 (1988b) 48-75.

——. 'How to Search Philo'. *SPhA* 2 (1990) 106-139.

——. 'Underneath Cohn and Colson: the Text of Philo's *De virtutibus*'. *SBLSPS* 30 (1991) 116-134, repr. in (1995c) 77-101.

——. 'A Note on Philo and Christian Heresy'. *SPhA* 4 (1992) 65-74, repr. in (1995c) 144-154.

——. *Philo in Early Christian Literature* (Assen-Minneapolis 1993).

——. 'Philo of Alexandria and the Beginnings of Christian Thought'. *SPhA* 7 (1995a) 143-160.

——. 'Why does Clement of Alexandria call Philo 'the Pythagorean'?'. *VC* 49 (1995b) 1-22, repr. in (1995c) 54-76.

——. *Philo and the Church Fathers. A collection of Papers*. VCSup 32 (Leiden 1995c).

——. 'Caesarea Maritima and the Survival of Hellenistic-Jewish Literature'. In: A. RABAN and K. HOLLUM (eds.). *Caesarea Maritima. A Retrospective after Rwo Millennia* (Leiden 1996) 476-495.

——. 'One of Us or One of Them? Christian Reception of Philo the Jew in Egypt'. (forthcoming).

SAFFREY, H.D. 'Pourquoi Prophyre a-t-il édité Plotin?'. In: *Porphyre: La vie de Plotin, II: Études d'introduction, texte grec et traduction française, commentaire, notes complémentaires, bibliographie*. Histoire des doctrines de l'antiquité classique 16 (Paris1992) 31-64.

SANDMEL, S. *Philo of Alexandria: an Introduction* (New York-Oxford 1979).

——. 'Philo Judaeus: an Introduction to the Man, his Writings, and his Significance'. *ANRW* II.21.1. 3-46 (Berlin-New York 1984).

SATRAN, D. Review of S. DANIEL-NATAF (ed.). Philo of Alexandria: *Writings* vol. 2. *Exposition of the Law, Part One*. *SPhA* 7 (1995) 225-226.

SCHERER, J. *Le commentaire d'Origene sur Rom. III. 5-V. 7 d'après les extraits du papyrus No 88748 du Musée du Caire et les fragments de la Philocalie et du Vaticanus gr. 762 : essai de reconstitution du texte et de la pensée des tomes V et VI du "Commentaire sur l'Epitre aux Romains"* (Le Caire 1957).

SCHOEDEL, W.R. 'Enclosing, not Enclosed: the Early Christian Doctrine of God'. In: W.R. SCHOEDEL, and R.L. WILKEN (eds.) *Early Christian Literature and the Classical Intellectual Tradition* (Paris 1979) 75-86.

SCHÜRER, E. *Geschichte des jüdischen Volkes im Zeitalter Jesu Christi*. Vol 2 (Leipzig 1886²).

——. *Geschichte des jüdischen Volkes im Zeitalter Jesu Christi.* Vol. 3 (Leipzig 1909[3/4]).

SCHÜRER, E., G. VERMES *et al. The history of the Jewish People in the Age of Jesus Christ (175 B.C. – A.D. 135).* 3 vols. (Edinburgh 1973-87).

SELAND, T. *Establishment Violence in Philo and Luke: a Study of Non-Conformity to the Torah and Jewish Vigilante Reactions* (Leiden 1995).

SHULER, P.L. 'Philo's Moses and Matthew's Jesus: a Comparative Study in Ancient Literature'. *SPhA* 2 (1990) 86-103.

SIEGERT, F. *Philon von Alexandrien, Über die Gottesbezeichnung "wohltätig verzehrendes Feuer" (De Deo): Rückübersetzung des Fragments aus dem Armenischen, deutsche Übersetzung und Kommentar.* Wissenschaftliche Untersuchungen zum Neuen Testament 46 (Tübingen 1988).

SIMONETTI, M. *Gregorio di Nissa Le vita di Mosè* (Milano 1984).

SLY, D. *Philo's Perception of Women.* BJS 209 (Atlanta 1990).

STAROBINSKI-SAFRAN, E. 'Exode 3, 14 dans l'oevre de Philon d'Alexandrie'. In: VIGNAU (1978) 47-55.

STERLING, G. '"The School of Sacred Laws": the Social Setting of Philo's Treatises'. *VC* 53 (1999a) 148-164.

——. 'Recherché or Representative? What is the Relationship between Philo's Treatises and Greek-speaking Judaism?'. *SPhA* 11 (1999b) 1-30.

STRICKERT, F. 'Philo on the Cherubim'. *SPhA* 8 (1996) 40-57.

STRITZKY, M-B. VON. *Zum Problem der Erkenntnis bei Gregor von Nyssa.* Münsterische Beiträge zur Theologie 37 (Münster 1973).

SWEENEY, L. *Divine infinity in Greek and Medieval thought* (New York 1992).

TARRANT, H. *Thrasyllan Platonism* (Ithaca-London 1993).

TERIAN, A. 'Back to Creation: the Beginning of Philo's Third Grand Commentary'. *SPhA* 9 (1997) 19-36.

TOBIN, T.H. Art 'Logos', in: *The Anchor Bible Dictionary* 4 (New York 1992) 348-356.

TOV, W. 'Die griechischen Bibelübersetzungen'. *ANRW* II.20.1 (Berlin-New York 1987) 121-189.

ULLMANN, W. 'Der logische und der theologische Sinn des Unendlichkeitsbegriffs in der Gotteslehre Gregors von Nyssa'. *Bijdragen* 48 (1987) 150-171.

VAGGIONE, R.P. *Eunomius. The Extant Works.* Oxford Early Christian Texts (Oxford 1987).

VIGNAU, P., (Ed.). *Dieu et l'être, exégèses d'Exode 3,14 et de Coran 20, 11-24* (Paris 1978).

VÖLKER, W. *Fortschritt und Vollendung bei Philon von Alexandrien* (Leipzig 1938).

———. review of J. Daniélou (1944). *Theologische Zeitschrift* 5 (1949) 143-148.

———. *Gregor von Nyssa als Mystiker* (Wiesbaden 1955).

WENDLAND, P. 'Philo und Clemens Alexandrinus'. *Hermes* 31 (1896) 435-456.

WESSEL, KL. Art. 'Durchzug durch das Rote Meer'. In: *RAC* 4 (Stuttgart 1959) 370-389.

WHITTAKER, J. 'The Value of Indirect Tradition in the Establishment of Greek Philosophical Texts or the Art of Misquotation'. In: J.N. GRANT. *Editing Greek and Latin Texts: Papers given at the Twenty-third Annual Conference on Editorial Problems University of Toronto 6-7 November 1987* (New York 1989) 63-95.

———. 'Catachresis and Negative Theology: Philo of Alexandria and Basilides'. In: S. GERSH, and C. KANNENGIESSER (eds.). *Platonism in Late Antiquity* (Notre Dame 1992) 61-82.

WILES, M. 'Eunomius: Hair-splitting Dialectician or Defender of the Accessibility of Salvation'. In: R. WILLIAMS (ed.). *The Making of Orthodoxy. Essays in Honor of Henry Chadwick* (Cambridge 1989) 157-172.

WILLIAMSON, R. *Philo and the Epistle to the Hebrews.* ALGHJ 4 (Leiden 1970).

———. *Jews in the Hellenistic World: Philo.* Cambridge Commentaries on the Writings of the Jewish and Christian World 200 BC to AD 200, I.ii (Cambridge 1989).

WINDEN, J.C.M. VAN. 'Quotations from Philo in Clement of Alexandria's *Protrepticus*'. *VC* 32 (1978) 208-213.

WINSTON, D. *Logos and Mystical Theology in Philo of Alexandria* (Cincinatti 1985).

———. 'Philo's *Nachleben* in Judaism'. *SPhA* 6 (1994) 103-110.

———. 'Sage and Super-sage in Philo of Alexandria'. In: D.P. WRIGHT, D.N. FREEDMAN, and A. HURVITZ (eds.). *Pomegranates and Golden Bells. Studies in Biblical, Jewish, and Near Eastern Ritual, Law, and Literature in Honor of Jacob Milgrom* (Winona Lake 1995).

WINSTON, D., and J. DILLON. *Two Treatises of Philo of Alexandria: a Commentary on De Gigantibus and Quod Deus sit immutabilis.* BJS 25 (Chio California 1983).

WOLFSON, H.A. *Philo: Foundations of Religious Philosophy in Judaism, Christianity and Islam.* 2 vols. (Cambridge MA 1947).

WONG, C.K. 'Philo's use of Chaldaioi'. *SPhA* 4 (1992) 1-14.

ZACHHUBER, J. *Human Nature in Gregory of Nyssa.* Philosophical Background and Theological Significance. VCSup 46 (Leiden 2000).

INDICES

1. *Biblical passages*

2. *Philonic passages*

3. *Passages in Gregory*

4. *Other passages*

Titles Available from Brown Judaic Studies

Brown Studies on Jews and Their Societies

Brown Studies in Religion